Learning, Speech, and the Complex Effects of Punishment

Essays Honoring George J. Wischner

George J. Wischner

Learning, Speech, and the Complex Effects of Punishment

Essays Honoring George J. Wischner

Edited by
Donald K. Routh

The University of Iowa
Iowa City, Iowa

Library of Congress Cataloging in Publication Data

Main entry under title:

Learning, speech, and the complex effects of punishment.

Includes bibliographies and index.
Contents: Introduction/Donald K. Routh—Biological contributions to the study of learning/Oakley Ray—Cognitive strategies in the discrimination learning of young children/Charles C. Spiker and Joan H. Cantor—[etc.]
1. Learning, Psychology of—Addresses, essays, lectures. 2. Punishment (Psychology)—Addresses, essays, lectures. 3. Speech, Disorders of—Addresses, essays, lectures. 4. Wischner, George J. I. Wischner, George J. II. Routh, Donald K.
BF318.L396 1982   153.1'5   82-18075
ISBN 0-306-40960-7

LC card number 82-18075

© 1982 Plenum Press, New York
A Division of Plenum Publishing Corporation
233 Spring Street, New York, N.Y. 10013

Printed in the United States of America

☐ Contributors

Joan H. Cantor, Department of Psychology, University of Iowa, Iowa City, Iowa

Harry Fowler, Department of Psychology, University of Pittsburgh, Pittsburgh, Pennsylvania

Sharon R. Garber, Department of Speech and Theater Arts, University of Pittsburgh, Pittsburgh, Pennsylvania

Judy Lynne Perlman, Department of Psychology, University of Iowa, Iowa City, Iowa

Oakley Ray, Veterans Administration Medical Center, and Departments of Psychology and Pharmacology, Vanderbilt University, Nashville, Tennessee

Donald K. Routh, Department of Psychology, University of Iowa, Iowa City, Iowa

Gerald M. Siegel, Center for Research in Human Learning and Department of Communication Disorders, University of Minnesota, Minneapolis, Minnesota

Charles C. Spiker, Department of Psychology, University of Iowa, Iowa City, Iowa

☐ Contents

CHAPTER 4

Learning Sets: The Pittsburgh Studies   71
Donald K. Routh

CHAPTER 5
Feedback and Motor Control in Stuttering   93
Sharon R. Garber and Gerald M. Siegel

CHAPTER 6
Facilitating Stimulus Effects of Reward and Punishment: Discriminability as a General Principle   125
Harry Fowler

1 Introduction

DONALD K. ROUTH

WHAT THIS BOOK IS ABOUT

A reader who happens onto this book on the library shelf may find the title a puzzle. Learning is one broad subject. Speech is another. And the "complex effects of punishment" might seem far afield from either. Perhaps, intrigued by this apparent diversity and wanting to discover what common theme underlies it, the reader may begin leafing through the chapters. The first one recounts a series of studies of rats—using learning techniques from the psychology laboratory, to be sure, but applied to the study of behavior genetics, sex differences, and aging. The second chapter has to do with young children's discrimination learning. Then, there is a chapter on learning sets. Next, there is a chapter on stuttering. Then the topic shifts back to the study of learning in rats. Then, there is a clinical chapter on punishment effects. Finally, there is a historically oriented essay on Iowa psychology graduates. Surely, by now the puzzled reader wants an explanation of why such diversity belongs between the covers of a single book.

   The answer is simply that the book is a *Festschrift* honoring a multifaceted man, George J. Wischner. Wischner combines in his interests and in his career all these diverse topics. As a broadly trained scientist, he was able to coexist comfortably with the University of Pittsburgh psychology department's biological emphasis and to train doctoral students like Oakley Ray to be full participants in biopsychology. Wischner would also not shy away from the label of *experimental child psychologist*. In fact, he once taught at the University of Iowa Child Welfare Research Station, where he knew Charles C. Spiker, co author of the second chapter. The third chapter, on learning sets, focuses on work done at Pittsburgh by Wischner and his colleagues and students. Why the chapter on

---

DONALD K. ROUTH ● Department of Psychology, University of Iowa, Iowa City, Iowa 52242.

stuttering? Wischner's Iowa doctoral dissertation, under Wendell Johnson and Kenneth W. Spence, concerned learning theory approaches to stuttering, and Wischner's articles based on this and subsequent research are classics in the field. Wischner has known Gerald M. Siegel, a speech pathologist and the coauthor of the stuttering chapter, from their Iowa days. What about the punishment chapters? Wischner began his interest in punishment effects on the rat with his M.A. thesis under Spence. The publication of this research, in fact, got Wischner involved in a controversy with the experimental psychologist Karl Muenzinger in the late 1940s. The chapter by Fowler details the history of Wischner and Fowler's long-term collaboration at the University of Pittsburgh in the study of reward and punishment effects on rodent discrimination learning. One should also not be surprised to find that a man with the above diverse interests and competencies was a clinical psychologist, which Wischner was and is. He was for many years director of the graduate program in clinical psychology at the University of Pittsburgh, where he supervised the training of many doctoral students in the clinical area. He is well known among Pennsylvania psychologists and once served as president of the Pennsylvania Psychological Association. Finally, one could probably not understand Wischner as a psychologist without some appreciation of the psychology department at Iowa that trained him. There was at that time, to be sure, the pervasive influence of Kenneth W. Spence. But the scientific rigor of the Iowa clinical psychology program and especially its unique ties to speech pathology were equally due to the influence of Carl E. Seashore, who laid the foundations of the department long before Spence's arrival and was the academic grandfather, so to speak, of Wendell Johnson. Surely Wischner's desire to chair a psychology department and thus his move to Cleveland after so many years at Pittsburgh were not uninfluenced by the example that had been provided by such powerful department heads as Seashore and Spence.

WISCHNER'S CAREER

To provide a brief chronological outline of his career, George Joseph Wischner was born April 14, 1914. He received his B.A. from Brooklyn College of the City University of New York in 1938. His M.A. thesis, at the University of Iowa in 1941, was entitled, "The Effects of Punishment on Discrimination Learning in a 'Non-correction' Situation." After serving as an aviation psychologist in the U.S. Army Air Corps from 1942 to 1946, Wischner returned to the University of Iowa to complete his Ph.D. in psychology. His 1947 doctoral dissertation was entitled, "Stuttering Behavior and Learning: A Program of Research." He served as assistant professor of psychology and as a psychologist at the student health service at the University of Missouri in 1947–1948. In

1948–1949 he returned to the University of Iowa as assistant professor of child psychology in the Child Welfare Research Station. From 1949 to 1952, he was assistant professor of psychology and speech at the University of Illinois. From 1952 to 1955, he was project leader and then director of research of the training methods division, Human Resources Research Office, George Washington University, Washington, D.C. From 1955 to 1972, he was professor of psychology at the University of Pittsburgh. Then, from 1972 until his retirement in 1979, he was professor and chairman of the department of psychology at Cleveland State University. Besides being a Fellow of the American Psychological Association and a former member of the editorial board of the *Journal of Consulting Psychology*, he is also a Fellow of the American Speech-Language-Hearing Association and a former member of the editorial board of the *Journal of Speech and Hearing Disorders*.

WISCHNER'S DOCTORAL STUDENTS

Wischner's list of Ph.D. students includes one at the University of Iowa, Martin R. Baron, whose 1949 doctoral dissertation was entitled, "The Effect on Eyelid Conditioning of a Speech Variable in Stutterers and Non-stutterers." He supervised 16 Ph.D. students during his years at the University of Pittsburgh. Below are listed their names, the dates on which their dissertations were defended, and the titles of the dissertations:

Ray, Oakley S., 1958, "Personality Factors in Motor Learning and Reminiscence."

Lepson, David S., 1959, "Speech Anxiety (Drive), Degrees of Response Competition and Mode of Response in a Forced-Choice Variation of Paired-Associates Learning."

Karpf, Bertram V., 1960, "An Investigation of the Effect of Speech Anxiety upon the Conditioning of a Finger Withdrawal Response."

Bowes, Anne E., 1962, "Problem Difficulty as a Factor in Learning Set Formation by Children."

Hall, Richard C., 1963, "Factors Influencing the Acquisition and Extinction of an Object Quality Discrimination Learning Set in Mentally Retarded Children."

McCreary, Joyce Y. B., 1963, "Factors Affecting the Attainment of Conjunctive and Disjunctive Concepts in Third Grade Children."

Gerben, Martin J., 1966, "Presolution Oddity Learning Set Training as a Variable in Oddity Discrimination Learning and Learning Set Formation by Children."

Routh, Donald K., 1967, "The Conditioning of Vocal Response Differentiation in Infants."

Ascher, L. Michael, 1968, "The Effects on Shock-Right Training of Various Schedules of Food and Shock in a Partial Reinforcement Situation."

White, Donna R., 1968, "The Selection and Experimental Study of Poor Readers in a Reversal-Nonreversal Shift Paradigm."

Friedman, Joanne Z., 1970, "Age Changes in Children's Syntagmatic and Paradigmatic Choices on a Forced-Choice Word Association Task and Their Relation to Reflection-Impulsivity."

Held, Mark L., 1970, "Ego Control and Pronounceability as Factors in Vocal Behavior in Conflict."

Peterson, Lawrence E., 1970, "Vocal Behavior in Conflict as a Function of Type of Conflict and Drive Level."

Colletti, Rose B., 1971, "Learning Set Formation in Brain-Damaged Patients with and without Aphasia as a Function of Problem Difficulty."

Egan, Mary, 1971, "Vocal Behavior in Conflict: The Effect of Reflection-Impulsivity and Response Strength on the Performance of Primary Grade School Children."

Filicki, Edward S., 1972, "Learning Set Formation in Process and Reactive Schizophrenics as a Function of Paradigm Difficulty."

THE SAN ANTONIO SYMPOSIUM

A dinner and symposium honoring Professor Wischner on the occasion of his approaching retirement were held at the time of the meetings of the Psychonomic Society at San Antonio, Texas, on November 10, 1978. On that occasion, papers were read by Oakley Ray, Harry Fowler, and the present author and also by Albert E. Goss, a fellow Iowa graduate and longtime friend of Wischner. A tape-recorded talk by George Shames, a speech pathology colleague of Wischner's, was also part of the program. This whole occasion was originally planned as a surprise, in collusion with Mrs. Mary Ellen Wischner. It almost had to occur without the guest of honor, since despite the urging of his wife, he was just not planning to attend the Psychonomic Society meetings that year. Finally, the only way to pursuade him to be in San Antonio was to let the secret out and tell him about the symposium and this planned *Festschrift.*

As students, colleagues, and friends of George J. Wischner, we present this volume to him in appreciation and respect for the man he is and for the contributions he has made to scientific psychology.

2 Biological Contributions to the Study of Learning

OAKLEY RAY

PROLOGUE

I never took a course from George Wischner. I was more fortunate. I had him as my adviser (Ray, 1959) and my friend. I could tell many George Wischner stories but will instead make only some general comments. As a graduate student, I was most impressed with two things about George. One was that he believed that graduate students were people and behaved that way, a most progressive attitude in the mid-1950s. We were invited to the parties at his home. That never happened with other faculty. The other characteristic that made an impact on me was his emphasis on doing it right: quality, not quantity. Sometimes, I would think it a bit much at the time, but in retrospect, it is the attention to detail and quality that saves most of us from ourselves. Those two features—a humanistic concern for people and a scientists's concern for quality—combined to make him a unique and valuable member of the psychology department at the University of Pittsburgh. He was, and is, the compleat psychologist: clinician, researcher (both animal and human), teacher, and administrator. He had our love and respect then—he has it now.

The graduate psychology program at the University of Pittsburgh provided students with the perfect background for the world ahead of us. As I remember it, all of us—experimentalists and clinicians—took the same courses except for some very advanced seminars. The only difference was that the experimentalists went to their laboratories outside class, and we clinicians went to our hospitals and clinics. The mold was the Boulder model, and we all fit it perfectly.

OAKLEY RAY ● Veterans Administration Medical Center, and Departments of Psychology and Pharmacology, Vanderbilt University, Nashville, Tennessee 37240.

After I completed my clinical training, I wanted to do some research and remember well talking with Larry Stein—newly arrived in Pittsburgh—about working in his laboratory. He had mixed feelings about a clinical student's working in an animal laboratory—especially when he learned that I had never seen a white laboratory rat (and my Ph.D. was only about five months away). In our conversation, though, he learned that even clinical students at the University of Pittsburgh knew about Clark Hull—so we could not be all bad (Charles Osgood's blue book was our Bible, even though we had frequent class discussions about which theoretician should have his words printed in red). I remember well the first study Larry and I worked on; we were testing one of Kenneth Spence's ideas about fluctuation at the threshold of a response. We were thus using the most modern of electromechanical equipment to study concepts that were even then dying on the vine.

Because of George Wischner's background at the University of Iowa, I knew well about Spence and the Iowa tradition. Probably everyone in graduate school in the 1950s and 1960s heard Spence say in a colloquium talk that if he had a gun with six bullets he could advance psychology 20 years. Not everyone heard a conversation I was able to hear over dinner at the Eastern Psychological Association meeting one year. Larry Stein invited me to go to dinner with Spence and him. I remember Spence's urging Larry not to go into physiological psychology: "I tried it once—there's nothing there." Larry and I both heard it; neither of us listened. Who knows? Spence may have been right.

BACKGROUND

In spite of Spence's admonition, I did move into the brain–behavior area. As I look back and remember it, my work as a clinical psychology trainee in several hospital settings had made me quite interested in the psychoactive drugs, those therapeutic agents that were being used successfully to decrease the number of inpatients in mental hospitals and thus set the stage, and the need, for the development of the community mental health movement. That interest in the effects of drugs on behavior dovetailed nicely with my graduate training, where the emphasis had always been on behavior.

I described myself as a humanistic behaviorist, which meant only that while I was concerned about and interested in people and their problems and potentials, I had the behaviorist's interest in the effects of varying events and contingencies in and around the animal and the situation being studied: varying the number of trials; the amount of reinforcement; the amount of deprivation; the distribution of trials, response complexity, drive, etc. My first research in the magnificent world of the animal laboratory (You know, the Law of Effect really works! It was also true that rats never lie.) combined those two background factors: the potential impact on human behavior and the control of experimental variables. I first focused on studying psychoactive drugs in a variety of behavioral situations (Ray, 1963, 1964a,b, 1965, 1966; Ray & Bivens, 1966a,b). It seems old hat now, but it warmed my heart (and, more importantly, was publishable) to be able to show that all the traditional behavioral concerns and concepts were important determinants of the effects of the psychoactive drugs. It was also true that the traditional psychological and behavioral concepts could be verified, expanded, and amplified by using psychoactive drugs as independent variables (Ray, 1978).

I will not belabor the results of the work done during those early years. I became more and more interested in the organization of the black box we call the brain, and in the relationship between the brain and behavior. Running a behavioral laboratory in a multidisciplinary research facility, as I did, had two excellent features. Since I was *the* psychologist, I regularly and repeatedly had to defend my ideas, concepts, and principles against potential attack by some very bright and aggressive neurophysiologists, pharmacologists, and biochemists. If my thinking got too sloppy, they chopped me down quickly, and everyone jumped in—smiling—for the kill. I learned to be nimble and cautious. I was also the person who knew least about biochemistry, pharmacology, and neurophysiology. That meant that I could and did learn a great deal over coffee and lunch and the operating table. They knew so much more than I did that I learned from everything they did—and did not do.

THE BIOLOGICAL ANALYSIS OF BEHAVIOR

Psychologists have typically reached up on the shelf, taken down the first rat they could grab, and proceeded with their analysis of behavioral variables (Ray & Barrett, 1975). This seems true, even though the joke in my graduate school days was that California rats had thoughts, plans, and expectancies, while Yale rats were the plodders of the world—just one response after another. For a number of reasons, I became interested in genetic factors as important determinants of behavior. This approach is certainly very much in line with today's Zeitgeist, but we started our work in the late 1960s (Barrett & Ray, 1970). Even then, we knew that our search must end in an analysis of brain chemistry. Because to many psychologists "a-rat-is-a-rat-is-a-rat," and because there have been few stories of a complete tracking from behavior to brain chemistry, I will sketch our exploration.

Figure 1 contains shuttlebox avoidance data from both sexes of eight strains of rats. The strains in the upper row were random-bred, while those in the lower row were inbred. There were obvious sex and strain differences. The superior performance by females in avoidance paradigms is well known, but not so the large strain differences. In a shuttlebox avoidance situation, the animal learns *when* to run. After a stimulus change, the animal must move to the other compartment within a certain period of time (10 sec here) to avoid foot shock.

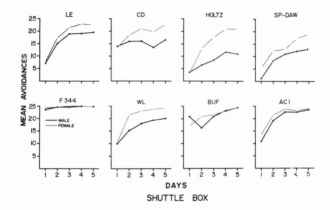

FIGURE 1. Mean number of avoidances across five days of testing in the shuttlebox. LE: Long Evans-black hooded (Simonsen Laboratories); CD: (Charles River Laboratories); Holtz: Holtzman (Holtzman Laboratories); SP-DAW (ARS/Sprague-Dawley Laboratories); F344; Fisher 344; WL: SF/f Mai; BUF: BUF/f Mai; AC1: AC1/f Mai (the last four were all inbred strains from Microbiological Associates).

FIGURE 2. Symmetrical aversive Y-maze in which rat avoidance and discrimination performance can be studied.

We had used a more complex behavior to study avoidance acquisition, and Barrett designed and built an automated Y-maze (see Figure 2), which we used in many studies. In the avoidance Y-maze, the animal not only had to learn *when* to run to avoid foot shock (within 10 sec of stimulus change) but also had to learn *where* to run to avoid foot shock: to the right or the left arm. Figure 3 shows the Y-maze data for the two strains that we have studied extensively. The F344 animals were an inbred strain, while the Zivic-Miller animals were a random strain.

Several things in Figure 3 need to be noted in particular: (a) there are clear sex and strain differences in avoidance behavior (upper panel); (b) there are no sex or strain differences in choice behavior (lower panel). Clearly, F344 animals are superior in knowing *when* to run, but they are no better than the Zivic-Miller animals in knowing *where* to run to avoid foot shock.

We did several studies to characterize, delimit, and define the strain–behavior interaction. Figure 4 presents data from a fostering and cross-fostering

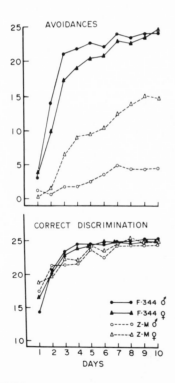

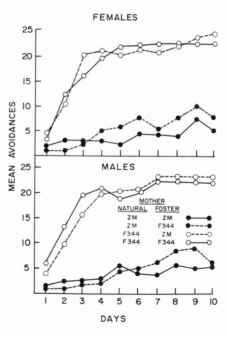

FIGURE 3. Mean avoidances and correct discriminations across 10 days with daily 25-trial sessions in the Y-maze.

FIGURE 4. Mean number of avoidances across 10 days of testing in the Y-maze for foster-care groups.

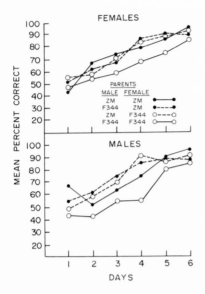

FIGURE 5. Mean percentage of correct responses across 6 days of testing in the appetitive Y-maze for the offspring of the indicated parents.

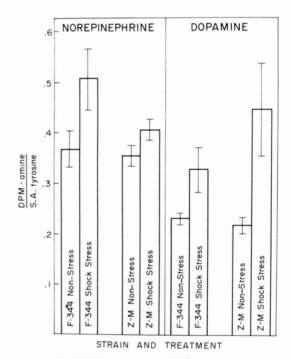

FIGURE 6. Mean conversion index (ratio of radioactive disintegrations per minute per gram of tissue of the monoamine to specific radioactivity of the precursor amino acid) of whole brain norepinephrine and dopamine under stress and no-stress conditions for male Z-M and F-344 animals. Vertical bars indicate the standard error of the mean.

study, which shows that the genetic difference, and not early maternal care, is the critical variable in these behavioral differences. Figure 5 shows that when animals from these two strains are tested in an appetitive Y-maze, there are no strain differences in the speed of response or the correctness of the choice behavior.

To shorten the story considerably: it was clear that Zivic-Miller animals responded to shock stress by "freezing," while the F344 animals responded by an increase in activity. Under the no-stress condition—as in Figure 5—there were no behavioral differences. Figures 6 and 7 contain brain biochemistry data for both strains under stress and no-stress conditions. Analysis of the brain biogenic amines under no-stress conditions yielded *no* strain differences. When animals were subjected to foot shock stress prior to analysis of their brain chemistry, large differences did appear.

The behavioral effects and greater increase in turnover in brain norepinephrine in the F344 animals under foot shock stress are congruent with present theorizing about the actions of norepinephrine. Similarly, the behavioral and brain biochemical responses (greater increase in serotonin turnover) of Zivic-Miller animals are those that would have been predicted from other research (Ray & Barrett, 1975). From our perspective as psychologists, there are some impor-

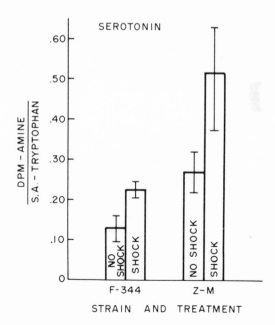

FIGURE 7. Mean conversion index (ratio of radioactive disintegrations per minute per gram of tissue of the monoamine to specific radioactivity of the precursor amino acid) of whole brain serotonin under stress and no stress conditions for male Z-M and F-344 animals. Vertical bars indicate standard error of the mean.

tant outcomes from the studies just described. One, certainly, is the relating of brain chemistry to behavior. Another is the separation of learning from performance. It is hoped that the most important result will be that psychologists will be encouraged and supported in selecting their animals with as much care as they use in selecting their behavior and control procedures.

Although sex differences are probably as important to psychologists as they are to the man-in-the-street, psychologists have not focused on them to any great extent. The next two studies to be discussed looked at male–female differences as another of the important biological determiners of behavior. Although there were no effects of cross-fostering on Y-maze behavior (see Figure 4), it might be that there are important effects of early experiences on animals with different genetic characteristics.

To explore that possibility, Betty Jo Freeman and I did a study (Freeman & Ray, 1972) that combined strain, sex, and rearing-environment differences. The two strains—F344 and Zivic-Miller—and the two sexes were separated from their natural mothers at the age of 28 days and placed in one of two environments for the next 60 days. We used Krech-type environments: 10 animals of the same strain and sex were placed in a large all-wire-mesh enclosure with many objects (ladder, seesaw, billiard balls, tunnels, swing), which were changed daily, and the entire enclosure was open to the many auditory and visual changes that occurred in the laboratory area; single animals were put in standard laboratory cages, which had insulating materials on the back and two sides and were housed in racks placed in rooms with constant low-level illumination and white noise. Food and water were provided *ad lib* in both situations. The large, group-cage condition was called the *enriched condition* (EC), while the single-cage condition was called the *isolated condition* (IC).

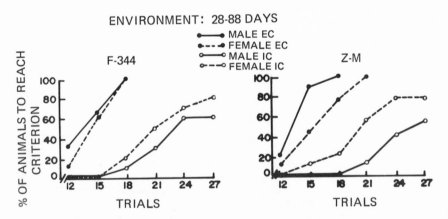

FIGURE 8. Percentage of animals to reach criterion in an appetitive Lashley III Maze as a function of strain (Zivic-Miller, F-344), sex, and rearing conditions.

SEXUAL DIFFERENTIATION IN THE RAT

CONCEPTION					BIRTH		
			xxxxxx			xxxxxxxxxxxxxx	
0	PRENATAL		16 17		21		
					0 POSTNATAL		5
DIFFERENTIATION			REPRODUCTIVE SYSTEM		NERVOUS SYSTEM		

GENETIC		MALE				FEMALE		
		RS	NS	BEH		RS	NS	BEH
NORMAL		M	M	M	NORMAL	F	F	F
CASTRATE DAY 1		M	F	F	TESTOSTERONE	F	M	M
CYPROTERONE		F	F	F	DAYS 1-5			

FIGURE 9. Time course, conception through postnatal Day 5, of sexual differentiation in the rat. (RS: reproductive system; NS: nervous system; Beh: behavior; M: male; F: female).

At the age of 90 days, the animals were run in a Lashley III Maze for food reinforcement. Figure 8 presents the results of that study. Two effects seem most important. One is the clear influence of the rearing environment: the animals from the EC reached the criterion of three successive errorless runs in fewer trials than those from the IC. Second is the differential effect on the sexes as a function of strain: the Zivic-Miller, but not the F344, males were obviously much more affected by the rearing environment than the females. This greater effect of environment on male than on female behavior is congruent with an early study of mine (Ray & Hochhauser, 1969) and with some reports on human subjects (e.g., Kasl, 1972) but has not really been very much followed up.

Those sex differences did become part of my accumulating evidence on male–female differences. I had early in my career been impressed with Cajal's observation that you can frequently learn more by studying the developing organism than by studying the adult. My developmental interests combined with my interest in male–female differences and were given focus by an article by Harris (1964). His work made it clear that there were differences in brain functioning in males and females and that those differences were manipulable in the rat. Figure 9 summarizes what was known about the sexual differentiation of the rat brain.

The phenomenon of sexual differentiation of the brain had a great impact on me: manipulations early in an animal's life have potent effects that appear in very different situations when the animal is much older! The basis for these strong effects is that the manipulations do not just transiently affect behavior; they permanently alter brain structure (Pfaff, 1966, 1968), and thus, function.

You do hop-skip-jump research when you are excited and just want to confirm that your direction is correct and that your technology and methods are satisfactory. If you castrate male rats within 24 hr of birth, does the probability of female sexual behavior increase in adulthood? If you administer testosterone to newborn females, is adult female sexual behavior decreased? Figure 10 shows that it is, and it has the graded effect that one would expect if brain organization is gradually developed over five or six days as was indicated in Figure 9. A graduate student (Goldman, 1969) later repeated (and confirmed) many of these findings in the nice, systematic way that is essential for dissertations.

If one is, in fact, changing brain organization and function, then other nonsexual but sex-related behaviors should also be affected. In the open-field task, females are more active than males. Figure 11 shows that neonatal manipulations have effects on adult open-field behavior that are in the directions one would expect. Similarly, Figure 12 shows that such effects can be demonstrated on sucrose ingestion.

The potency of the effects of these early changes in hormone levels brings home very vividly the importance of early experiences in affecting behavior that will not appear until much later in life. Critically, it is *not* that one can eliminate behavior or disrupt behavior—there are many ways of doing that. The important thing is that with specific early manipulations, one can change a class of well-organized behaviors from that typical of one sex to that typical of the other.

If one has an interest in human behavior, then it is frequently possible to do nice animal studies based on extrapolation from human data. There are many data (Wittig & Petersen, 1979) that suggest that at least two human sex-linked traits are genetically determined: the superior spatial-relations skills of males and the

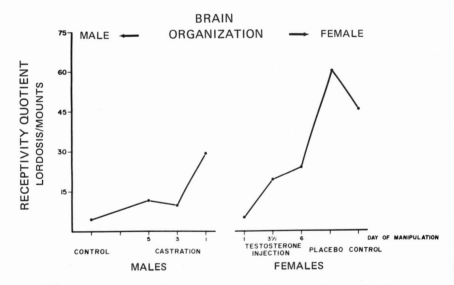

FIGURE 10. Hypothesized brain organization and actual female sexual behavior (following progesterone and estrogen priming) when paired with a proven vigorous male as a function of sex and day of postnatal manipulation (testosterone: 100 mg; placebo: peanut oil; control: no manipulation).

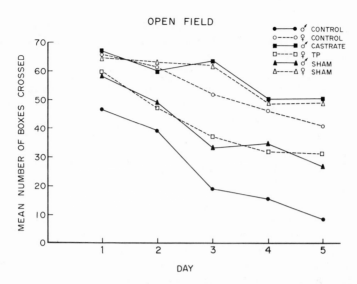

FIGURE 11. Open-field (4′ × 4′) activity (5 min/day for 5 days) in 60- to 70-day-old male and female Zivic-Miller rats as a function of postnatal manipulation (control: no manipulation; castrate: Day 1 castration; TP: 100 mg testosterone on day 1; male sham: Day 1 abdominal incision; female sham: peanut oil on Day 1).

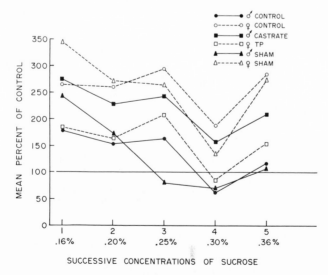

FIGURE 12. Sucrose intake compared with water intake in 60- to 70-day-old male and female Zivic-Miller rats as a function of sucrose concentration and postnatal manipulation (code as in Figure 11).

superior language skills of females. A graduate student and I decided to test one hypothesis in rats and to add the nicety of altering the sexual differentiations of the brain with early manipulations.

Figure 13 is a summary of a complex study on learning in the Hebb-Williams spatial maze; the study was completed in 1978 (Joseph, Hess, & Birecree, 1978). Take note that the effects of testosterone were prevented neonatally either by castration or by the administration of cyproterone, an androgen-blocking agent. No matter what technique was used, the results in this study were the same: if the neonatal actions of testosterone were blocked in genetic males, adult behavior was like that of normal genetic females; neonatal administration of testosterone to genetic females resulted in adult behavior similar to that of normal genetic males.

In spite of our ages, we really were interested in early experience effects other than those related to sex. Some of our studies involved the early administration of strychnine (Shaefer, Buchanan, & Ray, 1974) and the perinatal administration of growth hormone (Ray & Hochhauser, 1969). The effects were specific, discrete, and organized, not diffuse or chaotic.

I will take time here to mention one more series of studies that relate to the issue of biological influences on behavior. The process of aging is very much like sex differences in that it is everywhere and so all-pervasive that we frequently overlook it as a biological factor that has great impact on our behavior. We were

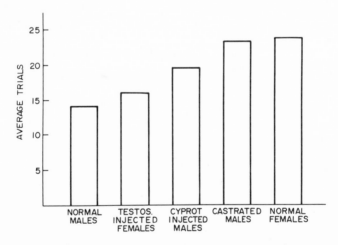

FIGURE 13. Average trials to criteria on Hebb-Williams Maze as a function of postnatal manipulation (normal: no manipulation; testosterone injected: females, 5 mg/0.10 ml testosterone on Days 1 and 4; cyproterone injected: males, 5 mg/0.05 ml cyproterone on Days 1, 4, 7, 10; castration: Day 1; testos. = testosterone, cyprot. = cyproterone). (Data derived from Table 1, Joseph *et al.*, 1978.)

fortunate in being able to house large numbers of animals for long periods of time without disrupting or curtailing the short-term studies that are the bread and butter of most laboratories.

I will comment on and present only one of those studies here (Ray & Barrett, 1974). Since we had a very nice procedure—Y-maze avoidance—that would separate learning and performance factors, we decided to look at those variables in a memory paradigm as a function of (a) age at time of acquisition and (b) age at time of retest for retention. There were two procedures: train at age 70 days, wait, retest at the ages indicated in Figure 14, or train at the age indicated in Figure 14, wait 24 hours, and retest. Four important points from this study need to be remembered: (a) no differences existed in retest performance as a function of the test–retest interval (for that reason we have combined the retest data from both procedures in Figure 14); (b) large differences existed in performance as a function of age at retest; (c) there were large differences in performance as a function of the number of acquisition trials; and (d) there were no differences in choice behavior as a function of age or of acquisition–retest interval (true in this study and in a follow-up study by Ray & Barrett, 1980).

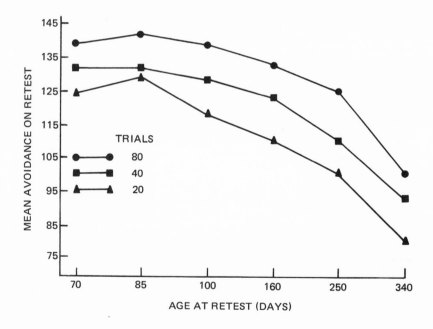

FIGURE 14. Mean number of avoidances as a function of age at time of testing during 150 retention trials on the Y-maze active-avoidance task.

SUMMARY OF POINTS AND ISSUES

The basic thrust in this paper has been to demonstrate the impact that nontraditional techniques and procedures can have on the study of learning and memory. Only in recent years have psychologists begun to appreciate the importance of genetic, early-experience, sex, and age differences as determinants of behavior. The use of a broad, multidisciplinary base in the study of behavior has led me to believe that (a) traditional behavioral concepts can be and have been verified and amplified by the use of psychoactive agents, electroconvulsive shock, and genetic differences among strains; (b) surgical, pharmacological, and hormonal manipulations in the early stages of development have effects that greatly alter the process of brain organization without disrupting it; (c) behavioral differences between genetically different strains of animals are every bit as great as, if not greater than, those induced by behavioral control procedures; (d) the genetically based behavioral differences that do exist can be analyzed in terms of differences in brain chemistry; and (e) learning and performance can be separated experimentally and are probably under the control of different factors.

POSTLOGUE

As I look at what George Wischner was and is, and reflect on the diversity of my career thus far, I am convinced of several things (Ray, 1978). Psychology will move forward only if it becomes less parochial and uses techniques from other areas; keeps in very close contact with behavior; and increases the correlations and relevance of animal research to human experiences. To do these things requires a broad-based graduate preparation and a faculty with a perspective on the past and an appreciation of the unknown quality of the future. A faculty made up of George Wischners.

As I close this chapter and wonder how George will respond, I can almost hear him say what he has said so many times before:

"Well, Oakley . . . "

REFERENCES

Barrett, R. M., & Ray, O. S. Behavior in the open field, Lashley III Maze, Shuttle-box, and Sidman avoidance as a function of strain, sex, and age. *Developmental Psychology*, 1970, *3*, 73–77.

Freeman, B. J., & Ray, O. S. Strain, sex, and environmental effects of appetitively and aversively motivated learning tasks. *Developmental Psychobiology*, 1972, *5*, 101–109.

Goldman, L. *The sexual behavior of adolescent and adult female rats treated with testosterone propionate in infancy.* Unpublished Ph.D. dissertation, University of Pittsburgh, 1969.

Harris, G. W. Sex hormones, brain development and brain function. *Endocrinology*, 1964, *75*, 627–648.

Joseph, R., Hess, S., & Birecree, E. Effects of hormone manipulations and exploration on sex differences in maze learning. *Behavioral Biology*, 1978, *24*, 364–377.

Kasl, S. V. Physical and mental health effects of involuntary relocation and institutionalization on the elderly—A review. *American Journal of Public Health*, 1972, *62*, 377–384.

Pfaff, D. W. Morphological changes in the brains of adult male rats after neonatal castration. *Journal of Endocrinology*, 1966, *36*, 415–416.

Pfaff, D. W. Autoradiographic localization of radioactivity in rat brain after injection of tritiated sex hormones. *Science*, 1968, *161*, 1355–1356.

Ray, O. S. Personality factors in motor learning and reminiscence. *Journal of Abnormal and Social Psychology*, 1959, 59, 199–203.

Ray, O. S. The effects of tranquilizers on positively and negatively motivated behavior in rats. *Psychopharmacologia*, 1963, *4*, 326–342.

Ray, O. S. The effect of central nervous system depressants on discrete trail approach-avoidance behavior. *Psychopharmacologia*, 1964, *6*, 96–111. (a)

Ray, O. S. Tranquilizer effects on conditioned suppression. *Psychopharmacologia*, 1964, *5*, 136–146. (b)

Ray, O. S. Tranquilizer effects as a function of experimental anxiety procedures. *Archives Internationales de Pharmacodynamie et de Therapie*, 1965, *153*, 49–68.

Ray, O. S. Behavioral analysis of drug actions. In P. Mantegazza & F. Piccinini (Eds.), *Methods in drug evaluation*. Amsterdam: North-Holland, 1966.

Ray, O. S. *Drugs, society, and human behavior* (2nd ed.). St. Louis: Mosby, 1978.

Ray, O. S., & Barrett, R. Interaction of learning and memory with age in the rat. In C. Eisdorfer & W. E. Fann (Eds.), *Psychopharmacology and aging*. New York: Plenum Press, 1974.

Ray, O. S., & Barrett, R. M. Behavior, pharmacological, and biochemical analysis of the genetic differences in rats. *Behavioral Biology*, 1975, *15*, 391–417.

Ray, O. S., & Barrett, R. Assessment of age related changes in learning and performance in the rat. In C. Eisdorfer & W. E. Fann (Eds.), *Psychopharmacology and aging*. New York: Spectrum Publications, 1980.

Ray, O. S., & Bivens, L. W. Chlorpromazine and amphetamine effects on three operant and four discrete trial reinforcement schedules. *Psychopharmacologia*, 1966, *10*, 23–43. (a)

Ray, O. S., & Bivens, L. W. Performance as a function of drug, dose, and level of training. *Psychopharmacologia*, 1966, *10*, 103–109. (b)

Ray, O. S., & Hochhauser, S. Growth hormone and environmental complexity effects on behavior in the rat. *Developmental Psychology*, 1969, *1*, 311–317.

Schaefer, G. J., Buchanan, D. C., & Ray, O. S. Effects of neonatal strychnine administration on active avoidance in rats. *Behavioral Biology*, 1974, *10*, 253–258.

Wittig, M. A., & Petersen, A. E. (Eds.). *Sex related differences in cognitive functioning*. New York: Academic Press, 1979.

3 Cognitive Strategies in the Discrimination Learning of Young Children

CHARLES C. SPIKER AND JOAN H. CANTOR

INTRODUCTION

Research on children's discrimination learning during the past 10 to 15 years has brought about some major changes in our theoretical conceptualizations about the way children solve such tasks. The role of mediating processes in children's learning has been prominent in theoretical viewpoints since the early work of Kuenne (1946). Research during the 1950s on the hypothesis of acquired distinctiveness of cues (see Cantor, 1965; Spiker, 1956, 1963, for reviews) represented an attempt to identify and describe the mediating mechanisms. The Kendler and Kendler (1962) theory of representational mediation was a recognition that the discrimination learning and concept identification of older children, at least, was strongly influenced by the development of dimension-specific mediating processes. The attentional theory of Zeaman and House (1963) also placed between the complex physical stimulus and the overt instrumental response an observing response on the part of the subject, whether infrahuman, human adult, or child, that determined which of the existing stimulus dimensions would become effective. Dimension-specific responding was also a feature of a modification of Spence's (1936) theory of discrimination learning that the present writers began to develop about 10 years ago (Spiker, 1970, 1971; Spiker & Cantor, 1973).

CHARLES C. SPIKER AND JOAN H. CANTOR ● Department of Psychology, University of Iowa, Iowa City, Iowa 52242. The research from the authors' laboratory reported here was supported in part by Grant BMS75-04334 from the National Science Foundation. Funds for the purchase of computer time were made available by the Graduate College of the University of Iowa.

Each theoretical viewpoint assumed that prior learning and experience determined which mediating response, observing response, or attentional response would occur on any given trial. Thus, children could be pretrained to attend to form, or to color, and it was expected that such training would transfer into the next task, there to facilitate, to interfere, or to be neutral. The paradigms designed to investigate the dimension-specific responding included the reversal and nonreversal shifts, the intradimensional and extradimensional shifts, and the optional shifts. The general strategy was to provide the child with an initial task and to determine how that task was learned by studying and analyzing his or her performance on a transfer task.

The empirical research resulted in a good deal of clarification about the way children learn discrimination problems. One of the dominant findings is that, with increasing chronological age, children are more and more likely to attempt to solve a new problem by utilizing the dimension that was relevant in previous problems. Moreover, the general ability of children to abstract dimensions from the various discriminanda seems to improve with increase in chronological age.

In the early 1960s, cognitive theories began to appear that were designed to describe and explain the discrimination learning and concept identification of human adults (e.g., Bower & Trabasso, 1964; Levine, 1963; Restle, 1962). The success that these theories enjoyed in the prediction of adult behavior (see Levine, 1975, for a review) assured that attempts would be made to extend them to the prediction of children's discrimination performance. The earliest attempts were made by Eimas (1969), Ingalls and Dickerson (1969), and Rieber (1969). There were strong hints in these experiments that children as young as first- and second-graders were making use of systematic strategies in solving discrimination problems. More thoroughgoing investigations were subsequently conducted by Levine and his colleagues (e.g., Gholson, Levine, & Phillips, 1972).

The primary purpose of the present chapter is to chronicle the efforts of the present authors in investigating the use of the systematic strategies by young children, particularly those of kindergarten and first-grade ages, and to review and summarize some of the research most relevant to our own that has been conducted by other investigators.

SOME BACKGROUND ON HYPOTHESIS TESTING IN YOUNG CHILDREN

The Blank-Trial Probe

The development of the blank-trial probe by Levine (1963) provided a major impetus to the study of the cognitive strategies of the human adult. Attempts to extend these techniques to the study of children's strategies were inevitable. It may be well to begin a discussion of the study of discrimination-learning strategies by presenting a summary of one of the earlier attempts to assess the strategies of children and adults.

Gholson, Levine, and Phillips (1972). This report contained two experiments, and we will begin with a summary of the first. The discriminanda consisted of two different black or white letters of two different sizes with a black bar either above or below the letter. On each trial (setting), two discriminanda were presented that differed from each other on all four attributes. With 4 bivalued dimensions, 16 different stimulus compounds can be constructed, and a total of 8 distinctive settings may be formed in which each compound differs from the other on all 4 dimensions. Four of these settings were selected for the blank-trial probes so that any one of the eight simple hypotheses (e.g., "black," "white," "bar over," etc.) would be revealed as three choices to the left and one to the right or three choices to the right and one to the left. The remaining four settings were used as the feedback trials that were inserted before and after the blank-trial probes.

The subjects were given four pretraining tasks in which the nature of the problems was exposed and the blank-trial probes were introduced on a gradual basis. Only subjects who solved at least two pretraining problems were kept in the experiment. If the subjects failed to solve a given problem in 16 feedback trials, the solution was provided, and the next problem was begun. After pretraining, each subject received six 76-trial problems in which there were fifteen 4-trial blank probes and 16 feedback trials. There were 50 subjects each from grades 2, 4, and 6, as well as the same number of college students.

The results showed that approximately 90% of all probes were of the 3–1, 1–3 patterns and were therefore consistent with the notion that simple hypotheses were determining the choices. From 88% to 93% of all the probe results were predictive of the choice on the next feedback trial. The subjects retained their hypotheses from 93% to 99% of the time following positive feedback and changed their hypotheses from 90% to 99% of the time following negative feedback. There were modest age trends with respect to all these indexes. Moreover, six second-graders, one fourth-grader, and no sixth-graders were eliminated from the experiment for failure to solve two problems in pretraining. Nevertheless, one of the most noteworthy results was the degree to which younger children approximated the performance of older children and adults. On approximately 90% of the trials, the children chose their next hypothesis from among the attributes that characterized the previous positive discrimination, a behavioral characteristic that has been called *local consistency.* The adult subjects had a somewhat higher index of local consistency (96%).

By examining the patterns of hypotheses and feedback outcomes over the first few trials, the authors attempted to determine whether there were systematic modes of generating the hypotheses, as well as to classify any such systematic patterns. They reported finding three systematic strategies that would lead to solution of the problems, as well as several systematic, stereotypical patterns that would fail to solve the problems. The strategies included *focusing*, reducing the number of potentially valid hypotheses by half on each feedback trial; *dimension checking*, reducing the number of potentially relevant dimensions by one on each negative feedback trial; and *hypothesis checking*, reducing the number of potentially valid hypotheses by one, on a dimension-by-dimension basis, on each negative feedback trial. Although the only frequent systematic stereotypical responding manifested by subjects in this experiment was the perseveration in choosing a specific stimulus attribute (e.g., the persistent choice of the larger one), other experiments have revealed other stereotypical modes of responding, including position alternation and perseveration.

The second experiment reported by Gholson et al. (1972) used 48 kindergarten and 48 second-grade children as subjects. The pretraining procedures were the same as in the first experiment, except that no child was removed from the experiment for failure to learn. There were nine experimental problems, each having 25 trials consisting of five 4-trial blank probes and 5 feedback trials.

The results for the second-grade children were quite similar in all respects to those for the second-grade children in the first experiment. The results for the kindergarten children were quite discouraging, providing little or no evidence of the presence of cognitive strategies in children of this age. The percentage of probes manifesting simple hypotheses was less than that expected by chance, with position perseveration and alternation accounting for 84% of those probes that did not signify simple hypotheses. Although the kindergarten children retained their hypotheses 79% of the time following positive feedback, they also retained their hypotheses 46% of the time following negative feedback. Only about 5% of the classifiable hypothesis-feedback patterns suggested a systematic strategy, and the remainder showed the stereotypical stimulus preference, position alternation, and position perseveration.

Methodological Problems in Blank-Trial Probing. The present writers found the results of the Gholson et al. (1972) study surprising on two counts. First, of course, we were surprised that so many second-grade children appeared to manifest systematic strategies in the solution of discrimination problems. Second, granted the performance of the second-graders, we were surprised that kindergarten children seemed to perform so differently. Having tested hundreds of children of these ages with discrimination learning tasks, we had no reason to believe that such important differences might obtain between the two age groups.

A detailed examination of the Gholson et al. (1972) methodology suggested several possible reasons that the kindergarten children might have failed to reveal themselves to be as sophisticated as second-graders in testing hypotheses. It should be noted that the authors did not report the number of subjects who learned a problem, in either experiment, although they reported the number of problems solved in each age group. No information was provided on either the number of problems solved or the number of problem solvers in the second experiment. Hence, it is not clear whether any of the kindergarten children solved a problem. Since only five feedback trials were administered, it is quite possible that too few trials were administered to permit the kindergarten children to solve many, if any, of the problems. Moreover, each child received a total of 13 problems, 4 pretraining and 9 experimental, in what was apparently a single testing session. If this surmise is correct, the rate of presentation of the settings must have been unusually rapid, a conjecture supported by the reported intertrial interval of 1 second. There were several other reasons to believe that the performance of the kindergarten children might not be representative of the performance of such children in our laboratories: the stimuli were projected two-dimensional images rather than three-dimensional objects; there were four non-spatial dimensions rather than the two or three dimensions characteristic of our discrimination problems; and the stimuli were composites of unitary features (e.g., a large white X) and separable or partitioned features (a disconnected bar over or under the letter), whereas ours were characteristically unitary stimulus objects.

There is still another possible explanation for the apparent difference in performance of the two age groups. A superficial reading of this report might give one the initial impression either that 80% of the second-grade children manifested systematic strategies while solving problems or that the second-graders used strategies on 80% of their problems. A more careful reading, however, reveals that these children used strategies on 80% of their *classifiable* problems. Two of the criteria that a problem protocol had to meet in order to be appropriate for the strategy-system analysis were that the first three or four probe patterns must represent simple hypotheses and that each of these hypotheses must be locally consistent (Gholson, Phillips, & Levine, 1973). Only 30% of the problem protocols met these (and other) criteria in the first experiment, and presumably a comparable percentage was obtained in the second experiment. Thus, it is possible that as few as 24% of the second-graders (i.e., 80% of the 30% of all protocols that were classifiable) produced all the protocols that showed systematic strategies. Since some of the criteria employed in selecting data for the analysis would undoubtedly produce a bias toward better performance (e.g., the local consistency requirement), it is not likely that the data are representative of the performance of all the second-grade children.

Considerably better performance of kindergarten children was reported in two additional experiments (Gholson & McConville, 1974; Gholson, O'Connor, & Stern, 1976), with an improved use of strategies, as well as better performance on the four-dimensional discrimination problems. Although Gholson and Mc-Conville reported that kindergarten children used strategy systems on 50% of their problems, an even more extreme selection of data for system analysis (18%) makes it unlikely that these strategy users were representative of the entire kindergarten group. In fact, as few as 9% (50% × 18%) of the children could have contributed all the protocols in which strategy systems were manifested. Gholson *et al.* (1976) reported that a group of kindergarten children, selected because they were clearly concrete-operational, used strategy problems in solving 75% of their problems. Since no more than 24% of the protocols were included in the analyzed data, as few as 18% of this intellectually superior group of kindergarteners may have contributed all the protocols in which strategy systems were identified. (Support for the accuracy of the above estimates is provided in a recent article by Tumblin, Gholson, Rosenthal, and Kelley, 1979, in which the numbers of children exhibiting strategies were reported.)

The selection of the problem, rather than the subject, as the unit of analysis does not permit answers to questions concerning the proportion of subjects in any condition who are using strategy systems in the solution of problems. Unfortunately, this practice has also led to another, more serious, consequence in the testing of the significance of differences among conditions with the chi-square statistic. Since each subject can contribute more than one observation (e.g., the subject solved Problems 1, 3, and 4 but did not solve Problems 2, 5, and 6), the frequencies entered in the chi-square table cannot be independent, as required by statistical theory (e.g., Winer, 1971, p. 855).

Irrespective of any methodological problems, the above studies demonstrate that at least some of the children of kindergarten age can use strategy systems in the solution of discrimination-learning problems. The blank-trial probe, however, is not well suited to younger children. The use of trials without feedback is potentially confusing to these children, and such trials add greatly to the total testing time. Perhaps for both of these reasons, there is a loss of large numbers of data, and a resulting possibility of serious bias in the results that can be used.

The Introtact Probe

The development of the introtact probe and its use with adults have been described by Phillips and Levine (1975). With this method, the subject is asked to predict, either before or immediately after each trial, what feature of the discriminanda is going to be correct on every trial. The predictive value of the blank-trial and introtact methods for the choice behavior of adults is entirely equivalent (Karpf & Levine, 1971; Phillips & Levine, 1975). For adults, the introtact probe has proved to be far more efficient—both in terms of the time required for data collection and in terms of the proportion of data lost—than is the more tedious blank-trial procedure. For these reasons, arguments have been made for the use of the introtact probe whenever possible (Cantor & Spiker, 1978; Kemler, 1978; Phillips & Levine, 1975).

Phillips (1974). The first published report on the use of introtact probes with young children is that by Phillips (1974, reported in Phillips & Levine, 1975). In this experiment, second- and sixth-grade children were queried prior to each choice as to the solution of the discrimination-learning problem. Other children from the same grades were given the same problem with blank-trial probes, and still others without probes of either type. With four-dimensional discriminanda, Phillips found no differences between the three groups of sixth-graders. The second-graders who had received the introtact probes, however, performed somewhat better than did those who did not receive the probes, who, in turn, performed somewhat better than did the subjects who received blank-trial probes.

Phillips found the introtact probe to provide better measures of the components of strategy than did the blank-trial probes. Thus, the proportions of times that the children chose the stimulus dictated by the previous hypothesis was greater for the introtact probes than for the blank-trial probes. The introtact probes produced a higher proportion of simple hypotheses than did the blank-trial probes. For the younger children, the introtact probes revealed a higher proportion for the retention of hypotheses following positive feedback, and for rejection of hypotheses following negative feedback, than did the blank-trial probes.

Kemler, Shepp, and Foote (1976). The next published use of introtacts with young children was that reported by Kemler, Shepp, and Foote (1976), although the basic methodology was attributed to an earlier experiment by Kemler (1972). These authors reported a successful use of the introtact probe with children as young as kindergarten age, but their methodology differed sufficiently from that of Phillips so as to render some of the results incomparable. For example, the kindergarten children had local consistency probabilities near unity in value, and they nearly always changed hypotheses following negative feedback. On the other hand, they chose in accordance with their previous hypothesis only about 60% of the time, and they retained their hypothesis following positive feedback only 45% of the time. Several features of this experiment will be discussed following a presentation of some of our early work with introtact probes.

Spiker and Cantor (1977). We (Spiker and Cantor, 1977) first used the introtact probe in an experiment in which we tested certain aspects of the previously mentioned modification of the Spence discrimination-learning theory. We provided the kindergarten children with a single, relatively simple simultaneous-discrimination problem as a pretraining task in which we administered introtact probes. The pretraining was designed to shape the children into effective responding to introtact probes that were to be administered prior to the first trial of each eight-trial block in the criterion task. For the criterion task, the stimuli were eight blocks differing with respect to three bivalued dimensions: color, form, and size. Each of the six cues was positive for an equal number of children. The criterion for learning was seven or eight correct choices in each of two successive blocks, except that a minimum of 32 trials was given to all children, and a maximum of 48 trials was administered to subjects who had failed to meet the criterion earlier.

The results of this experiment were in many respects quite encouraging. In order to assess the usefulness of the probe responses as predictors of discrimination performance, we classified the 108 children into subgroups in terms of the trial block on which they had first named a value from the relevant dimension as their prediction about the solution. When the proportions of correct responses per trial block were then subjected to analysis of variance, with the seven subgroups as a between-subjects factor, we found that the main effects of subgroups, trial blocks, and their interactions jointly accounted for 62% of the total variability of the criterion measure. Moreover, we were able to utilize this system of classification to assign theoretical parameters to the various subgroups in such a way that the modified Hull–Spence theory was able to account for nearly two-thirds of all the variability in the distribution of proportions of correct responses for the entire experiment.

Although there were clear indications that the introtact responses were predictive of the choice behavior, there was also evidence of a problem that was to persist over several future experiments. About 30% of the children restricted their probe responses to the values of a single irrelevant dimension, with concomitant failure to learn the discrimination. Since another 30% restricted their probe responses, from the very first query, to the relevant dimension, only about 40% of the 108 children referred to more than one dimension in their introtact responses.

Methodological Problems with Introtact Probes. The experiment just described provided indirect evidence that introtact probes may interfere with the discrimination learning of kindergarten children. Our next experiment (Cantor & Spiker, 1977) gave direct evidence that the use of introtact probes immediately prior to a choice trial may interfere with kindergarten children's learning of a discrimination problem. The discrimination task had form and color as irrelevant dimensions and size as the relevant dimension. Since none of the children referred to the size dimension on the initial introtact probe, it can be assumed that all the children were required to learn with their preferred dimensions as irrelevant. Of the 28 kindergarten children who received a single probe, 19 learned the problem, whereas only 8 of the 28 children who received probes prior to each trial met criterion. Of the 28 children given probes on each trial, 21 responded to the probes only with the names of the values on one of the irrelevant dimensions, a behavior pattern that we called *dimensional fixation* and Kemler (1978), in a similar context, referred to as "attribute perseveration."

Considerations up to this point seem to indicate that neither introtact nor blank-trial probes are entirely appropriate for kindergarten children unless some appropriate modification of the procedures used with older children can be developed. Phillips's (1974) work with second-grade children, however, strongly suggests that the introtact probe may be the more promising for younger children.

SOME CONSIDERATIONS IN THE STUDY OF HYPOTHESIS TESTING IN KINDERGARTEN CHILDREN

Implications of the Early Research

Phillips and Levine (1975), on the basis of their research review, concluded that second-grade children differ from adults only quantitatively in their use of strategy systems. The research reviewed above seems to support another conclusion of Phillips and Levine: Kindergarten children are qualitatively inferior to second-graders in their use of strategies. There are several possible interpretations of this evidence. First, there is the possibility that most kindergarten children simply do not have the strategy systems in their repertoires. Perhaps the level of cognitive development necessary for the practice of the strategies is still a year or two away for most 5-year-old children. This view is consistent with the fact that only a few such children, perhaps the most intellectually advanced, seemed to have employed the strategy systems identified by Gholson et al. (1972). Alternatively, kindergarten children may possess the strategies, but the blank-trial probes interfere with their use even more seriously than Phillips found to be true for second-graders. In this case, modification of the probe procedures may permit these children to manifest their strategies.

Other interpretations fall between these two extremes. It may be that kindergarten children have the basic cognitive skills to test hypotheses systematically, but that they are deficient or lacking in some of the component skills. Eimas (1969) suggested that first- and second-grade children may have some memory deficiencies that prevent them from manifesting the cognitive skills that they truly possess, and he presented some evidence supporting this interpretation. Tighe and Tighe (e.g., 1966) have argued that children become more proficient with age, through perceptual experience, in abstracting stimulus dimensions from multidimensional objects. Systematic testing of hypotheses, at least with the strategy systems described by Gholson et al. (1972), would seem to require that the subjects be able to respond selectively to the various dimensions present in the discriminanda. It may be that kindergarten children have not yet abstracted out the dimensions characteristically employed in standard discrimination problems. In this case, the use of other types of discriminanda, as well as a search for other strategy systems, might be successful in exposing the strategies that kindergarten children actually possess.

There is another possible interpretation of the inferior showing of kindergarteners with respect to problem-solving strategies. The dimensional fixation, or attribute perseveration, that seems to occur with high frequency among kindergarten children may signify that while these children can analyze the stimuli into dimensions, they are unable to shift freely from dimension to dimension as required by the strategy systems most appropriate for the standard problems. If this interpretation is correct, then the underlying strategies may be exposed by the development of discrimination problems that do not require the children to shift from dimension to dimension.

Finally, the relatively poor performance of kindergarten children may simply be the result of their failure to understand the nature of the task. If the older child or adult conceptualized the discrimination problem as a guessing game in which the correct discriminandum was randomly designated on a trial-by-trial basis, it is quite likely that no systematic problem-solving strategies would be observed. If this interpretation is the correct one, then giving kindergarten children extended experience with such problems (i.e., learning-to-learn experience) should result in marked improvement in their strategies.

Pilot Research in the Authors' Laboratory

After a review of the literature through 1975, our initial judgment was that kindergarten children probably do not differ fundamentally from second-graders in their capacities for testing hypotheses. We were inclined to attribute their poorer performance to interference from the probes, and we hoped to develop some procedures in pilot research that would permit us to probe for hypotheses without disrupting the children's presumed hypothesis-testing strategies. Our first attempt to minimize the disruption of performance by probes involved the use of pretraining tasks in which we guided the children through a hypothesis-testing routine. We used a standard discrimination problem as the criterion task with unitary stimuli as the discriminanda: stimulus blocks that varied in color, size, and form, with one relevant and two irrelevant dimensions, all varying within settings. Approximately one-third of the children given such tasks responded to the initial introtact probe with the name of one of the values of the relevant dimension, subsequently learning the task very rapidly. In order to maximize the amount of information about strategies that we obtained from each child, we adopted the practice of making relevant one of the dimensions that the child did not mention on the first probe request. This procedure resulted in a task of surprising difficulty, whether or not the probes were employed (Cantor & Spiker, 1979). *A nonpreferred dimension was assigned as relevant in all of the experiments to be reported below, a procedure that should be kept in mind when our results are compared with those obtained when the relevant dimension was assigned at random.*

The Problem of Dimensional Fixation. For the first pretraining tasks, we constructed discrimination problems with attributes or dimensions different from those to be used in the criterion task. Thus, we mounted on one block either a straight or a wavy line, with an arrowhead on one end or not, and with either a vertical or a horizontal orientation. The other block had opposite values on the three attributes. During pretraining, the experimenter guided the child through a series of hypothesis-testing moves by verbal instruction, asking the child to test one of the values (e.g., straight), suggesting retesting following positive feedback, calling attention to each disconfirmation of a value, and suggesting a new value for testing until the correct feature had been identified and confirmed on several successive trials. For convenience, this procedure is referred to here as *guided hypothesis testing*.

We soon found that while most of the children could follow the experimenter's instructions with respect to hypothesis testing, the vast majority of them were unable to transfer the strategy into the next pretraining task, not even into one involving the same stimulus elements. Dimensional fixation characterized their performance on the criterion task; that is, they restricted their hypotheses to the names of values of an irrelevant dimension. We suspected at this point that the failure to transfer reflected the children's difficulty in analyzing or dissecting the stimulus patterns into their various dimensional components (i.e., into straight, vertical, pointed, or into wavy, horizontal, blunt).

Our next tactic was to construct simpler pretraining tasks with only two nonspatial dimensions. The discriminanda were distributed stimuli (Silleroy & Johnson, 1973), in that the values on each dimension were spatially separated. For convenience, such stimuli are referred to here as *partitioned stimuli*, and the dimensions are usually referred to as *partitioned dimensions*; the more conventional discriminanda are referred to as *unitary stimuli*, and their dimensions are called *unitary dimensions*. In the present case, each value of a dimension was placed on the stimulus block in a unique location. Thus, one block would have a straight line with a single round dot above it; another would have a straight line with two round dots above it; a third would have a wavy line with one dot; and a fourth, a wavy line with two dots. The partitioned dimensions considerably simplified the pretraining for the children, and a larger proportion of them seemed to grasp the hypothesis-testing strategy, transferring it to the next pretraining problem with considerable success. Unfortunately, we found transfer into the criterion task, with its three-dimensional unitary stimuli, to be still negligible. Even after eliminating one irrelevant dimension from the criterion task, transfer was negligible and dimensional fixation on the criterion task was the rule.

The improvement that we observed in pretraining, following the introduction of the partitioned stimuli, reinforced our belief that the children's problem was in decomposing the dimensions. Our next move was to construct a criterion task with partitioned dimensions, in the expectation that the children would be better able to transfer the hypothesis-testing strategy from the pretraining tasks to the criterion task. Thus, irregularly shaped patches differing in color, geometric outlines differing in form, and an alphabetic letter in two different sizes were mounted on the tops of black blocks of uniform size and shape to construct discrimination tasks. The children were required to name all the features on each block prior to each pretraining task and prior to the first trial of the criterion task. For each child, the relevant dimension continued to be one not named in the initial introtact response. The children were given the three pretraining tasks and were then transferred to the new criterion task with partitioned stimuli. Most of the subjects still manifested dimensional fixation, however, and discrimination performance on the new task was little better than before. We found that many of the dimensionally fixated children were unable to respond to our requests for the names of the other features, particularly during the later trials of the criterion task. It appeared that they had forgotten the names that they had used at the beginning of the criterion task.

The Use of Memory Aids. Although the vast majority of children were able to follow the hypothesis-testing instructions, and even to assimilate them to the extent that the instructions were transferred from an early pretraining task to a later one, the routine seemed to break down in their attempts to solve the criterion task with new stimuli. We conjectured that a more concrete method of pretraining might better consolidate the strategy, facilitating its transfer into the criterion task. We constructed a set of cards, on each of which was one of the features of the partitioned discriminanda for the pretraining and criterion tasks. Forty-eight kindergarten children were given pretraining with the cards, during which they were taught to test the cards one by one. The children were trained to select a card from the stack, place it in full view on the apparatus, and choose from the first pair of blocks the one that had that feature on its top. They continued to select the block with that feature on succeeding trials unless its correctness was discon- firmed by a failure to find a marble inside the block. They would then remove the card, select another, and continue the process until the correct feature had been identified. Most of the children successfully transferred the technique into the second pretraining task, and by the third pretraining task, all of the children were able to use the procedure flawlessly. One-half of the children were given introtact probes prior to each trial in both the pretraining and the criterion tasks; the other half were queried only once prior to each task in order to determine the dimen- sional preference. One-half of each of these two groups were provided with cards for the criterion task, and the other half were not given cards.

The children who received cards during the criterion task performed nearly perfectly, transferring their newly acquired skills with very few errors. Of the 24 children who used cards, 22 learned the criterion task within the 40 trials allotted. Of the 24 children who did not have cards, only 6 met criterion. The children with cards appeared to be performing a mechanical task, which they seemed to enjoy thoroughly, but there was no apparent grasp of the hypothesis- testing strategy that the pretraining was intended to inculcate. Judging from the children who received introtacts without cards, the fate of most children without cards was the ubiquitous dimensional fixation. Since there were no differences at all between those who received probes and those who did not, it seems likely that the unprobed children also became dimensionally fixated.

The failure to find a difference in the performance of children who received probes and those who did not deserves comment in the light of the earlier experiment in which such differences were obtained for kindergarten children (Cantor & Spiker, 1977). The comment, however, will be delayed until the discussion of another experiment, in which, again, no differences between probe conditions were found (Cantor & Spiker, 1979).

Parrill-Burnstein (1978) provided one of her four groups of kindergarten children (Group 4) with training and memory aids that were quite comparable to those received by the children who had cards during the criterion task of the preceding experiment. She found that these children, like ours, performed nearly perfectly on the criterion task. She did not remove the aids, however, to see if the children could have performed without them; our results would suggest, unfortunately, that her children would have failed to transfer their strategy into the criterion task without the use of memory aids.

Estimates of Dimensional Fixation in Kindergarten Children

At this point in our pilot work on hypothesis testing, we had tested about 350 kindergarten children with different types of stimuli, with several different criterion tasks, and after having administered several different pretraining programs. The dimensional perseveration problem seemed to be inordinately robust for kindergarten children. After finding that the probed and unprobed children performed at about the same level in the preceding experiment, we began to entertain the hypothesis that relatively few kindergarten children ever change to another dimension from the dimension that they initially attend to. Since we were consistently assigning the preferred dimension as irrelevant, few of our subjects would therefore be expected learn. We noted that in experiments with intra- and extradimensional shifts, where the acquisition of an initial task was required, it was a common practice to give special training to children who had failed to learn after a prescribed number of trials (e.g., Shepp & Gray, 1971). The special training consisted of separating the positive and negative discriminanda and informing the child of which set was correct and which incorrect. Thus, the child could see that all the correct ones were, say, square and all the incorrect ones were round. Such a demonstration would seem to be an effective way of shifting the child's attention from an irrelevant dimension to the relevant one. The special training, incidentally, was found to produce transfer behavior entirely comparable to that obtained from subjects who learned without such help.

We attempted to check this hypothesis against some of our extant data by the following reasoning. Suppose that we have a discrimination problem constructed from the orthogonal arrangement of three bivalued dimensions (e.g., color, form, and size). Suppose further that one-third of a group of kindergarteners are randomly assigned to a color-relevant problem, one-third to a form-relevant problem, and one-third to a size-relevant problem. Let p_c, p_f, and p_s be the proportions of children who initially attend to the color, form, and size dimensions, where the p_i sum to unity. Now assume that the *attention principle* is true—that an initial attendance to the relevant dimension guarantees solution. Since the children were assigned their relevant dimension at random, one-third of the entire group would learn their tasks without ever having to shift attention from the original dimension, although the proportion who learned might vary among the three different groups because of the differential salience of the relevant dimensions.

From our files, we selected only those experiments in which the criterion task had three dimensions and in which the children began the task naive to discrimination problems. There were four independent experiments that met this criterion, with a total of 240 kindergarten children, of whom 123 met a learning criterion. The attention principle predicts that one-third (80) of the children would learn without shifting from the original dimension, leaving only 43 children (123 minus 80) of 160, or 26.9%, whose learning would require a shift of attention. Analogously, on a two-dimensional problem, with the relevant dimension assigned at random, half the children could learn without shifting dimensions. Two experiments contributed 108 kindergarten subjects, 71 of whom learned. The attention principle predicts that 54 of them would learn, leaving 17 of 54, or 31.5%, whose learning would have required shifting dimensions. Thus, these data provide an estimate that about 30% of the kindergarten children shifted dimensions.

Still further evidence was adduced for the proposition that few kindergarten children shift attention from the first dimension attended. In several of our experiments, children were given verbal pretraining in which they were required to name multidimensional stimuli with the values (e.g., "large," "small") of a dimension that was to be irrelevant in a subsequent discrimination problem. If it is assumed that such pretraining causes the children to attend to an irrelevant dimension on the subsequent task, then the proportion of children who learn in such groups provides a direct estimate of the proportion who shift dimensions. Our files contained the protocols of 520 kindergarten children who had received such pretraining, of whom 156, or 30.0%, learned the subsequent discrimination problem.

These estimates of the proportion of kindergarten children who fail to shift dimensions are consistent with those that can be estimated from experiments conducted by other investigators. For example, Shepp and Gray (1971) reported that 37 of 112 kindergarten children required special training to learn a two-dimensional task. Since 56 of the 75 children who learned without help would have been expected to learn by the attention principle, there were only 19 of the remaining 56 (.34) whose learning would have required a shift of dimensions.

Our realization that perhaps only a third of kindergarten children shift dimensions while attempting to solve discrimination problems led to another major tactical change. We conjectured that the difficulty the children were having with our procedures and tasks in the pilot work might not reflect a deficiency in either hypothesis-testing strategy or memory. Rather, the problem might arise from the difficulty they had in shifting dimensional attention. If a discrimination problem could be developed in which the shifting of dimensions was somehow facilitated, or in which the need to shift dimensions were minimized, kindergarten children might be able to manifest strategies more readily.

DEMONSTRATIONS OF COGNITIVE STRATEGIES IN YOUNGER CHILDREN

The Use of the "Story-and-Game" Context

An experiment by Kemler *et al.* (1976), in which kindergarten children served as subjects (Experiment 2), suggested that it might be possible to devise a task in which the shifting of dimensions was made easier. The discriminanda for their task consisted of identical pictures of two young girls with detachable articles of clothing and apparel, and the nature of the task was presented in the context of a story. The children were informed that the pictures were of identical twins, Amy and Betty, who could not be distinguished except by their clothing. They were told that the twins' teacher provided each of them with a distinctive set of articles of clothing (e.g., hats, belts, and hair ribbons), which they were to wear to facilitate their identification by others. The twins, however, played tricks on the other children by interchanging some of the articles of clothing. Each morning the twins would inform their teacher of which item would constitute their secret identifier for that day. The subjects were required to identify Amy on each trial in a series in which the irrelevant attributes were varied orthogonally to the relevant attribute. (It should be noted that these attributes are partitioned, or distributed, in the sense previously defined). After each choice, the experimenter identified Amy by placing an *A* on the appropriate picture. Immediately after the feedback, with the two pictures before them and with Amy's picture marked with *A*, the children were asked what they thought was the secret item that identified Amy.

The results for the kindergarten children were most remarkable. They met a rigorous performance criterion on a four-dimensional task with a mean trial of last error of 10.0. The local-consistency and lose-shift indexes were both near unity. Unfortunately, the win-stay index averaged only about .45, and the hypothesis predicted the next choice only about 60% of the time.

These results are perhaps more explicable when the point at which the probe was administered is taken into consideration. When the children were queried, both pictures were directly before them, the values of the various attributes were in place, and the correct (Amy) picture was clearly labeled. In order to choose one of Amy's present features for the next hypothesis, the subject needs to know

only which of the two pictures is Amy and which features constitute the population to be considered. The first piece of information is given by the A on Amy's
picture, and the second is provided by the conjunction of the picture and the
pretraining. Together, they virtually guarantee a choice that conforms with both
the local-consistency and lose-shift rules. The relatively low predictive value of
the hypothesis for the next choice (i.e., the response-consistency index) is
probably a consequence of giving the probe after feedback on Trial n rather than
in the usual position immediately before choice on Trial $n + 1$ (e.g., Karpf &
Levine, 1971; Phillips & Levine, 1975). With respect to the low win-stay index,
the child would have to remember which hypothesis was given on the preceding
trial in order to do better than chance in selecting the same hypothesis from
among Amy's current features. The relatively rapid solution of the problem
appears to result from the combination of an unusually effective set of training
procedures and the use of partitioned stimuli, an interpretation that will be
discussed in more detail below.

The Use of Pretraining and Unidimensional Tasks

The Kemler *et al.* (1976) procedures were subsequently to be much improved (Kemler, 1978), but our initial concern with the low response-consistency
index led us in another direction: an attempt to minimize the need to shift
dimensions. We began the construction of a new type of discrimination problem
by choosing a single dimension (e.g., color) and then selecting four values from
it (e.g., red, green, blue, and yellow). These four colors were arranged to form
two artificial bivalued dimensions (pseudodimensions) of the partitioned type.
Pairs of color patches were pasted on each of four black blocks of uniform size
and shape in such a way that red and green never appeared on the same block and
blue and yellow never appeared together. Red and green always appeared on one
side of the blocks (e.g., left) and blue and yellow always appeared on the other
side. The two pseudodimensions (red–green and blue–yellow) were thus
orthogonally arranged to form two different settings of a discrimination problem
that, together with their lateral reversals, produced a four-setting simultaneous-
discrimination problem with one dimension relevant and a second dimension
irrelevant and varying within settings.

A parallel task was constructed with geometric forms. Squares, circles,
triangles, and crosses were used to construct pseudodimensions (e.g., cross–
square and circle–triangle) with the same properties and relations as those
described for colors.

Our expectation for such a task was that kindergarten children would find it
easier to shift among the pseudodimensional hypotheses, which would refer to
the values of a single dimension (color or form), than to shift among hypotheses
that referred to values from two or more genuine dimensions. Further pilot work

with the new tasks was encouraging, and we began a formal experiment, which, for convenience, is referred to here as Experiment 1 (Cantor & Spiker, 1978).

Since the design used in this experiment is common to several studies to be reported in this chapter, it is described in considerable detail. One group (CON) was given the criterion task without any prior training. At the beginning of the task, however, all four blocks were shown to the child; each of the four features (colors or shapes) was identified by the experimenter through pointing and naming, and the child was required to repeat the names as the experimenter pointed to each feature in turn. The child was then informed that one of the features was special and could be used to identify which block would have the marble in it. The experimenter again repeated the names of all four features. The child was asked to predict which feature would indicate the marble each time, and the experimenter assigned as relevant that pseudodimension to which the child did not refer in the introtact response. A probe was given prior to each trial.

A second group (LTL) was given learning-to-learn training prior to the criterion task. With the same blocks to be used in the criterion task, the experimenter presented three problems in succession, introducing the first in the same way as for Group CON. Introtact probes were given prior to each trial in both pretraining and criterion tasks, with the initial response providing the basis for assigning the relevant pseudodimension. If the child had not solved the pretraining problem by the 10th trial, he or she was told the solution and was given an additional 6 trials to confirm it. The criterion task was presented immediately after completion of the third pretraining task, and the experimenter informed the child that the child would have to solve it by himself or herself.

The third group (HYP) was also given three pretraining tasks. During the first task, the experimenter gave guided training in what we have called *sequential hypothesis testing*. This strategy requires the consistent use of three component rules. The first rule requires that a hypothesis be maintained following positive feedback (the win-stay rule); the second requires that a new hypothesis be chosen following negative feedback (the lose-shift rule); and the third requires that the current hypothesis be one that has not been previously *explicitly* tested and disconfirmed (the valid-hypothesis rule). The experimenter designated the first feature to be tested and guided the child through a predetermined series of 12 trials in the following way. The first hypothesis tested was one of the values on the irrelevant dimension and was confirmed once before being disconfirmed; the second hypothesis was the other value on the irrelevant dimension and was confirmed twice before being disconfirmed; the third hypothesis was the negative cue and was immediately disconfirmed; and the final hypothesis was the positive cue, which was confirmed six times before the task ended. Throughout the task, the experimenter administered win-stay and lose-shift instructions whenever appropriate. An introtact probe was given for each trial by asking the child which feature was being tested. The second task was then administered, and the child was instructed to solve it in the same way as she or he had solved the first task. An introtact probe was given prior to each trial, which the first providing information for assigning the relevant pseudodimension. During the second and third task, the child attempted to solve the problems using the sequential hypothesis-testing strategy and was prompted by the experimenter to prevent errors in the use of the three rules. The criterion task was presented immediately after the third pretraining task, and the experimenter informed the child that the child had to solve it by himself or herself.

Then, 24 kindergarten and 16 first-grade children were randomly assigned to each of the three groups. Half the subjects in each group were trained on tasks constructed from colors, and the other half were trained on tasks constructed from forms. Training on the criterion task continued until 40 trials had been given, unless (a) the child gave seven consecutive correct choices with concomitant correct hypotheses within one block of eight trials, or (b) the child gave seven correct choices followed by eight correct choices in successive blocks of eight trials.

Analysis of the data revealed several interesting results. Since no statistically significant differences were found between the kindergarten and first-grade children with respect to any of the response measures to be reported, the data for the two age groups have been combined. For the three pretraining groups, the results are summarized in the first three rows of Table 1 for each of several dependent variables. The three groups may be compared first with respect to their performance on the discrimination task. (Throughout this chapter, a statistic is reported as significant only if the obtained probability was less than .05.) The main effect of pretraining was significant for the trial of last error (TLE), with Group HYP reliably superior to Group LTL, and with the latter reliably superior to Group CON. The fourth column of Table 1 shows the percentage of children who reached criterion in each group, with each of the three possible comparisons statistically significant. It is clear that the pretraining had a marked effect on discrimination performance, with explicit training in sequential hypothesis testing producing the best performance.

The main reason for the use of the unidimensional tasks with pseudodimensions was to reduce the incidence of dimensional fixation, and our qualitative observations suggested that we had been reasonably successful. To provide an objective index, a child was said to be dimensionally fixated if his or her introtact responses during the last half of the criterion-task trials referred only to the irrelevant cues. The percentages of children who were fixated, according to this definition, are shown for each group in the fifth column of Table 1. Although 40% of the Group CON children were fixated on the irrelevant pseudodimension, this percentage represented a substantial reduction relative to the percentages obtained in our pilot work with genuine dimensions. Moreover, the incidences in Groups LTL and HYP were both significantly below that in Group CON.

TABLE 1
Group Means for Discrimination Performance, Indexes of Strategy, and Strategy Errors for Experiments 1, 2, 3, and 4

	N	Grade	TLE (40 Max.)	Pct. crit.	Pct. fix.	Win-stay	Lose-shift	Valid-hyp.	% zero st. err.	% < 4 st. err.
Exp. 1 (2 P-Dim.)[a]										
Group CON	40	K,1	34.2	20	40	.30	.73	.32	0	5
Group LTL	40	K,1	17.3	65	20	.63	.77	.64	30	48
Group HYP	40	K,1	8.8	88	8	.89	.89	.84	58	82
Exp. 2 (2 P-Dim.)[a]										
Group CON	16	1	36.6	13	31	.24	.78	.31	0	0
Group LTL	16	1	9.9	81	25	.70	.84	.70	44	56
Group HYP	16	1	9.8	81	25	.87	.90	.75	44	81
Exp. 3 (2 Dim.)[a]										
Group CON	16	1	25.6	44	63	.28	.69	.32	0	6
Group LTL	16	1	20.3	63	58	.40	.66	.22	0	0
Group HYP	16	1	21.1	50	44	.60	.80	.51	25	44
Exp. 4 (3 Dim.)[a]										
Group CON	24	2,3	29.4	33	54	.36	.74	.35	4	4
Group LTL	24	2,3	11.8	88	13	.68	.87	.72	29	54
Group HYP	24	2,3	12.3	83	8	.95	.94	.78	46	71

[a]Number of pseudodimensions (P-Dim.) or genuine dimensions (Dim.) in the criterion task.

To assess the effectiveness of training on the various components of sequential hypothesis testing given to Group HYP, three conditional probabilities were computed for each subject in each group. To assess the child's adherence to the win-stay rule, we computed the precriterion probability that on Trial $n + 1$, the subject's hypothesis would be the same as that on Trial n, if the intervening feedback was positive. Adherence to the lose-shift rule was assessed by computing the probability that on Trial $n + 1$, the subject's hypothesis would be different from that on Trial n, if the intervening feedback was negative. Adherence to the valid-hypothesis rule was assessed by computing the probability that the hypothesis proposed by the child on Trial $n + 1$, if it differed from the one given on Trial n, was *not* one that had been explicitly proposed and disconfirmed by negative feedback on any previous trial.

The means of these three conditional probabilities are shown for each group in Columns 6–8 of Table 1. A multivariate analysis of variance (MANOVA) performed on the three indexes showed that the three groups differed significantly, and follow-up univariate tests indicated that Group HYP was superior to Groups LTL and CON with respect to all three measures, and that Group LTL was superior to Group CON on both the win-stay and the valid-hypothesis measures.

The utility (validity) of the indexes is in part confirmed by the clear-cut superiority of Group HYP (which was explicitly taught to use these three components of the strategy) with respect to all three indexes. The utility of these measures for kindergarten children is also indicated by the fact that the children's hypotheses predicted the choice on nearly every occasion; that is, the mean response-consistency index was nearly unity in each group. Moreover, if the children's stated hypotheses were truly reflecting an underlying strategy, rather than merely designating the child's next choice, then the indexes computed from the hypotheses should predict the general level of discrimination performance. The multiple correlations for Groups CON, LTL, and HYP between TLE as the dependent measure and the three indexes as independent measures were .83, .91, and .94, respectively. The multiple correlation for the three groups combined was .92. The appropriateness of the hypotheses obtained from the introtact probes for the study of kindergarteners' strategies seems well established.

The values of all three conditional probabilities would be unity for any child who followed the three component rules perfectly. Column 9 of Table 1 shows the percentage of children in each group who made no errors in applying the sequential hypothesis-testing strategy, with all three possible comparisons statistically significant. Column 10 of Table 1 gives the percentage of children in each group who made no more than three strategic errors (i.e., errors on any of the three component rules), with all possible comparisons again statistically reliable. The latter measure was devised to give the kindergarten child an occasional strategic error without denying her or him the status of a genuine user of the strategy.

It will be recalled that Group LTL received no instructions that were not also provided Group CON. The two groups differed only in that Group LTL was given an opportunity to solve three tasks similar to the criterion task, and if an LTL child did not solve a task, he or she was told the solution and given an additional six trials to confirm the correctness of the information. The differences between Groups CON and LTL, therefore, may be attributed to the standard positive transfer that has been called *learning to learn* (e.g., Reese, 1963). A detailed comparison of the hypothesis-testing behavior of the two groups provides an opportunity to throw some light on the source of that positive transfer. Examination of Table 1 indicates that the learning-to-learn training resulted in a lower incidence of dimensional fixation, coupled with a higher proportion of valid hypotheses. These related effects probably represent an improved ability of the LTL children to shift attention from the initially attended-to irrelevant dimension to the relevant one. The LTL children also learned to use the win-stay rule more effectively, and this learning may reflect a more general grasp of the solubility of the discrimination problems. The comparability of Groups CON and LTL with respect to the lose-shift index should not be taken too seriously. Subjects who guess which block is correct on a trial-to-trial basis would be expected to have a high lose-shift and a low win-stay index, a pattern that characterized many Group CON subjects.

Our success in teaching the sequential hypothesis-testing strategy to the kindergarten and first-grade children is evidenced by the statistically significant superiority of Group HYP with respect to Group LTL on each of the three indexes of the strategy. Moreover, the percentage of HYP children who used the strategy, either perfectly or with minimal errors, was significantly greater than was that of Group LTL. It is not too surprising, therefore, that Group HYP was also found to perform better than Group LTL on the discrimination problem.

Some Extensions and Limitations of the Methodology

Our next three experiments were conducted to explore the generality of the methodology we had developed. In Experiment 1, the children given pretraining received tasks that were identical to the criterion task except for the specific stimulus value that was designated as correct. Much of the superiority in the performance of Groups LTL and HYP, relative to Group CON, may have resulted from the similarity of their pretraining and criterion tasks.

Interdimensional Transfer in First-Grade Children. In Experiment 2, if the children were pretrained on tasks constructed from forms, they were tested on a criterion task constructed from color; if they were pretrained with color stimuli, they were tested with form stimuli. Sixteen first-grade children were randomly assigned to each of the three groups: CON, LTL, and HYP. Except for the shift from color tasks to a form task, or from form tasks to a color task, the conditions for the three groups were the same as for those in Experiment 1.

The major results of Experiment 2 are shown in Rows 4–6 of Table 1, where they may be conveniently compared with the results from Experiment 1. Although the differences among the three groups were significant for both TLE and the percentage of children meeting criterion, it is clear that these measures did not differ significantly for Groups HYP and LTL. The three groups did not differ significantly with respect to the incidence of dimensional fixation, although the percentage for Group HYP was considerably higher than for the same condition in Experiment 1.

The three indexes of strategy were analyzed with MANOVA, and a significant difference among the three pretraining groups was obtained. Follow-up univariate tests indicated that the three groups differed on both the win-stay and the valid-hypothesis measures, with Groups LTL and HYP superior to Group CON on both indexes, and Group HYP superior to Group LTL only on the win-stay index. Groups LTL and HYP, relative to Group CON, each had significantly more children who made no errors in using the sequential hypothesis-testing strategy. The same comparisons were significant for the percentages of children who made fewer than four strategic errors, although the differences between Group CON and Groups LTL and HYP were somewhat larger.

As in Experiment 1, the children's hypothesis predicted the next choice on nearly every occasion; the response consistency was virtually perfect. The multiple correlations for Groups CON, LTL, and HYP between TLE as the dependent measure and the three indexes as independent measures were .57, .69, and .95, respectively. The multiple correlation for the three groups combined was .86. Although the correlations for Groups LTL and CON were substantially below those obtained for these groups in Experiment 1, the indexes were still able to account for nearly three-fourths of the variance of the TLE for the three groups combined.

Experiment 2 thus demonstrates that the strategies developed in pretraining on a task constructed from one stimulus dimension (e.g., color) transfer to similar tasks constructed from another dimension (e.g., form). Although most aspects of Experiment 1 were replicated in Experiment 2, there was no significant difference between Groups LTL and HYP with respect to their discrimination performance, and they differed only with respect to the win-stay rule in their use of the rules of strategy. As will be seen from data to be presented below, a significant LTL–HYP difference has not always been obtained for first-grade and older children, presumably because many of them are capable of extracting the rules for sequentially testing hypotheses from learning-to-learn experiences.

The Transfer of Unidimensional Solutions to Two-Dimensional Tasks. Experiment 3 was conducted to determine whether first-grade children can transfer the sequential hypothesis-testing strategy from pretraining with tasks constructed from a single dimension to tasks in which two genuine stimulus dimensions are varying. In this experiment, we constructed a criterion task from the attributes that we had previously used in the unidimensional tasks. Thus, each of the four blocks had a color patch and a form outline, and the colors and forms were arranged orthogonally to form a simultaneous discrimination problem with one relevant and one irrelevant dimension. We again used three conditions, Group CON to provide a baseline, the learning-to-learn group (LTL), and a group given hypothesis-testing pretraining (HYP). Groups LTL and HYP were given three pretraining tasks, using the unidimensional tasks from Experiments 1 and 2, with half of each group being pretrained on a task constructed from colors and the other half on a task constructed from forms. Introtact probes, given prior to the first trial of each pretraining task and the criterion task, made possible the assignment of the child's nonpreferred dimension as the relevant one. Forty-eight first-grade children were randomly assigned in equal numbers to each group.

The results of Experiment 3 are shown in Rows 7–9 of Table 1. For the TLE, there were no reliable differences among the three pretraining groups. Moreover, the percentage of children meeting criterion did not differ significantly among the three groups. The incidence of dimensional fixation was about the same in all three groups, and, it should be noted, the incidence was considerably higher than in either of the two previous experiments. On the basis of these indexes alone, we would have to conclude that the pretraining given Groups LTL and HYP, with tasks constructed from a single stimulus dimension, failed to transfer to the criterion task, with its two genuine dimensions.

A MANOVA was conducted on the three indexes of strategy, and the main effect of pretraining the groups was found to be significant. Univariate follow-up tests showed only the win-stay index to be statistically significant, with Group HYP superior to the other two. The numbers of children who used rules of strategy without error were too few to warrant statistical analysis, but it should be noted that all four of these children were in Group HYP. Similarly, seven of the eight children who made fewer than four strategic errors were in Group HYP. Once again, there is minimal evidence that the strategy taught the HYP children, or that which the LTL subjects may have acquired on their own, transferred into the criterion task.

Response consistency for all three groups was virtually errorless, indicating that the children chose the stimulus indicated by their introtact response almost without exception. The multiple correlations between TLE as the dependent variable and the indexes of strategy as the independent variables were reasonably high, with correlations for Groups CON, LTL, and HYP of .84, .47, and .96, respectively.

The results of Experiment 3, at least at first glance, do not seem to be entirely consistent. On the other hand, the pretraining did not manifest itself in either TLE or in the percentage of children who met criterion in the critical task. On the other hand, there is some evidence that the pretraining improved the HYP children's strategies, and the indexes of strategy were highly correlated with TLE, particularly for Group HYP. A closer look at performance on the criterion task for individual children suggests a resolution for the apparent inconsistencies.

There were 8 of 16 children in Group HYP, 10 of 16 in Group LTL, and 7 of 16 children in Group CON who met criterion. The average TLE for the HYP children who met criterion was 3.1, whereas those meeting criterion in Groups LTL and CON averaged 9.7 and 9.6, respectively. The pretraining for neither Group LTL nor Group HYP was very successful in reducing the incidence of dimensional fixation in the task with two genuine dimensions. The HYP pretraining markedly improved the efficiency of those children who did not become fixated, and who were therefore probably destined to learn.

Although some of the first-grade children of Experiment 3 were able to transfer their pretraining strategies into a standard discrimination problem with two genuine dimensions, nearly half of those who had pretraining failed to do so. The incidence of dimensional fixation was quite high, and an examination of individual protocols suggests that dimensional fixation leads to two different behavior patterns. For one group, the fixation seems to inhibit the use of any successful strategy by leading the subjects into guessing on a trial-by-trial basis. It is possible, of course, that the causal sequence is in the reverse direction: that the guessing strategy leads the subject into a dimensional perseveration. The behavior of the second group of children argues against this latter interpretation, however. These children learn the problem but continue to tell the experimenter what their next choice will be, using the names of values on the irrelevant dimension. Phillips and Levine (1975) have called such children "describers."

Because so many of the first-grade children in Experiment 3 had become fixated on one of the genuine dimensions in the criterion task, we decided that pretraining with genuine dimensions might be necessary to prevent the development of fixation. In Experiment 4, pretraining on unidimensional tasks was supplemented by pretraining on a discrimination problem with two genuine, partitioned dimensions. The children given pretraining were then shifted to a criterion task with three genuine, partitioned dimensions. Once again, three groups (CON, LTL, and HYP) were constituted. Each subject in Groups LTL and HYP received pretraining on a unidimensional task constructed from forms, a unidimensional task constructed from colors, and a two-dimensional discrimination task constructed from forms and colors. The partitioned dimensions of the criterion task were form, color, and size of an arrowhead, with the latter irrelevant for all subjects.

Earlier pilot research had indicated that a discrimination task with three partitioned stimuli is quite difficult for kindergarten and first-grade children, particularly when the preferred dimension is made irrelevant. Children somewhat older were therefore chosen as subjects on the assumption that considerable dimensional fixation would still be present among those without pretraining and that the pretraining would minimize dimensional fixation in Groups LTL and HYP. From the available pool of subjects, 8 second-grade and 16 third-grade children were randomly assigned to the three groups.

None of the analyses conducted showed a significant grade effect, so the second- and third-grade data have been combined in this report. The major results of Experiment 4 are shown in the last three rows of Table 1. Groups LTL and HYP were significantly superior to Group CON with respect to TLE, although they did not differ from each other. A significantly greater number of subjects in Groups LTL and HYP met criterion than in Group CON, although again the two groups did not differ from each other. More than half the Group CON subjects were dimensionally fixated, whereas significantly fewer were fixated in both Groups LTL and HYP. Thus, in terms of general discrimination performance, Groups LTL and HYP were significantly better than Group CON, although the two pretraining groups did not differ from each other.

A MANOVA conducted for the three indexes of strategy yielded a significant effect for pretraining groups. Univariate follow-up analyses showed that the group effect was significant for all three indexes and that Groups LTL and HYP were superior to Group CON with respect to all three indexes. Group HYP was significantly better than Group LTL only with respect to the win-stay index. The numbers of children solving without strategic errors in Groups LTL and HYP were both significantly greater than that for Group CON, as was also the case for the numbers solving with three or fewer strategic errors. Groups LTL and HYP, however, did not differ significantly from each other with respect to either measure. Here, then, is firm evidence that the pretraining transferred to the criterion task with its three genuine, partitioned dimensions, although there is only weak evidence that it did so differentially for the two types of pretraining.

The response consistency indexes for all three groups in Experiment 4 were virtually perfect. The multiple correlation between TLE as the dependent variable and the three conditional probabilities as independent measures were .88, .94, and .97 for Groups CON, LTL, and HYP, respectively. The correlation for the three groups combined was .94. Clearly, the win-stay, lose-shift, and valid-hypothesis indexes predict the discrimination performance of the children with an impressive degree of accuracy.

It is evident from the performance of the children in Group CON that the dimensional fixation problem is quite serious, even for children up to age 10 years, when the preferred dimension is made irrelevant. Pretraining on a discrimination problem with genuine dimensions, however, greatly reduced the incidence of fixation for the subjects in Groups LTL and HYP. These results offer hope that the fixation problem may also be ameliorated for kindergarten children by appropriate pretraining.

SOME FACTORS AFFECTING THE SOLUTION OF DISCRIMINATION PROBLEMS

It is clear from the results of Experiments 1 and 2 that many kindergarten and first-grade children are capable of using one of the simpler problem-solving strategies. It is also clear that the incidence with which they manifest such strategies can be affected by the kinds of pretraining provided them. It is not yet clear, however, exactly which aspects of the children's problem-solving process have been affected by the LTL and HYP pretraining. In both conditions, the children received pretraining in which they had practice in responding to introtact probes. Given the earlier evidence that introtact probes interfere with discrimination learning (Cantor & Spiker, 1977; Spiker & Cantor, 1977), on one hand, it is conceivable that the "facilitation" of Groups LTL and HYP, relative to Group CON, was the result of a decrease in dimensional fixation or other interference induced by the probes. On the other hand, in our earlier experiment with memory aids, we failed to find a difference in performance between children who were and who were not given probes.

The Interaction of Age and Probe

Experiment 5 (Cantor & Spiker, 1979), had two major purposes. First, it was an attempt to extend downward to the kindergarten level the pretraining procedures of Experiment 4, which had been successful in getting second- and third-grade children to transfer their problem-solving strategies to a problem with genuine dimensions. Second, the experiment was designed to determine whether the introtact probes interfere with the discrimination performance of kindergarten and first-grade children. The three basic conditions, CON, LTL, and HYP, were factorially combined with the presence or absence of introtact probes during performance on the criterion task. In Experiment 5, 26 kindergarten and 24 first-grade children were assigned to each of these six combinations of pretraining and probe conditions. The first pretraining task for the LTL and HYP groups was a unidimensional discrimination task constructed from four colors; the second pretraining task was constructed from four forms; and the third pretraining task had two genuine dimensions, color and form. In each task, the dimensions were partitioned rather than unitary. The LTL and HYP groups were required to respond to introtact probes during all three pretraining tasks. During the criterion task, which also had color and form as genuine dimensions, only subjects in the introtact condition were required to respond to probes. Subjects in the no-introtact condition were required to respond to a probe prior to the first trial of the criterion task so that their preferred dimension could be determined. They were then informed that they need not respond overtly any longer.

The primary results of Experiment 5 are shown in Table 2, where the measures are shown separately for the kindergarten and first-grade children. The TLE means for the introtact groups are in the first column (I) and for the no-introtact groups, in the second column (NI). Since there was a statistically significant triple interaction among type of pretraining, grade, and presence or absence of introtact probes, separate analyses were conducted for the two grade

TABLE 2

Group Means for Discrimination Performance, Indexes of Strategy, and Strategy Errors for Experiment 5[a]

	TLE (40 Maximum)		Percentage criterion		Pct. fix.	Win-stay	Lose-shift	Valid-hyp.	% zero st. err.	% < 4 st. err.
	I	NI	I	NI						
Kindergarten[b]										
Group CON	28.8	31.0	31	35	62	.34	.73	.26	4	15
Group LTL	24.0	23.7	50	46	38	.72	.68	.43	23	38
Group HYP	21.4	20.2	54	54	46	.83	.69	.54	23	38
First grade[b]										
Group CON	29.8	24.2	33	50	46	.40	.76	.32	8	12
Group LTL	12.0	21.1	79	58	17	.83	.86	.68	46	58
Group HYP	8.7	21.9	92	50	0	.94	.85	.82	50	75

[a] All children received a criterion task with two genuine dimensions.
[b] There were 26 kindergarten children and 24 first-graders assigned to each of the six combinations of pretraining and probe conditions.

levels. For the kindergarten children, only the effect of pretraining groups was significant, with Group CON inferior to Groups LTL and HYP and the latter not differing from each other. For the first-grade children, there was a significant interaction between pretraining groups and the presence or absence of introtacts. A follow-up analysis indicated that there was no significant pretraining effect for the children who did not receive introtact probes, whereas the pretraining effect was significant for those who received probes, with Groups LTL and HYP superior to Group CON and not differing significantly from each other.

The percentages of children meeting criterion in the various groups are shown in Columns 3 and 4 of Table 2. The results on this measure were almost completely parallel to those on TLE. Groups LTL and HYP were superior to Group CON at both grade levels, but they did not differ reliably from each other. There was the same general equality of performance between the kindergarten introtact and no-introtact groups, coupled with the facilitating effect of the introtact probes on the first-grade LTL and HYP groups. The inherent difficulty of the task for kindergarten children is apparent in the fact that only slightly more than half of the HYP groups met criterion and only about a third of the CON children did so.

The incidence of dimensional fixation was significantly higher among the kindergarten children who received introtact probes than it was among their first-grade counterparts. Since the fixation condition is defined in terms of patterns of introtact responses, the amount of fixation among children who were not probed cannot be determined. There was significantly more dimensional perseveration in the CON groups at both grade levels than among the LTL and HYP groups. A comparison of the first-grade introtact groups from the present experiment with comparable children in Experiment 3 (see Table 1) provides some assessment of the effectiveness of pretraining on tasks with genuine dimensions in reducing dimensional fixation. Since the stimulus materials and procedures for the two experiments were entirely comparable, except for the use of the pretraining task with two genuine dimensions in Experiment 5, it seems reasonable to attribute the smaller incidence of fixation in Experiment 5 to the difference in type of pretraining.

It is quite clear from the TLE measure and from the numbers of subjects meeting criterion that the use of introtact probes did not interfere with the problem solving of either the kindergarten or the first-grade children. The superior performance of the LTL and HYP groups, relative to the CON groups, represents genuinely improved problem-solving rather than a reduction in the amount of interference produced by the probe procedures. The results of this experiment are in agreement, therefore, with the experiment in which memory aids were provided. The interference observed in the experiment reported earlier (Cantor & Spiker, 1977), however, requires some explanation. There are several methodological differences between the two experiments. For example, there was only one irrelevant nonspatial dimension in the present experiment, whereas there were two in the earlier study. Probably a more important difference, however, is that the stimulus dimensions in the earlier study were unitary, whereas those in the present study were partitioned. The assignment of a nonpreferred dimension as relevant requires the children to shift from the initially attended dimension to another one. The introtact probes may interfere more with the independent processing of unitary stimuli than with the processing of partitioned ones.

A MANOVA was conducted on the three indexes of strategy, with pretraining groups and grade level as between-subjects factors. The main effects of pretraining and grade were both statistically significant. Univariate follow-up tests indicated that the first-grade children were significantly better than the kindergarten subjects on all three indexes. Univariate tests also showed the main effect of pretraining to be significant for both the win-stay and the valid-hypothesis indexes, with Group HYP superior to Group LTL, and with Group LTL superior to Group CON. Groups LTL and HYP had a significantly greater incidence of errorless strategy than Group CON, as was also the case for the numbers of children solving with fewer than four strategic errors. Groups LTL and HYP did not differ significantly with respect to either measure.

Response consistency was virtually perfect in all six groups. The multiple correlations between TLE and the three indexes ranged from .87 for the first-grade CON group to .98 for the kindergarten LTL subjects. The multiple correlation for the six groups combined was .93.

Experiment 5 leaves no doubt that kindergarten and first-grade children can be trained to use hypothesis-testing strategies on standard discrimination problems with two genuine dimensions, provided only that they have been pretrained on such problems. The first-graders profited more from such training than did the kindergarten children, however. This experiment also shows definitely that the introtact probes, at least for the kinds of tasks used here, do not interfere with discrimination performance. Thus, the LTL and HYP pretraining produces a genuine facilitation of the problem-solving capabilities of these children.

The Story-and-Game Context

The finding that responding to introtacts does not interfere with the solution of discrimination problems by kindergarten children is consistent with that reported by Kemler (1978). Using procedures similar to those previously described for Kemler *et al.* (1976), Kemler investigated the hypothesis testing of kindergarten children (her Experiment 3). Three different experimental procedures were employed. In the standard condition, the children were given introtact probes immediately following feedback, and then the stimuli were set up for the next choice trial. In the choice-only condition, the children were not probed. In the hypothesis-only condition, the experimenter designated the correct choice on each trial and the child was required to state the hypothesis for the next trial. Six problems, each with four attributes (dimensions), were administered to each child, the first of which was a practice problem that was not included in the data analyses. All children were administered the final two problems under the standard condition. It is important to note that, for her Experiment 3, Kemler abandoned the practice, which she had employed in Experiments 1 and 2, of training the children against a dimensional preference.

Kemler found that 38 of the 48 kindergarten children solved four or more of their problems. Her finding that every child solved at least one problem is probably related to the chance assignment of the preferred dimension as relevant. The standard and choice-only conditions did not differ significantly in mean TLE, a result that is consistent with that of our Experiment 5 as well as with Kemler's earlier finding for 8-year-old and 11-year-old children (her Experiment 1). Kemler distinguished between "short-term efficiency" and "long-term efficiency" in solving problems. Short-term efficiency is manifested in high values for the win-stay, lose-shift, and local-consistency indexes. Long-term efficiency manifests itself in a low relative frequency of repeating the hypotheses that have been tried previously and disconfirmed. The kindergarten children manifested a high short-term efficiency, with .90, .99, and .99 for the values of the win-stay, lose-shift, and local-consistency indexes, respectively. Their long-term efficiency, measured by the relative frequency of repeating a previously disconfirmed attribute, was significantly worse than chance. Kemler's examination of the individual protocols revealed that the poor showing with respect to the long-term efficiency was a direct consequence of attribute perseveration; indeed, she found no evidence that would require the assumption that kindergarten children remember outcomes more than one trial back!

It should be noted that the win-stay index for the Kemler (1978) kindergarten children is considerably higher than that for the Kemler et al. (1976) children (up to .90 from .45). There was also some improvement in the percentage of time that the hypothesis predicted the next choice (up to 76% from 60%). Both improvements seem to have resulted from some changes in the instructions and procedures for the practice task.

Some Molar Factors Influencing Cognitive Strategies

The research described above demonstrates unequivocally that young children, including kindergarten and first-grade children, use hypothesis-testing strategies while solving discrimination problems. In our Experiments 1 and 5, the majority of kindergarten children were found to manifest hypothesis testing on specially constructed tasks after explicit training in testing hypotheses. This research does not indicate exactly which aspects of the training were responsible for the observed improvement, however. The next experiment (Spiker & Cantor, 1979a) was conducted in an attempt to identify factors that may account for the appearance of strategies in the problem solving of young children.

Analysis of the task requirements indicates that the most fundamental requirement for testing hypotheses, as opposed to a gradual, incremental acquisition, is that the subject recognize that the problem is solvable. That is, the subject must anticipate a high cue–reward relation. Without such an anticipation, there is no reason for any systematic "hypotheses" to be produced. Second, the child must attend to and perceptually identify the relevant dimensional components, and since there is a need to remember which components have been previously tested, readily available verbal labels for the various components should be helpful. Third, since the dimension initially attended to is not relevant, the subject must be able to shift attention to the relevant dimension. Finally, the most rudimentary hypothesis-testing strategy requires the subject to follow a win-stay rule, a lose-shift rule, and a rule that prohibits the use of a hypothesis that has been previously directly tested and disconfirmed (the valid-hypothesis rule).

In this experiment, we attempted to isolate each of these four molar factors and to determine their effects, if any, on the problem-solving strategies of kindergarten children. One group, CON, received no pretraining and provided a baseline against which all other groups might be compared. A second group, FAM, received specific pretraining that involved a familiarization with, and the naming of, the various dimensional components. These children were required to sort decks of cards, on each of which was one of the stimulus components (e.g., red, yellow, square, circle) of which the subsequent criterion task would be composed, and to name the stimulus component on each card as it was sorted. Group FAM children, then, received pretraining in perceptually identifying and naming the values on the relevant and irrelevant dimensions of the criterion task. A third group of children, SST, received pretraining in solving a series of simple simultaneous discrimination problems with a single relevant nonspatial dimension and no irrelevant nonspatial dimensions. The relevant cues of the pretraining tasks for subjects became the relevant and irrelevant cues for their subsequent criterion task. Prior to each pretraining trial, these SST subjects were required to predict which cue would always be correct in that problem. Group SST subjects, then, received training in which they learned about the invariant relation between a cue and the reward, in addition to their experience in naming and identifying the various values on the stimulus dimensions. The fourth group, LTL, received pretraining corresponding exactly to that given the LTL groups in the preceding experiments. Group LTL received three pretraining problems like the criterion task and were given the solution to each, if necessary, with additional trials to check the validity of the information. Since the subjects in this group were trained against their dimensional preference in each task, they were required to shift from the initially preferred dimension to another dimension in order to solve the problems. They also had practice in identifying and naming the various stimulus components, as well as in experiencing the invariant relation between cue and reward. Finally, a fifth group, HYP, received pretraining like that given the HYP groups of the previous experiments; that is, these subjects were taught during pretraining to conform to the win-stay, lose-shift, and valid-hypothesis rules, in addition to practicing identifying and naming the stimulus components, shifting from a preferred to a nonpreferred dimension, and learning to expect an invariant cue–reward correlation.

As the preceding paragraph indicates, a comparison of Groups CON and FAM permits an evaluation of the effectiveness of identifying and naming the stimulus components. Comparing Groups FAM and SST provides an assessment of the effect of learning about an invariant cue–reward relation. Comparing Groups SST and LTL permits an assessment of the importance of learning to shift from a preferred to a nonpreferred dimension. Finally, a comparison of Groups LTL and HYP offers a way to determine the effect of teaching the three component rules of the sequential hypothesis-testing strategy.

Each of the five groups received two experimental sessions, each administered on a different day. On the first day, all discrimination problems, pretraining as well as criterion, were constructed from four values of the form dimension. On the second day, the three pretraining tasks for Groups LTL and HYP were all constructed from both colors and forms. In all tasks, the stimulus dimensions were of the partitioned type. The second session was included so that we could determine whether additional pretraining would improve performance on genuine, two-dimensional tasks.

Thirty kindergarten children were randomly assigned to each of the five groups.

The results of the first session of Experiment 6 are shown in Table 3. The mean TLE for the five groups differed significantly, with Group SST significantly superior to Groups CON and FAM, which did not differ from each other. Groups LTL and HYP did not differ signficantly from each other, but each was significantly better than Group SST. The five groups also differed significantly in the numbers of subjects who learned. Group SST had a significantly greater number of learners than Groups CON and FAM in combination, and Groups LTL and HYP combined had a significantly higher proportion of learners than Group SST. There were no significant differences among the five groups in the numbers of subjects who were dimensionally fixated.

A MANOVA was conducted on the three conditional probabilities for the first session, and it indicated that the five groups differed significantly with respect to the indexes of strategy. Univariate follow-up analyses revealed that the five groups differed significantly with respect to each index. For the win-stay index, Group SST was significantly better than Groups CON and FAM in

TABLE 3
Group Means for Discrimination Performance, Indexes of Strategy, and Strategy Errors
for Experiment 6 (N = 30 Kindergarten Children per Group)

	TLE (40 Max.)	Pct. crit.	Pct. fix.	Win-stay	Lose-shift	Valid hyp.	% zero st. err.	% < 4 st. err.
Day 1 (2 P-Dim.)[a]								
Group CON	29.7	27	20	.43	.80	.45	10	20
Group FAM	29.3	33	23	.43	.76	.40	10	17
Group SST	21.4	53	30	.55	.81	.50	23	33
Group LTL	14.6	70	13	.76	.78	.69	37	63
Group HYP	10.3	80	7	.88	.92	.77	53	77
Day 2 (2 Dim.)[a]								
Group CON	28.2	37	43	.49	.68	.36	13	13
Group FAM	29.4	33	67	.52	.65	.34	13	23
Group SST	25.3	43	53	.60	.65	.39	20	23
Group LTL	20.0	53	43	.68	.71	.56	33	47
Group HYP	9.8	87	13	.91	.90	.73	47	73

[a]Number of pseudodimensions (P-Dim.) or genuine dimensions (Dim.) in the criterion task.

combination, and Groups LTL and HYP combined were significantly better than Group SST. Group HYP was significantly better than the other four groups with respect to the lose-shift index, and these four groups did not differ significantly from each other. With respect to the valid-hypothesis index, Groups LTL and HYP in combination were significantly better than the other three groups combined.

The percentages of subjects in the five groups who made no strategy errors showed essentially the same pattern as was the case for the various indexes of strategy. The percentage of these subjects in Groups LTL and HYP combined was significantly greater than the percentages in the other three groups combined. The distribution of the percentages of subjects who made fewer than four strategy errors was essentially the same as that for subjects who made no strategy errors.

The response-consistency indexes for the five groups were virtually perfect, since the children rarely failed to choose the discriminandum specified in their previous hypothesis. The multiple correlations between TLE as the dependent variable and the three conditional probabilities as independent variables ranged from .85 for Group HYP to .96 for Group LTL. The correlation for the five groups combined was .91.

The results for the second session are shown in the lower half of Table 3. It should be remembered that the criterion task for the second session was a task with two genuine, partitioned dimensions that followed three pretraining tasks that also had two genuine, partitioned dimensions. An analysis of variance of the TLE scores showed the five groups to differ significantly. Follow-up tests revealed Group LTL to be significantly superior to Groups CON, FAM, and SST combined, with Group HYP significantly superior to Group LTL. Groups CON, FAM, and SST did not differ significantly from each other. Group HYP had a significantly higher percentage of children who met criterion than did the other four groups in combination, and these four groups did not differ significantly from each other. Groups CON, FAM, SST, and LTL also did not differ significantly from each other with respect to the incidence of dimensional fixation, but the percentage of Group HYP children who were dimensionally fixated was significantly smaller than that for the other combined groups.

A MANOVA of the win-stay, lose-shift, and valid-hypothesis indexes yielded a significant effect for the five groups. Univariate follow-up tests gave significant group effects for each index. For both the win-stay and valid-hypothesis indexes, Group HYP was significantly superior to Group LTL, which was, in turn, significantly superior to Groups CON, FAM, and SST in combination. For the lose-shift index, Group HYP was significantly superior to the other four groups in combination. Groups HYP and LTL combined had a significantly higher proportion of subjects who solved without making any strategy errors than did the other three groups combined. For the percentages of subjects with fewer than four strategy errors, Group HYP was significantly superior to Group LTL, which was, in turn, significantly superior to the other three groups in combination.

The hypotheses continued to predict, almost without error, the choice for all five groups during the second session. Moreover, the multiple correlations between TLE as the dependent measure and the win-stay, lose-shift, and valid-hypothesis indexes as independent measures ranged from .75 for Group FAM to .95 for Group HYP. The multiple correlation for the five groups combined was .92.

In summary, there was no evidence that the familiarization pretraining improved either discrimination performance or the use of the component rules of the sequential hypothesis-testing strategy. Learning to expect an invariant cue–reward relation facilitated performance on the unidimensional tasks of the first session, and possibly that on the two-dimensional tasks of the second session. Learning to shift from an initially attended irrelevant dimension to the relevant dimension facilitated performance in both sessions, with respect to discrimination performance as well as in the use of sequential hypothesis-testing rules. Moreover, teaching the children to win-stay, to lose-shift, and to use valid hypotheses facilitated discrimination performance on the two-dimensional tasks of the second session and, quite possibly, on the unidimensional tasks as well. The degree of success in teaching the component rules of strategy was evident from the superior use of the rules by the HYP children, as well as from their effective handling of the two-dimensional tasks on Day 2. The incidence of dimensional fixation on Day 2 was more than double that on Day 1 in an apparent vindication of our initial decision to construct unidimensional tasks to relieve the amount of dimensional fixation.

The Influence of Task Complexity

In the preceding experiment, kindergarten children were brought to a highly efficient level of solving tasks with two genuine dimensions after one day of pretraining with unidimensional tasks and a second day of pretraining with two-dimensional tasks. The primary purpose of the last two experiments to be reported here was to determine whether a single session of pretraining with two-dimensional tasks could produce comparable levels of problem solving on two- and three-dimensional criterion tasks. A secondary purpose of the first of these two experiments (Experiment 7) was to test a hypothesis that an instructional prompt that had been given in HYP pretraining was a major factor in producing the general superiority of HYP pretraining over LTL pretraining. Since this hypothesis was not verified, it will not be described in further detail, and it will be ignored in the presentation of the results of this experiment.

If the experimental manipulation of the instructions is ignored, there were three pretraining conditions in Experiment 7: SST, LTL, and HYP. In this experiment, 20 kindergarten children and 9 first-grade children were assigned at random to Group SST, with 40 kindergarten and 18 first-grade children randomly assigned to each of the other two groups. In this experiment, Group SST served as a baseline against which Groups LTL and HYP were compared. The pretraining tasks were those used on Day 2 of the preceding experiment, and the pretraining procedures—except those for half of the children in Groups LTL and HYP, who received a variation from the standard instructions—were identical to those used in the second session of that experiment. The criterion task, also identical to that in the second session of Experiment 6, was constructed from two genuine, partitioned dimensions.

The results of Experiment 7 are shown separately for kindergarten and first-grade children in the upper portion of Table 4. It is clear that many children of both age groups were able to transfer their pretraining to the two-dimensional criterion task. Groups LTL and HYP were superior in all respects to Group SST, and the first-grade children were generally superior to the kindergarteners. The performance of the Group HYP kindergarten children of Experiment 7 was somewhat better than that of the kindergarten Group HYP in Experiment 5, who had two unidimensional and one two-dimensional pretraining tasks, but it was somewhat poorer than the performance of the kindergarten Group HYP on Day 2 of Experiment 6, who had three unidimensional and three two-dimensional pretraining tasks. The kindergarten LTL subjects from these three experiments differed very little on any of the performance indexes. The first-grade children in Groups LTL and HYP performed exceptionally well, performing somewhat better on their two-dimensional criterion task than did the second- and third-grade children of Experiment 4 on their three-dimensional task.

The purpose of Experiment 8 was to determine whether pretraining with two-dimensional stimuli would prepare first-grade children to solve three-dimensional problems. Once again, Groups SST, LTL, and HYP were constituted, with 21 children randomly assigned to each group. The criterion task was the same as that used for the second- and third-grade children of Experiment 4, in which, it will be recalled, the partitioned stimuli differed with respect to color, form, and size, with the latter irrelevant for all subjects. The pretraining tasks were the same as those used for Experiment 7.

The results of Experiment 8 are shown in the lower part of Table 4, where a statistically significant superiority in the performance of Group HYP, relative to that of Group LTL, appears once again. Perhaps the most remarkable finding in Experiment 8 was the poor performance of these children, compared with those of Experiment 7, presumably because of the extra irrelevant dimension. Nevertheless, 52% of the Group HYP children solved a three-dimensional discrimination problem in which an irrelevant dimension was their preferred dimension, and they made fewer than four strategy errors while doing so. An additional 19% solved the problem with four or more strategy errors.

TABLE 4

Group Means for Discrimination Performance, Indexes of Strategy, and Strategy Errors for Experiments 7 and 8

	N	Grade	TLE (40 Max.)	Pct. crit.	Pct. fix.	Win-stay	Lose-shift	Valid-hyp.	% zero st. err.	% < 4 st. err.
Exp. 7 (2 Dim.)[a]										
Group SST	20	K	32.1	25	65	.41	.68	.26	15	15
Group LTL	40	K	20.7	52	40	.69	.79	.47	30	48
Group HYP	40	K	17.9	62	32	.83	.82	.58	32	52
Group SST	9	1	19.6	56	44	.65	.58	.51	22	44
Group LTL	18	1	7.6	89	17	.75	.93	.71	44	66
Group HYP	18	1	9.9	83	11	.77	.82	.72	44	66
Exp. 8 (3 Dim.)[a]										
Group SST	21	1	36.2	14	67	.46	.66	.19	5	5
Group LTL	21	1	23.3	52	24	.57	.80	.43	14	24
Group HYP	21	1	15.8	71	19	.77	.82	.65	19	52

[a]Number of genuine dimensions (Dim.) in the criterion task.

DISCUSSION AND SUMMARY

The discussion is presented in three parts. First, an attempt is made to draw together the conclusions that can be obtained from the eight experiments from our laboratory, as well as from several of the experiments from other laboratories. Next, we present some tentative conclusions, which, since they are based on comparisons among several of the experiments, should probably be interpreted as suggestions for further research. Finally, we discuss some of the implications of these empirical findings for theories of children's discrimination learning.

Summary of Research Findings

The Usefulness (Validity) of the Introtact Probes. The responses of kindergarten and first-grade children to the introtact probes were highly predictive of their performance in the discrimination problems. The response-consistency index (the probability that the verbalized hypothesis named a dimensional value of the compound next chosen) was virtually perfect in all experiments. Moreover, the win-stay, lose-shift, and valid-hypothesis indexes, when used in a multiple-regression equation, typically accounted for between 80% and 90% of the variance of the TLE measure. The higher correlations were generally found for the LTL and HYP groups. That these three indexes were usually highest for the HYP groups, who were explicitly taught the win-stay, lose-shift, and valid-hypothesis rules, is further evidence for the validity of the measures.

Interference of Probes with Discrimination Learning. The evidence concerning the interference from introtact probes is not entirely consistent. The results of Experiment 5 indicate that introtact probes do not interfere with the learning of discrimination problems by kindergarten and first-grade children, at least with partitioned stimuli in tasks with no more than two nonspatial dimensions. Moreover, Kemler (1978) found no evidence of interference with kindergarten children on a task with as many as four partitioned dimensions. The use of introtact probes with unitary stimuli may be found to result in interference with the solution of such problems. Our Experiment 5, as well as the Phillips (1974) experiment, indicates that the probes may, in fact, facilitate the solutions of first- and second-grade children, possibly by reducing the production deficiency that such children have often been shown to manifest.

Dimensional Fixation. The use of introtact probes with young children reveals—but apparently does nothing to exacerbate—the phenomenon that we have called *dimensional fixation* (Cantor & Spiker, 1977). This phenomenon was also reported in kindergarten children by Kemler (1978), who called it "attribute perseveration." Kemler suggested that the high incidence of the fixation is a primary reason for the failure of her kindergarten children to manifest long-term efficiency in solving the discrimination problems. It is not entirely clear whether the fixation is a symptom of or a cause of the failure to solve the problem. It might be argued that the child finds a satisfactory method of communicating his or her future choice to the experimenter and continues to use that method, and that the self-confusion produced by saying the names of irrelevant cues prevents the solution for most children. Unfortunately, this argument would also entail the prediction that introtact probes should have interfered with solutions in Experiment 5. The ubiquitousness of this phenomenon is apparent in an examination of Table 1, where it can be seen that more than half of the second- and third-grade CON subjects were dimensionally fixated. Both LTL and HYP pretraining, and especially the latter, markedly reduced the incidence of dimensional fixation in nearly all of the eight experiments summarized in Tables 1–4.

The Effect of Pretraining on Children's Strategies. The vast majority of kindergarten and first-grade children can be trained to test hypotheses sequentially in the successful solution of discrimination problems. Up to this point, however, we have found the strategy to be relatively task-specific for most children of this age, in the sense that the strategy does not appear to transfer readily to problems more complex than those on which the pretraining was given. The incidence of positive transfer seems to be maximized by extensive pretraining on tasks that are of the same degree of complexity as the criterion task, although simpler pretraining problems may profitably precede the more complex ones.

A surprisingly high incidence of solutions to the criterion tasks occurs after the LTL type of pretraining. It should be noted that this training does not guarantee that a child will solve even one pretraining task on his or her own, although it guarantees that the subject will observe a solution sequence of choices and hypotheses. Since the child is trained against his or her dimensional preference, LTL pretraining also guarantees that his or her attention must be shifted from the initially attended dimension to the relevant one.

The relatively poor performance of the CON groups, which can be reviewed in Tables 1–3, testifies to the difficulty of these problems when the preferred dimension is made irrelevant. For example, even the second- and third-grade children of Experiment 4 (Table 1) had considerable difficulty with the three-dimensional stimuli in the absence of pretraining. Only one-third of the CON children met the solution criterion in 40 discrimination learning trials.

The Nature of Young Children's Strategies. Experiment 6 helped to identify several molar components of the strategies that the kindergarten and first-grade children used. We found that they could profit from having pretraining problems in which the presence of the stimulus–reward contingency could be detected (i.e., in the SST groups). The LTL groups benefited significantly from experience in shifting among the dimensions until the relevant dimension was discovered. And, of course, explicit training in the use of the win-stay, lose-shift, and valid-hypothesis rules was often, though not always, beneficial to the HYP groups. (One of the more surprising findings of this series of experiments is that many children of these ages who received only LTL pretraining spontaneously followed the rules for sequentially testing hypotheses.) On the other hand, sorting the stimuli on the basis of a single dimension at any one time, and the concurrent naming the stimuli with respect to the values on that dimension, did not facilitate subsequent solutions or solution strategies. It is possible that facilitation might be obtained with a more complex pretraining task, one that required the concurrent sorting and naming with respect to multiple dimensions.

One of the more important discoveries about young children's use of the sequential strategy is that many of them who obviously use the strategy do not do so without error. Of the kindergarten and first-grade children in all the HYP groups who solved the criterion problem, 85% made fewer than four strategy errors. For the LTL subjects, about 70% who solved the criterion problem did so with fewer than four strategy errors. Only about 40% of the CON children who solved the criterion task made fewer than four strategy errors. As Kemler (1978) has pointed out, any failure of children to use their strategies perfectly would result in their being incorrectly identified as unclassifiable, or worse, by a theoretical analysis that does not allow for the possibility of such errors (e.g., Gholson et al., 1972).

Short-Term and Long-Term Efficiency. Kemler (1978) introduced a valuable distinction between short-term strategies that make effective use of task-related information that is present at any point, and long-term strategies that integrate information that becomes available across trials. Thus, the win-stay and lose-shift indexes measure the extent to which the children are utilizing temporally local information efficiently. She also identified the local-consistency rule as a rule for the effective use of contemporary information. Her primary measure of long-term planfulness was an index of the child's tendency to repeat hypotheses that had been previously disconfirmed, a measure that is closely related to our valid-hypothesis index.

As previously indicated, Kemler found no evidence of long-term efficiency in the problem solving of her kindergarten children. A perusal of Tables 1–4 indicates that our LTL and HYP groups, especially the latter, had relatively high valid-hypothesis indexes. It is quite apparent that the LTL and HYP pretraining was effective, not only in improving the short-term efficiency of the kindergarten and first-grade children in these experiments, but also in producing a significant improvement in their long-term planfulness. On the other side of this coin, those children who failed to meet the learning criterion had relatively low valid-hypothesis indexes. The average of those who failed to meet criterion in the HYP groups, for example, was less than .10, an order of magnitude usually found to accompany dimensional fixation.

Implications for Further Research

It is inevitable that a series of related experiments, such as we have just reported, will raise as many questions as it has answered. Some of these questions are little more than hunches that we have enough faith in to share with others. Other questions are based on interexperimental comparisons, which are always subject to inadvertent procedural or sampling differences among the experiments, but which nevertheless constitute one of the richest sources of empirically based hypotheses.

The Effect of Type of Stimulus Materials. One of the more intriguing questions to arise in the course of this research concerns the construction of the stimuli. As a result of extensive pilot work, we concluded that the unitary stimuli that we were using were unsuitable for teaching the kindergarten children to test hypotheses systematically. Our next step was to construct the discriminanda from partitioned, or distributed, dimensions. Further pilot work indicated that even the partitioned stimuli eventuated in a high incidence of dimensional fixation. We then developed the pseudodimensional stimuli constructed from a single dimension (e.g., color or form). With such stimuli, we succeeded in teaching the vast majority of kindergarten and first-grade children to test hypotheses systematically.

To date, we have not yet compared unitary and partitioned discriminanda within the context of a single experiment. On the basis of our pilot experiences, we would expect that kindergarten and first-grade children would find the partitioned stimuli easier to use in testing hypotheses. The results that Kemler (1978) obtained are consistent with such an expectation. In Experiment 6, we compared discriminanda constructed from a single dimension (e.g., color) with partitioned stimuli constructed from two dimensions (e.g., color and form), but the effects of the two stimulus types were confounded with the amount of pretraining—the tasks with two genuine, partitioned dimensions having been administered on the second day. We would expect the pseudodimensional stimuli to be easier than the partitioned, genuine dimensions in a properly counterbalanced experiment.

The Effect of Task Complexity on Hypothesis Testing. In Experiment 3, and again in Experiment 8, we attempted to get first-grade children to generalize their pretraining to criterion tasks that had one more dimension than was present in the pretraining task. In Experiment 3, the children were pretrained on unidimensional tasks with pseudodimensions and then were shifted to tasks with two genuine, partitioned dimensions. In Experiment 8, the pretraining tasks had two genuine, partitioned dimensions and the children were shifted to criterion tasks with three genuine, partitioned dimensions. In both experiments, the amount of transfer was disappointing, with respect to both solution and the use of strategies. Even the HYP children, who were explicitly taught to use the sequential hypothesis-testing strategy, were plagued with a frequent incidence of dimensional fixation and numerous errors of strategy.

Although we are not clear as to exactly why the effects of pretraining tend to be restricted to criterion tasks of the type employed in pretraining, it seems a fairly safe bet that the answer has something in general to do with dimensional fixation. Perhaps our practice of training against dimensional preference in some way renders the addition of another irrelevant dimension particularly debilitating. There is a need to compare the performance of children trained against their dimensional preference with that of others who are trained toward their dimensional preference. In addition, the number of irrelevant dimensions could be profitably varied within a factorial design.

Pretraining in the Dimensionalization of Stimuli. Analysis of the testing of hypotheses in discrimination learning problems indicates that the subject needs to abstract the various dimensions from the complex discriminanda. Our attempt to improve this skill in Experiment 6 with the FAM pretraining was apparently not successful. Either the children already have such skills and do not need additional training, or the training was not appropriate. Given the high incidence of dimensional fixation, it is difficult to believe that the children do not need additional training in analyzing the stimuli into dimensions.

It will be recalled that the pretraining procedures that were used with the FAM children required them to sort stimulus cards that contained only one value on a single dimension. On the second day, for example, the FAM children sorted into four stacks cards that contained either a red blob, a blue blob, a square outline, or a circular outline, saying the name of each as it was placed in the appropriate one of the four stacks. A more complex pretraining task might well have been more effective. Consider a set of two-dimensional stimuli, of either the partitioned or the unitary type. The child could be required to name the values of both dimensions and to indicate in which two of the four stacks it would be "legitimate" to place each stimulus. Such a task should facilitate the analysis of complex stimuli into their dimensional components and would be more likely to produce positive transfer in the hypothesis-testing task.

The Locus of the Introtact Probe. In each of the experiments from our laboratory reported here, the introtact probe was administered immediately prior to the child's choice. Just before the child was allowed to choose a discriminandum, he or she was required to state a prediction about which stimulus would always be correct. Only if the child remembered the outcome of the preceding trial could he or she be locally consistent with more than chance frequency. In contrast to this procedure, Kemler *et al.* (1976) and Kemler (1978) administered the probe immediately after feedback on each trial. Thus, with the stimuli directly in front of him or her, and with the correct (Amy) stimulus specifically marked, the child was asked for a new hypothesis. A comparison of the indexes of strategy in the two experiments suggests that the two probe techniques produce somewhat different results. We typically obtained high indexes of response consistency, but relatively low indexes of local consistency. The Kemler experiments report high indexes of local consistency, but relatively low indexes of response consistency. An experiment in which the two probe locations were directly compared would be instructive.

Some Developmental Changes in Testing Hypotheses. None of the experiments from our laboratory has emphasized age comparisons, although several have involved subjects of adjacent grade levels. There are several apparent developmental trends that may turn out to be genuine. For example, given discrimination tasks of constant difficulty, the incidence of dimensional fixation appears to decrease with increasing chronological age, although its incidence among second- and third-graders (Experiment 4) is still astonishingly high. Moreover, if one holds constant the difficulty of the task, the effectiveness of the pretraining in testing hypotheses appears to decrease with increasing chronological age. For a given type of pretraining, older children are better than younger children in solving tasks of a given level of difficulty, and the difference in performance between different age groups seems to increase with an increase in the number of irrelevant stimulus dimensions. Experiments explicitly designed to test some of these developmental hypotheses would utilize several groups of children differing with respect to chronological age.

Some Molecular Components of Hypothesis Testing. In the present chapter, we have been primarily concerned with the molar components of the hypothesis-testing strategy. Thus, we have assessed the importance of practice in analyzing complex stimuli into dimensions and in naming the values of the various stimulus dimensions. We have studied the role of learning about the existence of cue–reward relations in such problems. We have conducted investigations to measure the learning to shift from dimension to dimension until the relevant dimension has been discovered. And, of course, each of the experiments reported from our laboratory has been concerned with teaching the win-stay, lose-shift, and valid-hypothesis rules for testing hypotheses sequentially.

It is now time to consider some of the more molecular abilities and skills that may be involved in testing hypotheses during the solution of discrimination problems. For example, one might entertain the hypothesis that the general inferiority of the strategies manifested by kindergarten and first-grade children is due to memory deficiencies. On the other hand, it may be somewhat gratuitous, if not presumptuous, to consider seriously a memory deficiency in children who have just acquired, in the short space of three or four years, a vocabulary with an average of 20,000–30,000 entries. The deficiency is more likely to be in the use of the memory than in the memory *per se.* In Experiment 5, we found that the first-grade children who were required to respond to the introtact probes were superior in performance to those who were not required to do so, a difference that may well reflect the production deficiency that has been assumed for children of these ages (e.g., Flavell, Beach, & Chinsky, 1966; Kendler, 1972).

Our frequent reference to the difficulty that children have with the dimensional analysis of complex stimuli reflects the importance that we attribute to this problem. One of our reasons for emphasizing this deficiency is obvious: hypotheses become available to the child only as the values of the various dimensions are detected and recognized. There is another consideration, however, that pertains more directly to the logic of the problem-solving technique. If the child selects the correct discriminandum on a particular trial, the outcome of that trial can be retained until the next trial in either of two obvious ways. The child may retain a visual representation of the correct compound that lasts until the next presentation of the discriminanda, or she or he may encode the correct compound as a verbal description that is retained until the next trial. After an incorrect choice, however, the child's options may be quite different. If the discriminanda are immediately removed, or if the child fails to orient immediately toward the positive discriminandum, the incorrect compound must be recoded into the positive compound in order for a representation of that positive compound to be available at the time of the next choice. This recoding might take place immediately, with the verbal description of the positive compound being retained over the next several seconds, or the child might retain either a visual image or a verbal description of the negative stimulus until the next trial and then attempt to recode in order to obtain the positive stimulus at that time. In either case, recoding would seem to require that the child be able to deal with the discriminanda on a dimension-by-dimension basis. At the present time, we have very little information about the young child's skills and abilities in recoding stimuli of this kind. Any research that would throw light on the ability of children to perform this type of recoding would be helpful in understanding the problem-solving strategies in the solution of discrimination problems.

Implications for Theoretical Formulations

Implications for Associative Theories. The demonstration of hypothesis-testing strategies in children as young as kindergarten age demands important changes in the associative theories that have been offered as explanations of the discrimination learning of children over the last 25–30 years. The changes over trials in associative processes that were permissible within associative theories, even within those postulating mediating mechanisms, were generally too slow to account for the behavior observed. If associative theories are to maintain their credibility as explanations for the discrimination behavior of, say, kindergarten children, the associative processes must be permitted much more rapid changes.

Appropriate modifications of the classical associative theories are not out of the question, however. As an example, consider an associative theory of the sort proposed nearly two decades ago by Zeaman and House (1963). In this theory, the orienting or observing response is dimension-specific. That is, associative processes determine which of the several stimulus dimensions present will be attended to. Other associative processes determine which of the stimulus values on the attended-to dimensions will be instrumentally selected. The rates of change in the associative processes are determined by rate parameters that may, in principle, be estimated from the data. A proper choice of these parameters can produce very rapid shifting among the dimensions to be attended to, as well as rapid shifts in the choice of stimulus values. In order to make complete contact with all the data from an experiment on hypothesis testing, however, it will be necessary to make explicit statements that will permit the deduction of the relations between the verbal hypotheses and the choice behavior.

The present writers have also offered an associative schema that was specifically designed to address the facts of experiments on hypothesis testing (Spiker & Cantor, 1979b). In this schema, too, the associative processes are speeded up by means of one-trial acquisition and extinction. The connections between verbal responses to stimulus compounds and the instrumental choices of the compounds followed principles that have been traditionally assumed to govern the operation of mediating mechanisms. The schema was then applied in an attempt to account for several of the well-known developmental trends, for several different types of stereotypes and strategies that have been observed in the context of hypothesis-testing experiments, and for some of the characteristic findings in the various dimensional-shift paradigms. Such a schema also provides predictions with respect to experiments that have not yet been conducted.

Implications for Perceptual Theories. The difficulty that many kindergarten and first-grade children seem to have in analyzing the stimuli into dimensions is a phenomenon that would be expected by some of the theories of discrimination learning that emphasize the importance of the perceptual processes. Tighe and Tighe (1966) conceptualized discrimination learning as a two-stage affair consisting of an initial differentiation of stimulus input, followed by the detection of the relation between the reward and relevant features of the discriminanda that have been previously differentiated. The first phase, perceptual learning, is characterized by the subject's increased sensitivity to the dimensions along which the stimulation varies. This perceptual learning phase is viewed as by far the most critical component of discrimination learning.

Advocates of this general viewpoint would be expected to point to several aspects of our findings as confirmation of their conceptualizations. They would probably attribute the prevalence of dimensional fixation to the fact that for these young children, the stimulus dimensions have not yet emerged. The improvement in performance as a result of LTL and HYP pretraining would probably be interpreted as evidence that the emergence of the dimensions is facilitated by such pretraining. The apparent improvement in performance with the use of partitioned dimensions or pseudodimensions would obviously be expected, since the emergence of such dimensions would require little or no perceptual learning. The perceptually oriented theories, however, appear to have no more basis than do the extant associative theories for predicting the occurrence of systematic hypothesis testing among young children.

Implications for Cognitive Theories. As noted earlier, the use of introtact probes for assessing the level of cognitive strategies utilized by children arose from the cognitive theory developed over several years by Levine (e.g., 1963) and his associates. The primary reference for the application of this formulation to the discrimination behavior of children is Gholson *et al.* (1972). This formulation describes three different strategy systems that lead ultimately to the solution of discrimination problems: focusing, dimension checking, and hypothesis checking. On the basis of their research with children, Gholson *et al.* reported the most frequent type of solution strategy to be dimension checking, with hypothesis checking and focusing running a relatively poor second and third, respectively.

Recently, the Gholson *et al.* analysis of strategies has come under sharp questioning. Kemler (1978) reported that an alternative model of discrimination learning, which assumes that the subject is locally consistent on each choice but has no memory for the outcome of any previous trial, predicts a pattern of responding comparable to those of the Gholson strategies, with relative frequencies that do not differ significantly from those reported by Gholson *et al.* for second-grade children. We find the Kemler alternative analysis quite attractive for two reasons. First, the dimension-checking strategy seems to be intellectually much too advanced for most second-grade children. Indeed, we have found it difficult to communicate an understanding of the strategy to advanced undergraduate students. Second, among the protocols of children who had been taught to use sequential hypothesis testing, and who were presumably doing so, we have found many sequences of hypotheses and choices that would qualify as "dimension checking." Whatever the merits of these two arguments, our data and those of Kemler (1978) indicate that no theory can be entirely correct if it fails to recognize that young children may follow a strategy and still make errors in the use of that strategy.

The errorless use of a strategy, of course, is not a necessary assumption in cognitive theorizing. A formulation such as that of Trabasso and Bower (1968), for example, predicts that the subject will make sequences of choices that would, in other frames of reference, be interpreted as "strategy errors." Unfortunately, the Trabasso–Bower theory in its original form does not describe the behavior of many children very well. One of the main difficulties is in accounting for the numbers of subjects who fail to learn in spite of rather extensive training.

One of the more innovative and promising ventures into cognitive theorizing is that described in a paper by Kendler (1979). This theorist, continuing a long history of two-level theorizing, has now proposed a gradual, incremental model of learning for younger children, a cognitive, saltatory model for older children and adults, and a probabilistic choice of models for children of intermediate chronological ages. It will be interesting to see whether such a structure can also incorporate the results of explicit hypothesis-testing experiments.

ACKNOWLEDGMENTS

We are extremely grateful to two school systems for their continuous participation in our research program. Both of them have contributed immeasurably to the research reported here. We are indebted to David L. Cronin, Superintendent, for permission to test children in the Iowa City Community School District, and to the principals and teachers at the Coralville Central, Hills Elementary, Hoover, Horn, Kirkwood, Lemme, Longfellow, Lucas, Penn Elementary, Sabin, and Shimek schools for their fine cooperation in many ways. We also express our deep gratitude to James A. Bayne, Superintendent, for permission to test children in the College Community School District, Cedar Rapids, and to Principal Eugene Holthaus of Prairie Elementary, Principal Charles Swaney of Prairie View Elementary, and their teaching staffs for their outstanding professional hospitality.

REFERENCES

Bower, G. H., & Trabasso, T. Concept identification. In R. C. Atkinson (Ed.), *Studies in mathematical psychology*. Stanford, Calif.: Stanford University Press, 1964.

Cantor, J. H. Transfer of stimulus pretraining in motor paired-associate and discrimination learning tasks. In L. P. Lipsitt & C. C. Spiker (Eds.), *Advances in child development and behavior*, Vol. 2. New York: Academic Press, 1965.

Cantor, J. H., & Spiker, C. C. Dimensional fixation with introtacts in kindergarten children. *Bulletin of the Psychonomic Society*, 1977, *10*, 169–171.

Cantor, J. H., & Spiker, C. C. The problem-solving strategies of kindergarten and first-grade children during discrimination learning. *Journal of Experimental Child Psychology*, 1978, *26*, 341–358.

Cantor, J. H., & Spiker, C. C. The effects of introtacts on hypothesis testing in kindergarten and first-grade children. *Child Development*, 1979, *50*, 1110–1120.

Eimas, P. D. A developmental study of hypothesis behavior and focusing. *Journal of Experimental Child Psychology*, 1969, *8*, 160–172.

Flavell, J. H., Beach, D. R., & Chinsky, J. M. Spontaneous verbal rehearsal in a memory task as a function of age. *Child Development*, 1966, *37*, 283–299.

Gholson, B., & McConville, K. Effects of stimulus differentiation training upon hypotheses, strategies, and stereotypes in discrimination learning among kindergarten children. *Journal of Experimental Child Psychology*, 1974, *18*, 81–97.

Gholson, B., Levine, M., & Phillips, S. Hypotheses, strategies, and stereotypes in discrimination learning. *Journal of Experimental Child Psychology*, 1972, *13*, 423–446.

Gholson, B., Phillips, S., & Levine, M. Effects of the temporal relationship of feedback and stimulus information upon discrimination-learning strategies. *Journal of Experimental Child Psychology*, 1973, *15*, 425–441.

Gholson, B., O'Connor, J., & Stern, I. Hypothesis sampling systems among preoperational and concrete operational kindergarten children. *Journal of Experimental Child Psychology*, 1976, *21*, 61–76.

Ingalls, R. P., & Dickerson, D. J. Development of hypothesis behavior in human concept identification. *Developmental Psychology*, 1969, *1*, 707–716.

Karpf, D., & Levine, M. Blank-trial probes and introtacts in human discrimination learning. *Journal of Experimental Psychology*, 1971, *90*, 51–55.

Kemler, D. G. *A developmental study of hypothesis testing in discriminative learning tasks*. Unpublished doctoral dissertation, Brown University, 1972.

Kemler, D. G. Patterns of hypothesis testing in children's discriminative learning: A study of the development of problem-solving strategies. *Developmental Psychology*, 1978, *14*, 653–673.

Kemler, D. G., Shepp, B. E., & Foote, K. E. The sources of developmental differences in children's incidental processing during discrimination trials. *Journal of Experimental Child Psychology*, 1976, *21*, 226–240.

Kendler, H. H., & Kendler, T. S. Vertical and horizontal processes in problem solving. *Psychological Review*, 1962, *69*, 1–16.

Kendler, T. S. An ontogeny of mediational deficiency. *Child Development*, 1972, *43*, 1–17.

Kendler, T. S. The development of discrimination learning: A levels-of-functioning explanation. In H. W. Reese & L. P. Lipsitt (Eds.), *Advances in child development and behavior*, Vol. 13. New York: Academic Press, 1979.

Kuenne, M. R. Experimental investigation of the relation of language to the transposition behavior in young children. *Journal of Experimental Psychology*, 1946, *36*, 471–490.

Levine, M. Mediating processes in humans at the outset of discrimination learning. *Psychological Review*, 1963, *70*, 254–276.

Levine, M. (Ed.). *A cognitive theory of learning*. Hillsdale, N.J.: Erlbaum, 1975.

Parrill-Burnstein, M. Teaching kindergarten children to solve problems: An information-processing approach. *Child Development*, 1978, *49*, 700–706.

Phillips, S. *Introtacts in children's discrimination learning*. Unpublished doctoral dissertation, State University of New York at Stony Brook, 1974.

Phillips, S., & Levine, M. Probing for hypotheses with adults and children: Blank trials and introtacts. *Journal of Experimental Psychology: General*, 1975, *104*, 327–354.

Reese, H. W. Discrimination learning set in children. In L. P. Lipsitt & C. C. Spiker (Eds.), *Advances in child development and behavior*, Vol. 1. New York: Academic Press, 1963.

Restle, F. The selection of strategies in cue learning. *Psychological Review*, 1962, *69*, 329–343.

Rieber, M. Hypothesis testing in children as a function of age. *Developmental Psychology*, 1969, *1*, 389–395.

Shepp, B. E., & Gray, V. A. Some effects of variable-within and variable-between irrelevant stimuli on dimensional learning and transfer. *Journal of Experimental Psychology*, 1971, *89*, 32–39.

Silleroy, R. S., & Johnson, P. J. The effects of perceptual pretraining on concept identification and preference. *Journal of Experimental Child Psychology*, 1973, *15*, 462–472.

Spence, K. W. The nature of discrimination learning in animals. *Psychological Review*, 1936, *43*, 427–449.

Spiker, C. C. Experiments with children on the hypothesis of acquired distinctiveness and equivalence of cues. *Child Development,* 1956, *27,* 253–263.

Spiker, C. C. Verbal factors in the discrimination learning of children. In J. C. Wright & J. Kagan (Eds.), *Basic cognitive processes in children. Monographs of the Society for Research in Child Development,* 1963, *28,* 53–69.

Spiker, C. C. An extension of Hull-Spence discrimination learning theory. *Psychological Review,* 1970, *77,* 496–515.

Spiker, C. C. Application of Hull-Spence theory to the discrimination learning of children. In H. W. Reese (Ed.), *Advances in child development and behavior,* Vol. 6. New York: Academic Press, 1971.

Spiker, C. C., & Cantor, J. H. Applications of Hull-Spence theory to the transfer of discrimination learning in children. In H. W. Reese (Ed.), *Advances in child development and behavior,* Vol. 8. New York: Academic Press, 1973.

Spiker, C. C., & Cantor, J. H. Introtacts as predictors of discrimination performance in kindergarten children. *Journal of Experimental Child Psychology,* 1977, *23,* 520–538.

Spiker, C. C., & Cantor, J. H. Factors affecting hypothesis testing in kindergarten children. *Journal of Experimental Child Psychology,* 1979, *28,* 230–248. (a)

Spiker, C. C., & Cantor, J. H. The Kendler levels-of-functioning theory: Comments and an alternative schema. In H. W. Reese & L. P. Lipsitt (Eds.), *Advances in child development and behavior,* Vol. 13. New York: Academic Press, 1979. (b)

Tighe, L. S., & Tighe, T. J. Discrimination learning: Two views in historical perspective. *Psychological Bulletin,* 1966, *66,* 353–370.

Trabasso, T., & Bower, G. *Attention in learning.* New York: Wiley, 1968.

Tumblin, A., Gholson, B., Rosenthal, T. L., & Kelley, J. E. The effects of gestural demonstration, verbal narration, and their combination on the acquisition of hypothesis-testing behaviors by first-grade children. *Child Development,* 1979, *50,* 254–256.

Winer, B. J. *Statistical principles in experimental design.* New York: McGraw-Hill, 1971.

Zeaman, D., & House, B. J. The role of attention in retardate discrimination learning. In N. R. Ellis (Ed.), *Handbook of mental deficiency.* New York: McGraw-Hill, 1963.

4 Learning Sets

The Pittsburgh Studies

DONALD K. ROUTH

INTRODUCTION

This chapter is a broad review of the learning set (LS) paradigm as a research tool in comparative, developmental, and clinical psychology. Its principal purpose is to place in context the contributions to this area of research by George J. Wischner, his students, and his associates at the University of Pittsburgh. During the 1950s, 1960s, and 1970s, Wischner and his group were among the most active researchers using this learning paradigm with human subjects, including normal children, familial and brain-damaged mentally retarded children, aphasic and nonaphasic brain-damaged adults, and schizophrenic patients. Considered together, these studies have uncovered some new phenomena related to LS, have reported on the effects of several important procedural variations, and have established the sensitivity of LS measures to cognitive development in children, to neuropsychological impairment, and to psychopathology. A number of these studies now exist, however, only in the form of M.A. theses and Ph.D. dissertations or as unpublished manuscripts. Thus, a somewhat detailed review of their nature and content may serve the useful purpose of making them accessible to the scientific community.

Definition and General Procedures

Following Harlow (1949), a learning set is defined as a marked positive transfer across problems of a similar type. Harlow, who was the most influential in stimulating research on LS, worked with rhesus monkeys, using the Wisconsin

DONALD K. ROUTH ● Department of Psychology, University of Iowa, Iowa City, Iowa 52242.

General Test Apparatus. He used long series of two-choice "object-quality" visual-discrimination learning problems, often for a fixed number of trials per problem. In an individual problem, the animal was confronted on each trial with a pair of laboratory-fabricated stimulus objects differing in multiple dimensions (size, shape, color combinations, etc.) but varying randomly from trial to trial in left–right position. One object of the two was arbitrarily designated as correct regardless of left–right position, and if the animal displaced the correct object, it was rewarded by finding a morsel of food in the well beneath. Choice of the incorrect object resulted in finding an empty food well and termination of the trial. On the first trial of such a problem, performance is at a 50% (chance) level of correctness. On Trial 2, an animal that has formed an object-quality LS could in principle be correct 100% of the time. Indeed, across problems, Trial 2 performance shows a systematic rise that defines the LS, or learning-to-learn, phenomenon.

Theory

Harlow presented LS as a way of resolving the controversy over trial-and-error versus insightful learning, since an inexperienced animal performs in random fashion, in contrast to the highly efficient behavior of an animal that has formed an LS. Harlow argues that the everyday experiences of both animals and humans offers many recurrent situations that permit LS formation, which thus might actually be considered more representative than isolated opportunities for discrimination learning.

In an early theoretical paper, Restle (1958) analyzed LS experiments as containing three types of cues. Type a cues are those that are valid (consistently reinforced) and common to all problems in the series, that is, the choice of "the object which was correct on the previous trial" (p. 89). Type b cues are valid only for a particular problem and not over the long run (e.g., the choice of the larger and more brightly colored of two objects). Type c cues are not consistently reinforced at any time and are thus invalid for the series of problems (e.g., the left–right position of the object). According to this analysis, LS formation consists of learning to respond to Type a cues and not to cues of Types b and c.

Harlow's (1959) "error factor" theory resembles Restle's analysis in part in ascribing LS formation to the extinction of incorrect response tendencies such as response shift, "the strong tendency of the monkey to respond to both stimuli" (p. 516) rather than staying with one stimulus object that has been associated with reward. To some, including the present author, Harlow's error–factor theory seems too one-sided, leaving no room for new behaviors to develop. It is rather like describing the behavior of a sculptor as merely removing the excess marble from the preexisting shape of a statue.

Levine (1959), a student of Harlow, soon began to develop a more detailed model of the particular systematic response tendencies, or "hypotheses," involved in animal and human LS formation. In a series of object-quality discrimination problems, for example, Levine's "win-stay-lose-shift (with respect to object)" hypothesis will generate correct problem solution behavior, while other hypotheses will not. Examples of maladaptive hypotheses in object-quality learning would include position preference, position alternation, stimulus preference (regardless of reinforcement), stimulus alternation, and both win-stay–lose-shift (position) and lose-stay–win-shift (position). Schusterman (1962) soon produced experimental evidence that a win-stay–lose-shift strategy with respect to objects, however it was acquired, seemed to be a sufficient basis for one-trial discrimination learning in chimpanzees.

Levine (1975) went on to elaborate his hypothesis-testing model considerably in the study of discrimination learning, learning set, and concept formation in adult humans. He and others also developed more direct ways of assessing hypothesis behavior in humans. One of these is the "blank-trials" procedure, in which a number of trials are given with no feedback to the subject, in order to assess patterns of responding over several trials uninfluenced by feedback. The other major procedure is the "introtact," in which the subject is asked for verbal statements of hypotheses between trials (Phillips & Levine, 1975). One interesting finding of research with animals (e.g., Ricciardi & Treichler, 1970) as well as humans using such hypothesis models is that the two parts of win-stay–lose-shift responding are somewhat independent of each other. Across a series of problems, subjects may begin to engage in consistent lose-shift behavior considerably earlier than they engage in win-stay behavior.

LS AND SPECIES DIFFERENCES

One reason for the boom in LS research in the late 1950s was the empirical demonstration in comparative studies that the LS paradigm was sensitive to species differences. At that time, at least, the opinion seemed credible that the performance of animals on LS problems in terms of slope and asymptotic level was representative of their degree of cerebral cortical development and their general place on the phylogenetic scale. Miles (1957), for example, published a widely reproduced graphic comparison of the results of several studies showing the rhesus monkey to be superior in its LS performance to the squirrel monkey, and both to be superior to the marmoset.

For a time, the LS paradigm appeared to be the comparative psychologist's equivalent of an IQ test, a way of lining different species up according to a single dimension of adaptive psychological functioning. According to Harlow (1949), for example, by and large the phylogenetic data demonstrate that LS formation is closely related to evolutionary position, as conventionally described, and to cortical complexity in so far as this characteristic has been effectively measured. (p. 508).

Of course, like early concepts of the IQ, such views of the universality of the LS task as a comparative yardstick proved to have been oversimplified. Different species are adapted to diverse ecological niches, and their performances in laboratory learning situations may therefore differ in important qualitative ways, not just quantitatively. Thus, monkeys are relatively adept visually, and the use of visual discrimination problems in the study of LS gave them perhaps an unfair advantage over, for example, rats, which handle olfactory LS problems far better than visual ones (Slotnick & Katz, 1974), or the dolphin, whose LS formation abilities seem to be best observed with series of auditory discrimination problems (Herman & Arbeit, 1973). The tree shrew, an insectivorous species, does not initially approach a discrimination problem with strong position habits like most animals that have been studied—perhaps because its insect prey in the natural habitat do not tend to stay in one place—so the shrew's laboratory learning and LS formation (if any) would necessarily be qualitatively different from those of other animals (Leonard, Schneider, & Gross, 1966).

But this is just good hindsight. At the time Wischner and his associates began their LS research, and still during the mid 1960s, when the present author was a graduate student, the paradigm seemed to have excellent possibilities as a measure of phylogenetic status. It also seemed to have potential as a measure of cortical function or pathology, analogous perhaps to the sorting tasks used by Weigl (1927/1941) in his experiments with human patients with cerebral damage, normal adults, normal and retarded children, and compared by him to other tasks used in research with nonhuman primates.

LS AND CHILD DEVELOPMENT

Research with children on positive transfer across a series of similar problems actually antedates LS research with nonhuman primates. For example, Roberts (1932, 1933) gave a series of matching-to-sample problems with color as the relevant dimension to 43 preschool children. The 2-year-olds did not improve across problems, but the older children did. Interestingly, Roberts found something of a dissociation between the children's choices and their verbal behavior. Some who chose correctly could not verbalize the basis of their solutions to the problem, while others verbalized correctly but then did not behave accordingly.

Koch and Meyer (1959), studying a sample of 33 preschool children, found their LS acquisition rate markedly superior to that of rhesus monkeys on comparable problems. They also found a $-.59$ correlation between days to LS criterion and the children's Stanford-Binet mental ages. It is interesting that about the same time, Harlow, Harlow, Rueping, and Mason (1960) reported a study of infant rhesus monkeys in which there seemed to be a maturational threshold below which LS formation did not occur. In general, Harlow *et al.*'s older monkeys (like Koch and Meyer's older children) were found to form LS more effectively than younger ones. Fagen (1977), whose 10-month-olds are so far the youngest human subjects in the literature to show significant interproblem learning, found that every one of these infants was somewhat hindered in reaching criterion by strong position preferences.

The most definitive studies of LS formation as a function of developmental status in humans are those of Levinson and Reese (1967), Berman, Rane, and Bahow (1970), and Gholson (1980), all of which provide support for hypothesis-testing models of LS formation.

Levinson and Reese (1967) studied discrimination LS formation in cross-sectional samples of preschool children, fifth-graders, college freshmen, and aged subjects. In general, LS formation became increasingly more efficient with age through adolescence but was impaired in the aged relative to most of the younger groups. The somewhat better LS acquisition among a subgroup of the aged who were highly educated and had held professional positions makes it difficult to be sure whether there is really a decline in LS formation ability with adult age or merely a relationship of aptitude at this task to level of education. Longitudinal study will be necessary to clarify this point.

The Levinson and Reese study analyzed the subjects' patterns of performance in terms of the Levine (1975) and Bowman (1963) models of hypothesis behavior. As Reese (1963) had also found and as was confirmed in the Berman *et al.* (1970) study, lose-shift–object behavior tended to appear earlier in the learning sequence than win-stay–object response patterns. A similar finding with nonhuman primates was noted above.

One new feature in the Levinson and Reese (1967) study in comparison to previous ones was the use of "backward" LS curves for homogeneous subgroups of subjects who reached LS criterion on the same day. These curves were generally biphasic. For preschoolers, there tended to be an initial gentle rise, interpretable perhaps in terms of the acquisition of lose-shift–object responding, and a final steep rise, perhaps corresponding to the addition of win-stay–object behavior. For college student subjects, the short initial phase was flat, followed by an abrupt change to criterion. Levinson and Reese commented that backward LS curves plotted on the basis of data from rhesus monkeys were not biphasic like those obtained from human subjects but instead showed a single prolonged period of gradual improvement.

On the basis of his own work and a review of the literature on position responses, object responses, and LS in children, Gholson (1980) hypothesized a three-tiered developmental process seen over the approximate ages of 2½–6 years. The youngest children operated in terms of "response sets," in which they stayed with one position or object or alternated without regard to the reinforcement contingencies in the problems. Second, the children separated their responses to winning and losing; for example, a child might develop a lose-shift pattern with respect to position or object while remaining with the response set after a win. Finally, there was a reconsolidation of task-relevant information (cues, response rules, and feedback) so that integrated hypotheses could emerge.

As was the case in the literature on LS and species differences, our present views on developmental processes in LS formation are now considerably more refined than they were in the late 1950s and early 1960s.

LS AND MENTAL RETARDATION

If LS formation is more efficient in older than in younger normal children, one would expect mentally retarded individuals to perform at a lower level than nonretarded persons of the same chronological age. Stevenson and Swartz (1958), for example, reported such findings. If speed of LS formation is related to mental age (MA) in normal children, one would also expect MA level to be predictive of the efficiency of LS formation within samples of retarded individuals. Ellis (1958), among others, reported such a finding.

Going a step further, one might find retarded individuals of at least some subgroups to be more impaired than even nonretarded comparison groups matched for mental age. Girardeau (1959), studying children with Down syndrome, found them impaired in LS formation compared with nonretarded children of the same mental age, perhaps because of the inattentive behaviors noted to be especially characteristic of these Down syndrome children.

Ellis, Girardeau, and Pryer (1962), working with a group of institutionalized mentally retarded individuals with IQs below 25, found that the asymptotic level of their average performance was even below that of rhesus monkeys on comparable problems.

In summary, even by the early 1960s, it was evident that the LS paradigm was sensitive to the phenomenon of mental retardation in humans, and the task of understanding why this was so and how to remediate such defective performance became of interest.

The Kaufman and Peterson Studies

As part of their 1955 Ph.D. dissertations at the University of Pittsburgh (just before Wischner's arrival there), Kaufman and Peterson (1958) studied object-quality LS formation in groups of normal and mentally retarded children matched for age (9–12 years) and sex. The Trial 2 performance of the retarded across problems was inferior to that of the nonretarded subjects, at least by one of the statistical tests carried out, and the retarded made significantly more stimulus perseveration errors than the controls. Kaufman and Peterson's (1965) second study, with some of the same subjects, involved a set of more difficult conditional discrimination problems (later labeled "Weigl problems" by Wischner and his associates), in which the correct object depended on the color of the background tray on a particular trial. Object A was always correct on a white tray, and Object B was always correct on a black tray, regardless of the left–right position of the objects. The age-matched normal control group did significantly better than the retarded children across a series of 96 of these six-trial conditional discrimination problems. In fact, there was no overlap between the scores of the members of the two groups.

THE PITTSBURGH STUDIES BY WISCHNER AND HIS ASSOCIATES

The stage has now been set for the presentation of a series of somewhat more detailed accounts of 14 studies carried out at the University of Pittsburgh by Wischner and his colleagues and students.

Bowes (1959)

One of the innovations that Harlow (1949) introduced when he established the discrimination LS paradigm was the practice of giving each problem in the series for only a limited number of trials (e.g., six), rather than requiring mastery of each problem before proceeding to the next. Braun, Patton, and Barnes (1952) found that even the use of three trials per problem with rhesus monkeys permitted efficient LS formation. The Bowes (1959) thesis concerned the mastery of varying numbers of early problems as a factor in the formation of object-quality LS. The subjects were all institutionalized mentally retarded children, including 28 diagnosed as "familial" and 32 children with Down syndrome. Groups matched on age, intellectual level, and diagnostic status were randomly assigned to one of four experimental conditions in which they received either 0, 3, 12, or 60 object-quality discrimination problems to a mastery criterion before being exposed to a final series with a constant three trials per problem.

In general, the more early problems these children had learned to mastery, the fewer additional three-trial problems they required to demonstrate LS formation. The use of problem-mastery pretraining of this kind seemed to be more essential for the Down syndrome children, who in the no-pretraining condition performed significantly worse than the "familial" retarded subjects. The use of such pretraining also seemed to attenuate or eliminate the correlation between LS formation and mental age and IQ. It is unfortunate that the design of the study did not permit one to sort out the effect of a given number of trials, whether part of the problem-mastery pretraining series or part of the subsequent three-trials-per-problem routine, on subsequent performance. Levine, Levinson, and Harlow (1959), working with rhesus monkeys, compared the effects of 3 and 12 trials per problem in the formation of LS. They found the critical variable to be the number of trials the animal received, regardless of how these were distributed into problems.

Hall

Hall's (1959) thesis concerns object-quality-discrimination LS formation by children with and without neurological involvement. The subjects, matched for age and IQ, attended special education classes in public schools; 13 had neurological difficulties manifested by cerebral palsy, epilepsy, and other such diagnoses. The others were considered "familial." All were given up to 120 three-trial discrimination problems.

Contrary to expectation, there was no significant difference in LS formation between the two groups of children: in each group, 9 of the 13 children reached LS criterion and 4 did not.

The only findings supportive of the hypothesized difference between the "familial" and the neurologically impaired groups were correlational ones. For the neurologically impaired group only, high scores on the Children's Manifest Anxiety Scale predicted LS errors, and teacher ratings on the Pascal and Zax (1955) scales of low educability and low cooperativeness also predicted LS errors. Thus, among neurologically impaired children, those who were anxious, or who were considered less educable and less cooperative, had poorer LS performance. Pascal and Zax (1955) had previously found significant relationships between their teachers' rating scales and performance on a double alternation task among cerebral-palsied children.

Patterson

The Patterson (1961) thesis concerned the effect of verbal pretraining on the learning of a single Weigl conditional discrimination problem. It will be recalled that Kaufman and Peterson's (1965) second study, discussed above, demonstrated highly divergent performances by normal and retarded children, aged 9–12 years, in conditional discrimination LS problems. But Kaufman and Peterson's subjects had had extensive prior experience with object-quality and discrimination-reversal LS. Later, when Wischner and his students tried to study Weigl LS formation in normal and retarded children with approximate MA levels of 9–10 years, they found that not only did LS formation fail to occur, but the children showed little evidence of improvement on a single Weigl problem in which Object A was correct with one background tray color and Object B correct with the other tray color. Some of the children, after failing to solve the problem, were asked to describe the stimuli verbally. This procedure seemed to facilitate their subsequent performance in that pilot work. Thus, the Patterson study was a systematic attempt to learn how to facilitate Weigl conditional discrimination learning.

The verbal pretraining used by Patterson was based on the principle of acquired distinctiveness of cues (Miller & Dollard, 1941). It was expected that learning distinctive verbal labels for the two background tray colors would make the subjects more likely to use this information in subsequent learning. One pretraining group thus learned to give nonsense syllable names (*gov* and *rem*) to the two trays, presented in random order. A second pretraining group learned to name the two trays, which were in this case presented with 1 pair of objects on them in random order, and a third pretraining group learned to name the trays presented with 10 different pairs of objects in random order. One of the two control groups had no pretraining, only the Weigl problem itself. The other control group had pseudopretraining involving no verbal labeling but only repeated presentation of the black and white trays with instructions to look. The subjects were 50 fourth- and fifth-grade normal elementary-school children, assigned randomly to the different experimental conditions.

It proved to be relatively easy for the children in the pretraining groups to learn to name the background trays, although the addition of objects to the stimulus display significantly increased the difficulty of the pretraining task. In general, almost all the children who had verbal pretraining learned the conditional Weigl discrimination task, while most of those in the control groups did not, as predicted. Those given verbal pretraining with the stimulus objects present on the trays performed significantly better than those whose pretraining involved the trays alone. Thus, the results of the study clearly supported the hypothesis of acquired distinctiveness of cues as applied to conditional discrimination learning.

Hall

An unpublished study by Hall (cited in Gerben, 1964) replicated the procedures of Patterson (1961) with mentally retarded children matched for mental age with Patterson's normal children. Hall's findings indicated that verbal pretraining also enhanced subsequent Weigl-problem learning in retarded children.

Gerben

The Gerben (1964) thesis was a comparison of the effects of verbal and motor pretraining on the learning of a single Weigl conditional-discrimination problem by normal and retarded children.

Patterson (1961), in her discussion section, had remarked that

> one might develop discriminative motor responses during pretraining . . . . It may well be that with certain kinds of subjects, such as retarded children, motor pretraining could be as effective as verbal pretraining. (p. 44)

Such a nonverbal procedure could be useful, given the language difficulties the retarded often experience. It was essentially this hypothesis that Gerben (1964) set out to test.

The subjects were 30 "familial" retarded children attending special education classes and 30 normal children attending third or fifth grade, matched for mental age with the retarded subjects; 10 retarded and 10 nonretarded children were randomly assigned to each experimental group (i.e., verbal pretraining, motor pretraining, or no pretraining). The apparatus used in this study permitted the presentation of color slides of the objects on either red or green backgrounds. For the two types of pretraining, the subjects were presented with pairs of such slides with the background colors varying randomly from trial to trial, and a different pair of objects was presented on each trial, chosen from a set of 10 object pairs. Verbal pretraining subjects learned to say *gov* for one background color, *rem* for the other. Motor pretraining subjects used a movable T-bar mounted on a triangular wooden box; they learned to press this bar upward for one background color and downward for the other. After pretraining (if any), each subject was given a single Weigl discrimination problem.

Although the verbal pretraining task seemed slightly easier than the motor pretraining one, the difference was not statistically significant. The normal children mastered both types of pretraining task significantly more easily than the retarded children did.

Interestingly, for the normal children, the verbal and motor pretraining procedures were essentially equivalent in their effects: both types of training facilitated subsequent Weigl discrimination learning relative to the no-pretraining condition. For the retarded subjects, contrary to prediction, the results of the two types of pretraining were different: while the verbal pretraining significantly facilitated subsequent Weigl discrimination learning, the motor pretraining did not have effects that differed significantly from those of the no-pretraining condition. One way of accounting for these results would be to hypothesize that some kind of overt or covert labeling of the background cues is what is really necessary, and that the normal subjects accompany their motor pretraining with such a label (e.g., "up" or "down"), while the retarded do not. Of course, additional research is needed to assess the validity of such a speculation.

Routh and Wischner

The Routh and Wischner (1970) study was an attempt to extend Patterson's (1961) findings concerning verbal pretraining effects from a single Weigl conditional-discrimination problem to Weigl LS formation. The subjects were 50 children of average intelligence, aged 7–11 years, assigned randomly to one of five experimental conditions. The overall control group received only the LS series of 90 six-trial Weigl problems. The verbal pretraining group first learned to say *gov* for one background tray color and *rem* for the other, regardless of the stimulus objects present, as in the Patterson (1961), Hall (cited in Gerben, 1965), and Gerben (1964) studies, and they then received the LS series. The single-problem group received verbal pretraining, then a single Weigl problem to mastery, and finally the LS series. Two other experimental conditions were introduced in an attempt to control for the effects of sheer experience involved in the single-problem mastery. The subjects in the "random" single-problem group first received verbal pretraining, then a number of trials on one Weigl problem equal with those in the single-problem group subject for subject, but with random, approximately 50% reinforcement (i.e., either both or neither of the food wells was baited with M&M candy on predetermined trials), and then the LS series. The subjects in the "yoked" single-problem group first received verbal pretraining, then a number of trials on the single problem equal to those of the single-problem group and yoked to these subjects in trial-for-trial reinforcement patterns rising to 100% at the end, and then the LS series.

The subjects in the "yoked" single-problem control group must have acquired some type of interfering response tendencies as part of their single-problem experience, for they did poorly on the final LS series although they had previously received verbal pretraining. The other results showed that verbal pretraining significantly facilitated Weigl LS formation, as expected. Learning a single Weigl problem to criterion before the six-trial-per-problem LS series did not have any additional facilitating effect.

Bowes (1962)

Bowes's (1962) dissertation examined object-quality LS formation in normal first- and third-grade children as a function of the degree of similarity of the pairs of stimuli making up the discrimination problems and as a function of shifting from one level of stimulus similarity to another. Superior LS performance was found in the children on the easier discrimination problems (low stimulus similarity within pairs) as compared with those assigned difficult (high-stimulus-similarity) problems. Also, shifting from one level of difficulty of problem to another was found to facilitate LS performance at the other level of difficulty. And most interestingly, in terms of the goal of training children to form LS efficiently, the children shifting from easy to difficult discrimination problems performed better on the latter than the subjects who had worked only on difficult problems from the beginning.

Wischner, Braun, and Patton

The Wischner, Braun, and Patton (1962) study was a demonstration of the long-term retention of an object-quality LS by retarded children over a period of approximately six months. This study was noteworthy in part because there had been hardly any previous information in the literature on the long-term retention of LS.

The subjects were 32 mentally retarded children attending special classes. Their mental ages ranged from approximately 4 to 11 years, and it was of interest that mental age was found to be significantly correlated with LS errors only in the group with MAs below 8 years. Evidently, object-quality LS is not a sufficiently challenging task to produce correlations at higher MA levels.

The children were originally given a series of up to 120 discrimination problems with three trials per problem. In all, 20 of the 32 subjects reached the LS criterion within the initial maximum of up to 10 days of training. Better than half the noncriterion subjects had comments in their school records indicating possible neurological involvement, while no such entries were found in the records of the children who reached criterion.

The retention testing five to seven months later showed only a small decrement in performance, and two days of additional practice were sufficient to bring the subjects' Trial 3 performance back to where it was at the termination of the original learning. The subjects who had not reached criterion during the original learning continued to perform poorly at the time of the retention test, though they seemed to have learned and retained something, which produced performance a bit above a chance level.

Wischner and O'Donnell

The Wischner and O'Donnell (1962) study involved a novel paradigm of concurrent or serial LS formation. In this procedure, instead of presenting a single pair of objects for a predetermined number of trials, then another pair for the same number of trials, and so on, there was a single presentation of all pairs of objects before any of the objects was presented for the second trial. A *trial* was thus defined as one complete presentation of all the pairs to be discriminated. The procedure was therefore in some ways analogous to paired-associate learning, but in this case, the object pairs were presented in a constant sequence.

The subjects were 10 normal and 11 mentally retarded children matched for mental age. Each child learned, successively, five concurrent problems, each containing either 5 or 10 object pairs. Both the normal and the retarded children formed concurrent LS. The retarded were unexpectedly significantly superior to the normals on the first concurrent problem, but then the normal children were significantly superior to the retarded on all subsequent problems. The most interesting finding of this study, however, was a significant serial-position effect seen in the retarded children only. They performed better on the first and last few stimulus-object pairs within problems than on the pairs that were in the middle. This is a phenomenon worthy of further investigation.

deHaan and Wischner

The deHaan and Wischner (1963) study was of some methodological importance in comparing two different types of LS training apparatus used in the University of Pittsburgh laboratory. One apparatus was the traditional Wisconsin General Test Apparatus adapted for use with children, in which actual three-dimensional stimulus objects were presented to the subject on a tray; the subject responded by displacing one of the objects to find either an M&M candy or an empty foodwell underneath. The other apparatus was an automated version of the LS procedure involving the rear projection of photographs of the same objects (color slides) onto screens. The subject responded by pressing a lever beneath one of the screens, a correct response being followed by the delivery of an M&M candy to a central well.

The subjects were 70 institutionalized retarded children, half of whom received up to 120 problems on the traditional version of the Wisconsin General Test Apparatus, the other half on the automated version of the apparatus. The performance of these two groups was highly similar, providing some reassurance that studies using these different types of apparatus may be regarded as comparable. Readers interested in a fuller discussion of some of the theoretical points addressed in this study (e.g., spatial contiguity between cue, response, and reward) may refer to the original published version.

Hall

The Hall (1963) dissertation, like several others that have been discussed, examined the effects of learning a single problem to mastery on subsequent LS formation, and it used institutionalized retarded children as subjects. It also introduced two rather novel elements. One of these was the "extinction" of single-problem or LS discriminative responding, that is, termination of all reinforcement of responses until a subject had dropped from 100% "correct" back to a 50%, or chance, level of responding to either object. The other novel procedure, introduced only during the LS problems, involved either always rewarding the first object chosen on Trial 1 and then pairing that object with a new object on subsequent trials (called a *reward procedure*) or never rewarding the object chosen on Trial 1, then pairing the object chosen with a new one on subsequent trials (called a *non-reward procedure*).

The design of the study was a 3 (type of pretraining) × 2 (type of Trial 1 procedure) factorial one. The first group of 20 subjects received no pretraining problem, only the LS series of up to 100 problems at six trials per problem, and then LS extinction. The second group of 20 subjects received a single discrimination problem to mastery, then the LS series, then LS extinction. The third group of 20 subjects learned the single discrimination problem, then was extinguished on that problem, then received the LS series, and finally LS extinction. Within each of these groups during the LS series, half the subjects had the reward and half the nonreward procedure on Trial 1 of each problem.

The results are not easily summarized or placed in theoretical context. Single-problem learning clearly facilitated subsequent LS performance, in line with previous results. However, for some reason, the group that was "extinguished" on the single problem after learning it did the best of all in subsequent LS acquisition—by some measures, significantly better than the group that learned only a single problem without undergoing "extinction." Perhaps it was helpful to extinguish the response to what Restle (1958) called Type *b* cues (i.e. those that are valid only for a particular problem).

In general, the subjects who were always given a reward on the first trial of LS problems did better on the LS series than those given a nonreward on each LS Trial 1. One speculation that occurs to the present author is that the first-trial reward procedure might have helped by facilitating the learning of win-stay–object responding.

LS extinction seemed abrupt by some measures (i.e., an immediate return to chance level responding), but a closer look at Trials 2 and 3 suggested a more gradual process and one that was complexly influenced by the previous first-trial reward or nonreward procedures.

The whole question of the processes underlying the extinction of a discrimination problem and of LS responding raised by Hall's study is an intriguing one and is in need of considerable further study and theoretical analysis.

Gerben

Gerben's (1966) dissertation examined once more the relationship between the mastery of single discrimination problems and LS formation, but it reversed the order of presentation. That is, in Gerben's study the pretraining procedures consisted of varying numbers of four-trial LS problems, and the subsequent performance measures were several discrimination problems, each learned to mastery.

The subjects were 50 kindergarten children of average intelligence, randomly assigned to one of five different experimental conditions: 0, 18, 36, or 54

LS problems before exposure to a series of four discrimination problems, each learned to mastery; or LS problems alone, given until a criterion of errorless performance was reached. In this case, all of the discrimination problems were three-choice rather than two-choice ones and were based on the oddity principle, in which the subject had to learn to choose Object A when presented with two examples of Object B, and to choose Object B when presented with two examples of Object A.

Although the subjects in the groups with 18 and 36 preliminary LS problems did not reveal any sign of learning or LS formation during these problems, there was a significant relationship between the number of pretraining LS problems given (0, 18, 36, or 54) and the number of trials needed to learn the first two mastery problems. That is, the LS problems facilitated single-problem learning and transfer. However, in contrast to the findings of, for example, Levine et al. (1959) using monkeys and object quality LS, Gerben found that the average amount learned per mastery trial was significantly greater than the average learned per LS trial. The greatest overall learning efficiency in achieving errorless performance was therefore found in the group given no LS pretraining problems before being given the four mastery problems.

Gerben examined the course of a number of systematic response tendencies during learning and found evidence for the following general sequence: position-oriented responding, then object-oriented responding, and finally, responding oriented toward the similarity–oddity dimension embedded in the problems. Of course, in a three-choice oddity-discrimination problem, position-oriented responses produce only 33% reward on the average. Win-stay–lose-shift (object) responses, like other object-oriented responses in this type of problem are not maximally adaptive, producing at best 50% reward on the average. In order to master an oddity problem, the subject must learn systematic observation and comparison of all three stimuli and the choice of the odd object rather than the position- or object-based response.

Colletti

The Colletti (1971) dissertation investigated three types of LS formation (in order of presumed increasing difficulty: object quality, oddity and Weigl LS) in adult male neurological patients. The subjects were 12 brain-damaged patients with right hemiplegia and aphasia; 12 nonaphasic, left-hemiplegic brain-damaged patients; and 12 hospital control patients with no neurological or psychiatric impairment. The groups were matched on age. The study of aphasic and nonaphasic brain-damaged patients might, it was hoped, throw some light on whether successful LS formation in humans necessarily involves linguistic mediational processes, as opposed to some abstract capacity factors represented in the brain but transcending language.

Colletti employed a new LS procedure with these adult subjects, using a memory drum rather than the Wisconsin General Test Apparatus; low-meaningful nonsense syllables rather than three-dimensional objects as stimuli; and verbal reinforcement ("right") for correct responding, rather than candy. This procedure, which permitted the presentation of more LS problems per day, had previously been used in unpublished research with retarded children by Wischner and Gerben. They found evidence of LS formation with it.

For each of the three types of LS studied, 100 four-trial problems were presented to the subjects, following initial pretraining on a single object-quality-discrimination problem. The sequence of administration of the three types of LS series was counterbalanced across subjects.

The two brain-damaged groups and the controls performed similarly on the initial-pretraining discrimination problem; that is, intraproblem learning of this kind was insensitive to their neuropsychological status. There was no consistent correlation of IQ and performance on discrimination learning or LS procedures among the three groups of subjects.

As expected, the subjects found the object-quality LS easiest, had increasing difficulty with the oddity LS, and found the Weigl LS the most difficult. The two brain-damaged groups performed more poorly than the controls on all types of LS formation, but the aphasics did not differ significantly from the left-hemiplegic group. The oddity LS and especially the Weigl LS were relatively more difficult for all of the brain-damaged patients than for the controls.

The results of the Colletti study appear to be in line with previous studies of children by Wischner and his associates already reviewed (i.e., Bowes, 1959; Wischner et al., 1962) and with considerable animal research in indicating the sensitivity of LS procedures to neurological impairment. Thus, this study extended the implications of the previous research to adult humans with acquired brain lesions. These LS procedures seem to be tapping something about the capacities of the brain beyond what is measured by IQ tests. However, there is little support in the Colletti study for the specific importance of linguistic mediational processes in LS formation, since the aphasics did as well as the nonaphasic brain-damaged patients.

Filicki

The final study in the series carried out by Wischner's students at Pittsburgh, the Filicki (1972) dissertation, applied LS procedures to process and reactive schizophrenic patients. The same general paradigm was used as in the Colletti (1971) study but, in this case, with different subjects receiving object-quality, oddity, and Weigl LS procedures. The memory drum version of these tasks was used, with "yes" and "no" feedback from the experimenter for correct or incorrect responding. This was evidently the first study using LS procedures with a schizophrenic subject population. Filicki hypothesized that because of the impairment in their ability to abstract, schizophrenics, especially process schizophrenics, would perform more poorly than control subjects on these LS tasks.

The subjects were 108 Veterans Administration patients, including 72 from a neuropsychiatric hospital with an unequivocal diagnosis of schizophrenia and 36 from a general medical and surgical hospital with no known psychiatric difficulty. The schizophrenics were subdivided into process and reactive groups of 36 each, using Phillips Scale ratings. Within these groups, 12 subjects were randomly assigned to each of the experimental LS conditions.

The three types of subjects did not differ significantly on an initial single-object–quality-discrimination learning problem given as a pretraining task. Although the process schizophrenic subjects were significantly older than the reactive schizophrenics, age was not generally a significant correlate of discrimination learning or LS performance.

Over all types of subjects, the object-quality LS problems were the easiest, the oddity problems of intermediate difficulty, and the Weigl problems the most difficult, as expected. Also, as predicted, the process schizophrenics were the most impaired of the three groups in their performance, particularly on the Weigl LS. The control subjects' performance was the best, and the performance of the reactive schizophrenics was intermediate. In general, the performance of the reactive schizophrenics was closer to that of the controls than to that of the process schizophrenics. An analysis of systematic response tendencies revealed few significant differences among the groups.

Although Filicki explained these schizophrenics' difficulties with LS problems in terms of their impaired abstract abilities, he noted that their level of LS performance was still superior to that of the brain-damaged patients studied by Colletti (1971).

CONCLUSIONS AND IMPLICATIONS

This chapter began with a broad review of the animal and human LS literature and proceeded to present the series of studies carried out by Wischner and his associates. It remains to pull together the main conclusions from the Pittsburgh studies and to discuss them in relation to some other developments in the field.

The following conclusions seem to follow from the Pittsburgh LS studies:

a. LS procedures can be adapted for subjects of widely varied age, level of mental functioning, and psychopathology. Harlow's basic Wisconsin General Test Apparatus can be adapted for use with children and can be automated or translated into a memory drum procedure for use with adults without seeming to produce any marked alteration in the processes involved in LS formation (Colletti, 1971; deHaan & Wischner, 1963; Filicki, 1972).

b. Pretraining in the form of learning single discrimination problems to mastery can generally be expected to facilitate children's LS formation more than an equivalent number of trials in a fixed trials-per-problem procedure (Bowes, 1959; Hall, 1963; and especially Gerben, 1966).

c. Verbal pretraining involving the labeling of the background cues facilitates the learning of a Weigl conditional-discrimination problem by normal and retarded children, whereas motor pretraining of the same kind seems to be effective only with normal children. Verbal pretraining also facilitates Weigl LS formation (Gerben, 1964; Hall, 1962; Patterson, 1961; Routh & Wischner, 1970).

d. Learning a series of easier discrimination problems and then shifting to more difficult ones may facilitate LS formation more than beginning with high-difficulty problems (Bowes, 1962).

e. LS formation seems to be associated with excellent long-term retention in retarded as well as normal children (Wischner et al., 1962).

f. The concurrent LS paradigm may produce serial position effects, at least in certain populations and circumstances (Wischner & O'Donnell, 1962).

g. Given problems of suitable difficulty, LS performance seems to be sensitive to various aspects of neurological impairment. This is not generally true of performance on single discrimination problems. Pertinent studies consistent with these conclusions include those of Bowes (1959), Wischner et al. (1962), and Colletti (1971).

h. The sensitivity of LS procedures to levels of mental retardation in children as indexed by mental age or IQ seems clearest at mental age levels below 8 (Wischner et al., 1962). In adulthood, LS performance seems relatively unrelated to IQ differences (Colletti, 1971).

i. Impairments in LS formation may be associated with severe psychopathology (Filicki, 1972).

None of the Pittsburgh studies made use of methods such as the blank-trials or introtact procedures or the plotting of "backward" LS curves for homogeneous subgroups of subjects. As the study by Levinson and Reese (1967) discussed in the introduction to this chapter, as well as the previous chapter in this volume by Spiker and Cantor, makes clear, such techniques can add significantly to one's understanding of the processes underlying discrimination learning and learning sets. It is therefore recommended that any who attempt to build on the work begun by the Pittsburgh studies take note of these important new methods. They may help in elucidating some of the puzzling findings reported above.

Nevertheless, the Pittsburgh studies have significantly advanced knowledge in this field, and their results need to be more widely disseminated.

During recent years, there has been a rather precipitous decline in the number of LS studies being published, as new research fads have lured investigators away to other paradigms. Nevertheless, as the work of Levine (1975),

Gholson (1980), and others has shown, LS phenomena can easily be integrated into contemporary cognitive approaches in psychology.

Speaking as a clinical psychologist, the present author would find it sad if researchers neglected the potential of the LS paradigm in studying psychopathology. To highlight this potential, it may be suitable to close the chapter with a few intriguing examples of clinically oriented LS research (other than the Pittsburgh studies) that have appeared over the last 20 years.

Restle, Andrews, and Rokeach (1964), using Rokeach's Dogmatism Scale to select their subjects, studied the performance of open- and closed-minded college-student subjects on reversal LS problems and oddity problems. To a sophisticated and open-minded human subject, reversal learning, in which the correct object is changed from Object A to Object B and back again at unpredictable times, must seem rather arbitrary if not downright authoritarian. Such a subject may do poorly if he or she keeps looking for some nonexistent rational principle to use as a basis of response. Closed-minded subjects, who are used to accepting authority passively, were found by Restle *et al.* (1964) to perform better on reversal LS problems than did open-minded subjects. Oddity problems, which can be solved on the basis of a rational principle, were learned better by open-minded subjects.

Pearson (1969) explored the use of object-quality-discrimination learning problems as a measure of academic potential among a group of cerebral-palsied children 2–3½ years old. Children whose IQ test performance was poor but who were rated "not retarded" by their teachers did significantly better on the LS series than children with similar test scores rated "retarded" by their teachers.

Levin, Rapin, Costa, and Tourk (1971) studied the acquisition of a conditioned matching LS in 64 children in a school for the deaf. A follow-up study of a subgroup of these children with communication disorders showed that LS performance significantly predicted their academic achievement one year later.

Finally, Prior and Chen (1975) studied the object-quality LS performance of 19 autistic children compared with that of MA- and IQ-matched control groups of normal and retarded children. The limiting factor for the autistic children in demonstrating LS mastery seemed to be their amount of negativistic, withdrawn, and psychotic behavior during the task, a matter of "style" rather than intellect. Still, the autistic children's performance was better than one would have expected in terms of their measured MA levels, suggesting that their true level of mental development might be higher than that obtained with standard measuring techniques.

In short, LS procedures seem to tap into human higher mental processes with a sensitivity that is exceeded by few, if any, other nonverbal laboratory tasks available to the psychologist. It is predicted that this fact will eventually lead to a renaissance in their use by researchers.

REFERENCES

Berman, P. W., Rane, N. G., & Bahow, E. Age changes in children's learning set with win-stay, lose-shift problems. *Developmental Psychology*, 1970, *2*, 233–239.

Bowes, A. E. *Mastery of varying numbers of early problems as a factor in the formation of object-quality learning sets in two types of mentally retarded children.* Unpublished M.S. thesis, University of Pittsburgh, 1959.

Bowes, A. E. *Problem difficulty as a factor in learning set formation by children.* Unpublished Ph.D. dissertation, University of Pittsburgh, 1962.

Bowman, R. E. Discrimination learning set performance under intermittent and secondary reinforcement. *Journal of Comparative and Physiological Psychology*, 1963, *56*, 429–434.

Braun, H. W., Patton, R. A., & Barnes, H. W. Effects of electroshock convulsion upon the learning performance of monkeys: I. Object-quality discrimination learning. *Journal of Comparative and Physiological Psychology*, 1952, *45*, 231–238.

Colletti, R. B. *Learning set formation in brain-damaged patients with and without aphasia as a function of problem difficulty.* Doctoral dissertation, University of Pittsburgh, 1971.

deHaan, H. J., & Wischner, G. J. Three-dimensional objects versus projected color photographs of objects as stimuli in learning-set formation by retarded children. *Journal of Comparative and Physiological Psychology*, 1963, *56*, 440–444.

Ellis, N. R. Object-quality discrimination learning sets in mental defectives. *Journal of Comparative and Physiological Psychology*, 1958, *51*, 79–81.

Ellis, N. R., Girardeau, F. L., & Pryer, M. W. Analysis of learning sets in normal and severely defective humans. *Journal of Comparative and Physiological Psychology*, 1962, *55*, 860–865.

Fagen, J. W. Interproblem learning in ten-month-old infants. *Child Development*, 1977, *48*, 786–796.

Filicki, E. S. *Learning set formation in process and reactive schizophrenics as a function of paradigm difficulty.* Doctoral dissertation, University of Pittsburgh, 1972.

Gerben, M. J. *A comparison of the effects of motor and verbal pretraining on the learning of a single Weigl discrimination by normal and retarded children.* Unpublished M.S. thesis, University of Pittsburgh, 1964.

Gerben, M. J. *Presolution oddity learning set training as a variable in oddity discrimination learning and learning set formation by children.* Unpublished Ph.D. dissertation, University of Pittsburgh, 1966.

Gholson, B. *The cognitive-developmental basis of human learning: Studies in hypothesis testing.* New York: Academic Press, 1980.

Girardeau, F. L. The formation of discrimination learning sets in Mongoloid and normal children. *Journal of Comparative and Physiological Psychology*, 1959, *52*, 566–570.

Hall, R. C. *Object-quality discrimination learning-set formation by children with and without central organic involvement.* Unpublished M.S. thesis, University of Pittsburgh, 1959.

Hall, R. C. *Factors influencing acquisition and extinction of an object quality discrimination learning set in mentally retarded children.* Unpublished Ph.D. dissertation, University of Pittsburgh, 1963.

Harlow, H. F. The formation of learning sets. *Psychological Review*, 1949, *56*, 51–65.

Harlow, H. F. Learning set and error factor theory. In S. Koch (Ed.), *Psychology: A study of a science*, Vol. 2. New York: McGraw-Hill, 1959.

Harlow, H. F., Harlow, M. K., Rueping, R. R., & Mason, W. A. Performance of infant rhesus monkeys on discrimination learning, delayed response, and discrimination learning set. *Journal of Comparative and Physiological Psychology*, 1960, *53*, 113–121.

Herman, L. M., & Arbeit, W. R. Stimulus control and auditory discrimination learning sets in the bottle-nose dolphin. *Journal of the Experimental Analysis of Behavior*, 1973, *19*, 379–397.

Kaufman, M. E., & Peterson, W. M. Acquisition of a learning set by normal and mentally retarded children. *Journal of Comparative and Physiological Psychology*, 1958, *51*, 619–621.

Kaufman, M. E., & Peterson, W. M. Acquisition of a conditional discrimination learning-set by normal and mentally retarded children. *American Journal of Mental Deficiency*, 1965, *69*, 865–870.

Koch, M. B., & Meyer, D. R. A relationship of mental age to learning-set formation in the preschool child. *Journal of Comparative and Physiological Psychology*, 1959, *52*, 387–389.

Leonard, C., Schneider, G. E., & Gross, C. G. Performance on learning set and delayed-response tasks by tree shrews (*Tupaia glis*). *Journal of Comparative and Physiological Psychology*, 1966, *62*, 501–504.

Levin, G. R., Rapin, I., Costa, L. D., & Tourk, L. Acquisition of a learning set by children with communication disorders. *Journal of Communication Disorders*, 1971, *4*, 83–98.

Levine, M. A model of hypothesis behavior in discrimination learning set. *Psychological Review*, 1959, *66*, 353–366.

Levine, M. (Ed.). *A cognitive theory of learning: Research on hypothesis testing*. Hillsdale, N.J.: Erlbaum, 1975.

Levine, M., Levinson, B., & Harlow, H. F. Trials per problem as a variable in the acquisition of discrimination set. *Journal of Comparative and Physiological Psychology*, 1959, *52*, 396–398.

Levinson, B., & Reese, H. W. Patterns of discrimination learning set in preschool children, fifth graders, college freshmen, and the aged. *Monographs of the Society for Research in Child Development*, 1967, *32* (Serial No. 115).

Miles, R. C. Learning set formation in the squirrel monkey. *Journal of Comparative and Physiological Psychology*, 1957, *50*, 356–357.

Miller, N. E., & Dollard, J. *Social learning and imitation*. New Haven, Conn.: Yale University Press, 1941.

Pascal, G. R., & Zax, M. Double alternation performance as a measure of educability in cerebral palsied children. *American Journal of Mental Deficiency*, 1955, *59*, 658–665.

Patterson, J. R. *The effects of verbal pretraining on the learning of a single Weigl problem*. Unpublished M.S. thesis, University of Pittsburgh, 1961.

Pearson, D. Object-discrimination learning set acquisition in young cerebral palsied children in relation to tested and rated intelligence. *Journal of Consulting and Clinical Psychology*, 1969, *33*, 478–484.

Phillips, S., & Levine, M. Probing for hypotheses with adults and children: Blank trials and introtacts. *Journal of Experiment Psychology: General*, 1975, *104*, 327–354.

Prior, M. R., & Chen, C. S. Learning set acquisition in autistic children. *Journal of Abnormal Psychology*, 1975, *84*, 701–708.

Reese, H. W. Discrimination learning sets in children. In L. Lipsitt & C. C. Spiker (Eds.), *Advances in child development and behavior*. New York: Academic Press, 1963.

Restle, F. Toward a quantitative description of learning set data. *Psychological Review*, 1958, *65*, 77–91.

Restle, F., Andrews, M., & Rokeach, M. Differences between open- and closed-minded subjects on learning-set and oddity problems. *Journal of Abnormal and Social Psychology*, 1964, *68*, 648–654.

Ricciardi, A. M., & Treichler, F. R. Prior training influences on transfer to learning set by squirrel monkeys. *Journal of Comparative and Physiological Psychology*, 1970, *73*, 314–319.

Roberts, K. E. The ability of preschool children to solve problems in which a simple principle of relationship is kept constant. *Journal of Genetic Psychology*, 1932, *40*, 118–133.

Roberts, K. E. Learning in preschool and orphanage children. *University of Iowa Studies in Child Welfare*, 1933, *7*, No. 3.

Routh, D. K., & Wischner, G. J. Effect of verbal pretraining and single-problem mastery on Weigl learning-set formation in children. *Developmental Psychlogy*, 1970, *2*, 176–180.

Schusterman, R. J. Transfer effects of successive discrimination-reversal training in chimpanzees. *Science*, 1962, *137*, 422–423.

Slotnick, B. M., & Katz, H. M. Olfactory learning-set formation in rats. *Science*, 1974, *185*, 796–798.

Stevenson, H. W., & Swartz, J. D. Learning set in children as a function of intellectual level. *Journal of Comparative and Physiological Psychology*, 1958, *51*, 755–757.

Weigl, E. On the psychology of so-called processes of abstraction. *Journal of Abnormal Psychology*, 1941, *36*, 3–33. (Originally published 1927.)

Wischner, G. J., & O'Donnell, J. P. Concurrent learning-set formation in normal and retarded children. *Journal of Comparative and Physiological Psychology*, 1962, *55*, 524–527.

Wischner, G. J., Braun, H. W., & Patton, R. A. Acquisition and long-term retention of an object-quality learning set by retarded children. *Journal of Comparative and Physiological Psychology*, 1962, *55*, 518–523.

5 Feedback and Motor Control in Stuttering

SHARON R. GARBER AND GERALD M. SIEGEL

For speech production to proceed smoothly, the timing and coordination of a variety of complex movement patterns must be programmed and carried out in a precise fashion. During the moment of stuttering, this process is disrupted, and the stutterer may appear to be struggling in the grip of an uncontrollable spasm or seizure. For this and other reasons, early theorists attempted to identify some underlying physical abnormality as the root cause of stuttering. The earliest programmatic research in stuttering involved comparisons of stutterers and non-stutterers on a great variety of physiological, motor, and perceptual variables. After many years of such research, the accumulated evidence was at best suggestive, and no constellation of physiological variables emerged that could unequivocally be identified with either the person who stutters or the moment of stuttering (Bloodstein, 1975).

Partly because of these negative findings and partly because the intellectual atmosphere changed, there was a switch in emphasis to behavioral or environmental explanations of stuttering. During this era, stuttering was analyzed within the context of psychoanalytic theory (Glauber, 1958), diagnosogenic theory (Johnson, 1959, 1967), and several variations of learning theory (Brutten & Shoemaker, 1967; Goldiamond, 1965; Wischner, 1950, 1952).

In recent years, there has been a renewed interest in a physiological explanation for stuttering, motivated, perhaps, by the failure of behaviorism to provide a satisfactory explanation of stuttering and by the development of new theories and

SHARON R. GARBER ● Department of Speech and Theater Arts, University of Pittsburgh, Pittsburgh, Pennsylvania 15260. GERALD M. SIEGEL ● Center for Research in Human Learning and Department of Communication Disorders, University of Minnesota, Minneapolis, Minnesota 55455.

more sophisticated analyses of motor performance. Two major orientations have emerged, one dealing with stuttering as a disorder of the feedback system, and the other concerned with various aspects of motor control, with particular emphasis on laryngeal control. These two approaches to stuttering form the basis of the present chapter.

FEEDBACK

In his model of speech as a servosystem, Fairbanks (1954) suggested that speakers monitor their output to determine whether errors have occurred and to correct these errors when necessary, much as a heating system self-corrects when the temperature deviates from the thermostatic setting. A fault in some part of the feedback system, it was presumed, might cause a breakdown in performance. About the time that Fairbanks's paper came out, Lee (1951) discovered that normal persons who hear their voices fed back with a short delay evidence a disruption in speech that is very reminiscent of stuttering. Taken together, the Fairbanks and Lee papers suggested that stutterers may have an internal distortion of the feedback system that leads to the stuttering behavior. A huge amount of research followed, and it led Yates (1963b) to the optimistic conclusion that a major breakthrough had been made in the understanding of stuttering. As will be evident, the study of feedback processes in normal speakers and stutterers proceeded vigorously, but the breakthrough that seemed to be imminent has not occurred.

In part, the fault seems to be in the basic model. In the servosystem model proposed by Fairbanks, speech is constantly monitored by some combination of air- and bone-conducted auditory feedback and, presumably less importantly, tactile and proprioceptive feedback. The role accorded to auditory feedback appears now to be unwarranted because of speed limitations. Fairbanks did not specify the unit of monitoring in his system. If the unit is understood to be a phoneme or even a syllable, continuous auditory regulation appears unlikely. By the time auditory feedback could be processed, it would be too late to make corrections, and the feedback system would thus appear to have little value in the regulation of speech. The speed limitations are eased if control is relegated to the proprioceptive feedback system (MacNeilage, 1970) or if the model is extended to include unconscious control. In the Fowler, Rubin, Remez, and Turvey (1980) theory of speech production, muscle coordination and regrouping occur at a reflexive level, with the muscles feeding information to each other and then coordinating and regrouping according to the context of the situation. However, in the model proposed by Fairbanks, the logic of the timing constraints would seem to argue against the degree of regulation accorded to the auditory feedback loops.

In addition, the results of systematic research suggest that while auditory feedback may be necessary for speech development (Fry, 1966; Van Riper, 1971), adults do not ordinarily require auditory feedback: witness their ability to speak intelligibly in the presence of extremely high levels of noise. Peterson and Shoup (1966) pressed the issue even further and suggested that adult speech is free from all forms of feedback control. There have been numerous studies of normal adults in which high levels of noise have been combined with oral desensitization, with only minimal loss of speech intelligibility (Ringel, 1970), this despite the probability that the nerve block procedures inadvertently introduced involvement of the motor or central nervous system (Abbs, Folkins, & Sivarajan, 1976; Borden, Harris, & Catena, 1973; Locke, 1968).

In summary, the Fairbanks model did not sufficiently acknowledge the time constraints in the auditory feedback system and seems to imply a much greater degree of feedback control than is necessary for speech production. If adults do use feedback during speech production, it is doubtful that it is used constantly, or that all feedback channels are used in the same way. For example, auditory feedback may be used to monitor prosodic features such as vocal intensity, while proprioceptive feedback may be important in the monitoring of articulation. Consonants and vowels may require different types of monitoring, since vowels are relatively steady-state, while consonants are generally dynamic and fleeting. It may be that feedback monitoring is normally minimal but becomes active when communication is at risk (Siegel & Pick, 1974). Though the model originally proposed by Fairbanks no longer seems entirely adequate as a way of accounting for normal speech production, it did raise some intriguing and influential possibilities for conceptualizing the problem of stuttering as an interference with the feedback loop (Mysak, 1960; Van Riper, 1971; Yates, 1963b). The effects of various feedback manipulations on normal speech are explored in the next section, with a particular concern about the possibility that speech disruptions that are observed may serve as an analogue to stuttering.

Feedback Disruptions in Normal Speakers

Auditory masking alters vocal intensity, fundamental frequency, and speech rate (Lane & Tranel, 1971), but there is no report of stuttering behaviors resulting from such masking (Lane & Tranel, 1971; Van Riper, 1971). Nor does filtering of the speaker's feedback affect fluency (Garber & Moller, 1979). Interference with tactile or proprioceptive feedback by topical or local anesthesia in the oral cavity has a much greater effect on articulation than does masking, but again, these procedures do not appear to interfere with fluency (Lane & Tranel, 1971; Ringel, 1970).

Thus, though several feedback alterations have been studied in normal speakers, only delayed auditory feedback (DAF) appears to produce stuttering-like behavior, most markedly when the delay is in the vicinity of 200 msec. Individuals differ in their susceptibility to DAF, in terms of both the kind and the extent of their reactions (Burke, 1975a; Yates, 1963a), but attempts to determine what factors dispose certain speakers to be susceptible have not been fruitful (Burke, 1975a), and, indeed, no satisfactory explanation has yet been offered as to why DAF should be disruptive to any speaker.

Work in the area of vision has shown that subjects adapt to almost any sort of perceptual distortion as long as the distortion is constant. For example, adults soon adapt to a prism that turns their visual world topsy-turvy (Held & Freedman, 1963). DAF also imposes a constant distortion on the speaker, though a temporal rather than a spatial one, but speakers seem to adapt little, if at all (Atkinson, 1953; Tiffany & Hanley, 1956; Winchester, Gibbons, & Krebs, 1959). It should be noted that these studies all involve relatively short durations of exposure to DAF and that adaptation may require much longer experience with DAF. The extent to which normal speakers would ultimately adapt to other feedback manipulations, such as sidetone amplification, noise, or masking, is not yet known.

Delayed feedback also produces perturbations in nonspeech tasks. Chase, Rapin, Gilden, Sutton, and Guilfoyle (1961) found that the key-tapping responses of adults were disrupted by delayed light flashes, tactile pulses, or auditory feedback. No attempt was made to determine whether these perturbations would adapt. Delayed visual feedback has also been shown to disturb visual tracking (Smith, 1962), but again, exposures were too short to test for adaptation. Thus, it appears that delayed sensory feedback is disruptive to a variety of behaviors, including speech, but it is not yet clear whether the speech disruptions induced by DAF are different from the perturbations caused in other modalities, or even from other feedback manipulations applied to speech. These possibilities deserve further research.

It should be noted that the vast majority of feedback research has involved static alterations in feedback. Recent work by McClean (1977) suggests that the effects on speech may be quite different when alterations are introduced in random fashion. McClean's work involved the effects of random noise presentation on lip movement. This work should be extended to other types of measurements and feedback disruptions. Perhaps with this technique, fluency disruptions will emerge in domains other than the temporal.

Feedback Processes in Stuttering

The fact that some normal speakers respond adversely to DAF and that the responses are not readily dissipated even with extended exposure would seem to make even more compelling the possibility that stutterers are continually forced to cope with an abnormal feedback system. Several accounts of stuttering have been offered that build on such a possibility. Van Riper (1971) and Gruber (1965) suggested that the stutterer may have failed to make the transition from auditory to tactile monitoring. Lane and Tranel (1971) raised the possibility that stutterers are excessively attentive to their auditory feedback. These are interesting speculations, but it is not clear why excessive monitoring of one or all feedback channels should result in stuttering. Yates (1963b), drawing on the research of Cherry and Sayers (1956), argued more specifically that stutterers suffer from an abnormal discrepancy between their air- and bone-conducted feedback and that the deviation lies primarily in the bone conduction. Neilson and Neilson (1979) have suggested that stutterers have difficulty coordinating auditory information and movement. Others have suggested of stutterers that there may be an abnormality in phase relationships between the two ears (Stromsta, 1972), that the reflex mechanisms involved in their speech production may be abnormal (Wyke, 1974), or, more particularly, that their auditory feedback may be distorted because of a malfunction of the stapedial reflex of the middle ear (Webster & Lubker, 1968). None of these theories, it should be noted, gives a satisfactory explanation for certain occasions when stuttering is reduced or absent, as when the stutterer addresses a pet or a young child or suddenly experiences unaccountable periods of complete fluency before again lapsing into stuttering.

There is a final point that should be made concerning the analogy that is drawn between stuttering and the effects of DAF on normal speakers. In part, the motivation for thinking of stuttering as a feedback failure comes from the severe disruptions to speech that occur when speech is delayed. However, it is not clear how the effects of DAF in normals correspond to the various feedback theories of stuttering. For example, there is no indication of how the effects of an abnormal stapedial reflex should be related to the phenomena underlying DAF. Thus, while the effects of DAF on normal speakers are offered as evidence for a feedback explanation of stuttering, it is seldom the case that the stuttering theories look back to the normal speaker or make any attempt to integrate the findings from normal speakers with those from stutterers.

Perceptual Processes in Stutterers

If stutterers do suffer from some abnormality in the feedback system, it might be the case that the abnormality would be reflected in some basic perceptual defect, and especially one that might interfere with self-monitoring. The relevant studies are reviewed below.

Tactile and Proprioceptive Processes. There have been surprisingly few studies of the oral tactile or proprioceptive skills of stutterers. Class, as reported by Moser, LaGourge, and Class (1967), found that stutterers made significantly more errors on oral form recognition than normal speakers, but the magnitude of the difference was very small. Jensen, Sheehan, Williams, and LaPointe (1975) found no difference between stutterers and nonstutterers on tests of oral form identification, two-point discrimination, weight discrimination, and interdental thickness discrimination. Gunderson (1972), on the other hand, found that on an oral-form-discrimination task, severe stutterers produced more errors than mild stutterers, who produced more errors than normal speakers. As is so often the case when stutterers and normal speakers are compared, the results were equivocal. The Gunderson study is intriguing, however, in that it does go beyond a simple comparison between normal and stuttering speakers and reveals an ordered set of results.

None of these studies involves sensory judgments accompanying movement of the oral structures. An interesting study of this type was conducted recently by Jordan, Hardy, and Morris (1978) on articulatory defective children. An artificial palate with several contact plates was constructed for each subject. The subjects' task was to touch each plate on command. The task was performed in the presence and the absence of anesthesia. Articulatory-defective children performed more poorly than the normal children during the initial testing but improved over time. Unfortunately, the effects of anesthesia were confounded with a learning effect. This is an interesting task as it requires an interpretation of sensory input accompanying lingual movement. This type of study on the stuttering population would be of interest.

Auditory Processes of Stutterers. There is no reason to expect that stutterers differ systematically from normals in standard audiometric evaluations, and the evidence bears this out (Brown, Sambrooks, & MacCulloch, 1975; Gregory, 1960; Hugo, 1972). On other tests comparing stutterers and nonstutterers, the usual mélange of contradictory results arises. Brown et al. (1975) found that stutterers had a lower threshold for auditory discomfort than nonstutterers. Hall and Jerger (1978) compared stutterers and normal speakers on a battery of tests designed to assess central auditory function. The stutterers differed from the controls on three of the seven audiometric tests, but the investigators cautioned that the differences were quite subtle and only suggestive of central auditory dysfunction. Toscher and Rupp (1978) also reported that stutterers performed more poorly than nonstutterers on tests of synthetic sentence identification. Karr (1977) found no differences between stutterers and controls on perception of (CID) sentences or spondaic words. These early findings suggest that there is reason to look more deeply at the central auditory functioning of stutterers, but it should be noted that the research seems to stem more from a random search for a possible difference between the two populations than from a theoretically motivated hypothesis about why stutterers and normals should differ in these functions.

Tests of dichotic listening, on the other hand, are directly related to one of the earliest theories of stuttering. According to the Orton–Travis theory of cerebral dominance, stuttering occurs because one of the cerebral cortices, usually the left, has failed to acquire functional dominance over the other, resulting in a failure of coordination of neural impulses to the paired midline structures involved in speech. In the early 1930s, the theory seemed handsomely supported by the numerous but uncontrolled observations of left-handedness or arbitrarily changed handedness among stutterers. Both of these conditions, it was presumed, were related to confused cerebral dominance. When the initial enthusiasm had waned, however, it soon became apparent in more methodologically adequate studies that stutterers did not differ in any significant way from nonstutterers in terms of handedness and that change of handedness did not in itself appear to be related to stuttering. Finally, therapeutic attempts based on changing or restoring natural handedness had no especially beneficial effects on stutterers. In recent years, the theory has languished.

Interest in the cerebral dominance theory of stuttering resurfaced when Kimura (1961) introduced the dichotic listening test as a safe and convenient alternative to the intracarotid sodium amytal (Wada) test of cerebral dominance for language. In the dichotic test, different speech stimuli are presented simultaneously to the ears, and the subject is asked to identify what he or she hears. Generally, the stimuli presented to the right ear are identified correctly more often than those presented to the left ear. Presumably, this right-ear advantage (REA) occurs because the left hemisphere is dominant for speech and the neural connections between the right ear and the left hemisphere are prepotent (Kimura, 1961). A lack of cerebral dominance would be reflected in a weak or nonexistent right-ear effect. At present, the results comparing stutterers and nonstutterers are equivocal. In four studies, stutterers had a smaller REA than their controls (Brady & Berson, 1975; Curry & Gregory, 1969; Perrin & Eisenson, 1970; Sommers, Brady, & Moore, 1975), but in five additional studies, no differences were found (Cerf & Prins, 1974; Dorman & Porter, 1975; Quinn, 1972; Sussman & MacNeilage, 1975). Despite the attractions offered by the dichotic paradigm, there are numerous problems associated with its interpretation; for example, the variability among subjects is very large, the effect itself is typically quite small, and it is affected by numerous task variables (Speaks & Niccum, 1977).

Sussman and MacNeilage (1975) have reported an interesting variation of the dichotic test. The subject hears a continuously varying tone in one ear. In the other ear, the subject hears a second tone, which changes as she or he moves the lower jaw. The task is to track the tone in the first ear by making appropriate jaw movements. The normal subjects performed better when the tone controlled by the jaw was presented to the right ear than when it was presented to the left. On this task, the nonstutterers were found to exhibit a larger REA than the stutterers. When the groups were compared on conventional dichotic listening, however, they did not differ. Both showed an REA. Sussman and MacNeilage concluded that stutterers may have a selective lack of cerebral dominance for production tasks. Neilson and Neilson (1979) attempted to replicate this study but failed to find a difference between stutterers and nonstutterers in the tracking task. However, Neilson and Neilson added a measure of time lag between stimulus and response signals, essentially a reaction time measure, and found that the stutterers had significantly greater reaction times than the nonstutterers. Thus, ultimately, both studies found some difference between the normal speakers and the stutterers on skilled auditory-motor performance. Intuitively, this type of task seems more directly related to speech than the usual perceptual tasks and is well worth exploring further.

Given the Neilson and Neilson data, studies by McFarlane and Prins (1978) and Cross and Luper (1979) are of considerable interest. Cross and Luper reported that stutterers had longer reaction times than nonstutterers when asked to initiate voicing immediately after hearing a tone, though it did not matter whether the ear receiving the tone was the right or the left. McFarlane and Prins found that stutterers had longer reaction times than nonstutterers when asked to initiate lip movement to an auditory stimulus. Once again, these tasks are interesting in that they involve an integration of auditory perception and motor activity in a way that seems close to speech and to the normal interplay between hearing and speaking that characterizes feedback control.

Reference was made earlier to the role of the stapedial reflex in stuttering. Shearer and Simmons (1965) demonstrated that the stapedial reflex occurs 65–100 msec before phonation in both stutterers and nonstutterers. They reported no differences between groups. Webster and Lubker (1968) speculated that stutterers may experience unstable contraction of the stapedius muscle, thereby attenuating auditory feedback in a way that contributes to stuttering. More recently, Horovitz, Johnson, Pearlman, Schaffer, and Hedin (1978) found that when stutterers were asked to imagine anxiety-producing situations, their acoustic reflex thresholds were altered, while those of nonstutterers were not. In the control situation, the reflex in the two groups did not differ. Though it would be interesting to pursue this line of research further, it is not clear how a variation in the reflex would lead to stuttering. Perhaps a study of random variations in masking or sidetone amplification in normal speakers would be a reasonable analogue. It is difficult to see why such variations would lead to anything like the DAF effect in normal speakers.

A study by Stromsta (1972) comes closer than most to identifying a difference between the auditory systems of normal and stuttering speakers that may be related to auditory feedback. He presented a bone-conducted tone to stutterers and nonstutterers. While the subject heard the tone, the phase of bilateral air-conducted tones was altered between the ears until the signals canceled and the subject could no longer hear the tone. According to Stromsta, this procedure provides a measure of interaural phase disparity. Stutterers reportedly needed a greater interaural phase disparity to reach cancellation than did the nonstutterers. Given the possible implications of this finding, it is unfortunate that no replication has been reported.

Studies of auditory localization (Asp, 1965), imperceptivity during stuttering blocks (Froeschels & Rieber, 1963; Martin & Starr, 1967), and auditory–visual integration (Cohen & Hanson, 1975) fail to provide any consistent evidence of auditory disorders in stutterers.

To summarize, attempts to establish gross differences between stutterers and nonstutterers on most perceptual tasks have come to naught. Attempts to assess reaction time and tracking ability in auditory motor tasks are among the more interesting recent methodological approaches to stuttering and may uncover a perceptual defect that can somehow be correlated with stuttering behavior. It would also be interesting to assess stutterers' self-perception during speech by using methods such as autophonic scaling of loudness (Lane, Catania, & Stevens, 1961).

Feedback Disruptions in Stutterers

If it is assumed that stutterers have a disorganized feedback system, it might be helpful to interfere with that system in such a way as to redress the inherent anomaly. For example, if air and bone conduction are abnormally discrepant, then an external noise that eliminates the discrepancy might be expected to restore fluency. If the relationship between tactile and auditory feedback is at fault, then perhaps nerve blocks to the oral cavity will result in fluency. To the extent that such procedures reduce stuttering, they provide some test of a theory, but the relationship between any successful manipulation and a relevant theory is not entirely self-evident. For example, if intense masking should succeed in reducing stuttering, it might be because the stutterer can no longer monitor the auditory feedback because she or he can no longer hear the discrepancy between air and bone conduction, because the interaural phase disparity has been eliminated, or because the stutterer is listening to the noise (rather than not listening to himself or herself).

Predictions concerning the effects of DAF on stuttering are even more problematic. Why should an externally presented delay correct an intrinsic delay? How could one arrive at a prediction concerning the proper delay values that would cancel the stuttering? Further, it is still not known why DAF disrupts normal speakers, and some more than others. It is not a simple matter of air-conducted feedback's being delayed compared with bone-conducted feedback. According to Stromsta (1962), there is a natural delay among feedback modes even in normal conditions. If it is the air–bone discrepancy that causes the disruptions under DAF, why do the effects not disappear as the air-conducted signal is increasingly amplified over the bone-conducted signal? If it is the discrepancy between the air-conducted signal and tactile or kinesthetic cues that gives rise to the DAF effect, then why does the effect not disappear when the speaker's oral cavity is desensitized (McCroskey, 1958)? These are the sorts of questions that must be kept in mind as we proceed to interpret studies in which the stutterer's feedback is experimentally disrupted in the effort to restore fluency.

Masking. During auditory masking, a noise or tone is presented while the stutterer talks. To interfere maximally with feedback, the masking stimulus should be on continuously, and it should be sufficiently intense and in an appropriate frequency range to compete with speech. One would expect the effects of masking to increase as these conditions are more closely approached. Shane (1955) was the first to test stutterers with noises of different intensity levels. Stutterers read aloud in quiet, in 25-dB white noise, and under 95-dB white noise (referenced to the threshold of the "average, normal ear"). Stuttering decreased substantially under 95-dB noise but was unaffected by 25-dB noise. Several more recent studies confirm that greater reductions in stuttering are achieved as noise intensity is increased (Adams & Hutchinson, 1974; Conture, 1974; Maraist & Hutton, 1957). Binaural presentation is more effective than monaural noise (Yairi, 1976), presumably because binaural masking is more complete. These studies suggest that as self-perception becomes more difficult, stuttering decreases. However, Maraist and Hutton found substantial decreases in stuttering even when the noise was 50 dB with reference to the "normal noise detection threshold," and clearly not enough to eliminate self-perception.

Cherry and Sayers (1956) were the first to test the relative effects of masking noises of different frequency bands. Stutterers spoke under white noise that was low-pass filtered with a cutoff frequency of 500 Hz, or under white noise that had been high-pass filtered with a cutoff frequency of 500 Hz. The low-pass noise was particularly effective in reducing "breakdown time," a finding that led Cherry and Sayers, and many others (e.g., Yates, 1963b), to conclude that the noise works through differential masking of the low-frequency bone-conduction component of the stutterer's auditory feedback. However, attempts to replicate this finding by May and Hackwood (1968) and Conture (1974) have been unsuccessful, thus casting doubt on the thesis that stuttering is caused by some disturbance in the bone-conducted aspect of auditory feedback.

The temporal relationship of the noise to the speech has also been examined. If noise is effective because it reduces feedback, it should be most successful when presented continuously while the person is talking. However, Sutton and Chase (1961) reported that noise introduced by means of a voice-operated relay during intervals of silence was as effective in reducing stuttering as noise presented so as to overlap with speech. Webster and Dorman (1970) refined the experimental procedures so as to ensure that the timing of the noise and speech would be properly synchronized, and they found results similar to those of Chase and Sutton.

More recently, Altrows and Bryden (1977) arranged for greater durations between the noise-on and the noise-off conditions and reported reductions in stuttering only when the noise coincided with speech. Altrows and Bryden concluded that it was the greater precision in synchrony between the noise and the speech that resulted in the differential effects they had obtained, in contrast to earlier experiments. Synchrony is very difficult to achieve in experiments of this sort, however, and even in Altrows and Bryden, there was the likelihood of some error since the experimenter introduced the noise by means of a handswitch when the first speech sound was judged to have occurred, excluding inaudible stuttering. The opportunity for uncertainty and delay is obvious.

The reduction in stuttering achieved by noise increases as the duration of the noise is lengthened. Murray (1969) reported that continuous noise resulted in a greater decrease in stuttering than noise presented in random bursts or contingent on moments of stuttering. Burke (1969) also found that noise was most effective when it was on throughout the speech episode.

In general, the masking studies indicate that the presentation of an intense, wide-band noise during phonation results in decreased stuttering, but there are ambiguities even in this broad generalization. Though effectiveness seems to covary with intensity, substantial reductions have been found with low noise levels (Barr & Carmel, 1969; Maraist & Hutton, 1957). It seems likely that the noise must be present during some portion of phonation to be effective, but the exact relationship is in dispute. The effect of different noise bands, particularly those that have been equated for loudness, is still uncertain. An approach using several noises matched alternatively for intensity and loudness, like the approach of Garber, Siegel, Pick, and Alcorn (1976) in studying the Lombard, would seem appropriate for stuttering as well.

Garber and Martin (1974) evaluated the long-term effects of noise on three stutterers. Once the stuttering stabilized in base rate, each subject was run for a series of 50-min sessions in which the noise was alternately on for 5 min and off for 5 min. The noise could not be kept on continuously for fear of acoustic damage to the subjects' ears. All three subjects decreased their stuttering during the first 5-min noise segment. Beyond the first 5 min, however, they responded very differently. Subject 2 was given 100-dB SPL of white noise over four 50-min sessions and showed a slight increase in stuttering. Subject 3 participated in four sessions under 100-dB noise and showed no change. Only Subject 1 consistently decreased stuttering under noise. These results are puzzling, but they certainly do not argue for a feedback explanation of stuttering. Nor can they be dismissed by appealing to individual differences. It seems very unlikely that three such prototypically different stuttering types would have been selected for the study by the operation of chance factors. Nor is it in any way obvious which individual differences would dispose a stutterer to decrease stuttering or to be unaffected by the noise. It is interesting that in a group experiment involving 20 stutterers, Martin and Haroldson (1979) obtained a significant mean reduction in percentage of stuttering/under 100 dB of white noise as compared to a no noise control condition, but that 20% of the individual stutterers did not decrease their percentage of stuttering under the noise, and 50% of the stutterers increased their stuttering duration under the noise.

Delayed Auditory Feedback. The literature on the effects of DAF on stuttering is large and has been reviewed elsewhere (Soderberg, 1969; Van Riper, 1971; Yates, 1963b). It appears at first glance that DAF causes stuttering to decrease, but more careful analysis indicates that the effects are variable, and that mild stutterers respond to DAF more as do normal speakers, with decreased fluency, while severe stutterers find DAF ameliorative (Burke, 1975b; Naylor, 1953; Soderberg, 1960). The type of measurement may also affect the results. It is difficult to differentiate between moments of stuttering and the repetitions or prolongations induced by DAF, but there is evidence that these response classes may respond differentially. Hayden, Scott, and Addicott (1977) reported that "stuttering blocks" were greatly decreased under DAF, but that "disfluencies" (primarily prolongations) increased. The problem of distinguishing stutterings from nonfluencies is not simple in any circumstance and is especially complicated in the case of DAF, where the experimental procedure may simultaneously be increasing certain kinds of disfluencies and decreasing others.

The effects of DAF also vary according to the age of the subjects, the delay interval, and the speech task. According to Burke (1975b), young stutterers were more affected by DAF than older stutterers, perhaps because the younger children have more of the sorts of nonfluencies discussed above by Hayden *et al.* (1977). It is interesting that the delay intervals used with stutterers have tended to fall in the same range as those used to disrupt normal speech, around 200 msec. Lotzmann (1961) reported considerable variation in the response of individual stutterers to DAF, but the smallest interval used was 50 msec, and there was no attempt to make a fine-tuned match between delay interval and subject characteristics. Burke (1975b), Novak (1978), and Timmons and Boudreau (1978) also reported variation in the effect of DAF depending on delay interval. DAF effects also may be influenced by the speech task. Burke (1975b) found that on a spontaneous speech task, stuttering was reduced in DAF; on a sentence-reading task, stuttering increased.

Despite its early promise, and particularly the enthusiasm that greeted Goldiamond's (1965) introduction of DAF as a therapeutic technique, DAF's clinical uses have shed little light on the nature of the stuttering disorder. To that extent, the view that stuttering is essentially a problem of internally delayed feedback must be regarded as significantly weakened.

Stutterers versus Nonstutterers. The concept that stuttering and DAF-induced disfluencies are comparable responses, based on similar underlying processes, did not sit comfortably with the prevailing diagnosogenic theory (Johnson, 1959) that stuttering is the outcome of an evaluational system that is acquired gradually, over a period of time during which the speaker learns to react to his or her normal nonfluencies with concern, anxiety, and struggle. Surely such evaluational attitudes could not come and go with the flick of the switch on a tape recorder. The most systematic attack came from Neelley (1961), working under Wendell Johnson's guidance. Neelley found that both stutterers and non-stutterers were disrupted by DAF, but that the responses of the two groups were qualitatively distinguishable. He concluded that stuttering disfluencies and DAF disfluencies did not implicate the same underlying processes at all. Yates (1963b) was quick to respond that Neelley did not use optimal delay intervals and, perhaps more importantly, that it was not sensible to compare the responses of a stutterer, who presumably has had years of coping with his or her internal delays, with the responses of a normal speaker experiencing delay for the first time.

The issue has been joined, though by no means resolved, by others. Novak (1978) found that stutterers increased their fluency under DAF both before and after a period of therapy. Freeman and her colleagues (Borden, Dorman, Free-man, & Raphael, 1977; Freeman, 1977), using electromyographic (EMG) tech-niques, studied the muscle coordination of stutterers under normal feedback and that of normal speakers under DAF. The stutterers displayed patterns of incoor-dination that never occurred in the group of nonstutterers. In particular, the stutterers appeared to have difficulty with the transitional adjustments from voiceless to voiced states and vice versa, while normal speakers under DAF had little difficulty in initiating voicing but rather prolonged the voiced state or repeated it.

These findings, like those of Neelley (1961), suggest that stutterings are basically different from responses to DAF, but it is still possible that this finding reflects a difference in experience with the timing disruption, rather than a difference in underlying etiology. The question is not readily resolved, but it would be interesting to track the EMG responses of normal speakers over an extended period of exposure to DAF.

Another way to study the relationship between stutterings and DAF re-sponses is to subject them to similar manipulations. For example, it is now well documented that a brief time-out period is generally very successful in reducing the frequency of stuttering (Martin & Haroldson, 1979), but it is not known whether the same procedure would have any effect on the disfluencies occa-sioned by DAF. Brandt and Wilde (1977) took somewhat this approach when they presented normal speakers with DAF in one ear and then, in the other, either noise, the ticking of a metronome, or a tape recording of someone reading the same passage that the subject was to read. In the last two conditions, the subject was instructed to pace himself or herself with the metronome or the speaker. The paced reading and the metronome conditions were quite successful in reducing speech disruptions under DAF, as compared with the noise. This is an interesting result because much the same effect has been reported with stutterers (Azrin, Jones, & Flye, 1968; Cherry & Sayers, 1956; Fransella & Beech, 1965). Perhaps an even stronger test might be made by presenting the DAF binaurally, as is usually done, and applying the metronome as a tactile pulse or a visual flash, so that it does not interfere with audition.

Other Feedback Alterations. There are a few studies in which feedback manipulations other than DAF or masking were used with stutterers. Andrews and Ingham (1971) and Harris (1955) amplified stutterers' voices and reported reductions in stuttering. Curtis (1961) and Ham and Steer (1967) filtered the feedback, with a high-pass cutoff of 800 Hz. Curtis found no change, while Ham and Steer reported reductions in stuttering. Hutchinson and Ringel (1975) tested stutterers in a control condition, in a condition involving nerve-block injections to the oral cavity, and in a placebo condition in which the injections were given but no anesthesia was administered. The stuttering reportedly increased in the anesthetization condition. This finding is entirely contrary to what would be expected if stuttering is viewed as a conflict between tactile and auditory feedback, since the anesthetization should have removed the discrepancy. Webster and Gould (1975) anesthetized the internal branch of the superior laryngeal nerve of one adult stutterer and found a decrease in stuttering. McCroskey (1958) and Burke (1975a) found no lessening of the effects of DAF on normal speakers when the oral cavity was anesthetized.

Comparison among Feedback Conditions with Stutterers. Masking and DAF have been used clinically, and the masking apparatus has been miniaturized to allow the stutterer to carry his or her treatment with him or her. Since these methods involve some modification of feedback, it is instructive to note their relative effectiveness and the extent to which they intercorrelate when applied to the stuttering problem. The most comprehensive study was reported by Martin and Haroldson (1979). The experimental treatment conditions involved: 100 dB SPL of white noise; 250 msec of DAF; metronome; time-out contingent on stutterings; "wrong" contingent on moments of stuttering. Each of 20 adult stutterers was rotated through the five treatment conditions and appropriate baserate sessions. The conditions each consisted of a 50-min session. The largest overall reductions occurred in the time-out and metronome conditions, though all of the treatments were effective to some extent. Correlations among the conditions revealed no readily interpretable patterns. It was not the case that some stutterers were very amenable to all treatment conditions while others were characteristically resistant. Of special interest in the current discussion, the correlation between the effects of noise and DAF was a relatively high .60, and the correlation between DAF and the metronome was .64. Both of these correlations were significant, while noise correlated with the metronome only a nonsignificant .34. Nor were these the highest correlations. Time-out, a response-contingent operant procedure, correlated .79 with the metronome and .80 with DAF, neither of which involved any contingency. The pattern is not simple.

In a related study, Hutchinson and Norris (1977) compared the effects on stuttering of noise, DAF, and rhythm among 12 subjects who read and spoke spontaneously under all conditions. In the reading task, stuttering decreased under all conditions. In spontaneous speech, the largest decrease in stuttering was again with the metronome, but the decrease in the DAF condition was quite small and was nonexistent under masking. Intercorrelations among the conditions were not reported. Brayton and Conture (1978) also obtained greater reductions of stuttering under rhythm than under masking.

Summary of Feedback Studies

The fact that speech disruptions that are very much like stutterings can be created simply by delaying a normal speaker's auditory feedback, and that these effects seem to square nicely with a servosystem model of speech, cannot be ignored, and it is easy to see why Yates should have been prompted to enthusiasm concerning the eventual role of feedback theory in solving the riddle of stuttering.

However, data on the stutterer's feedback system do not support such enthusiasm. Perceptual studies provide no convincing evidence of a defect in the self-monitoring system. Studies of feedback alterations are difficult to interpret. Stuttering often is decreased in the presence of high-intensity white noise, but the long-term studies available do not indicate that the effect is consistent over time. DAF is sometimes reported to reduce stuttering, but the results are complex and inconsistent. It may be that stuttering is related to perceptual difficulties. Long-term analyses of self-perception or of the relationship between perception and motor planning may uncover evidence of such a deficit. At the present time, however, one cannot conclude on the basis of empirical data that stuttering results from a disordered feedback system.

In the early 1970s, the feedback explanation of stuttering began to lose ground as researchers became frustrated in the attempt to find direct evidence of a perceptual disorder. A search began for alternate explanations of the fact that stuttering often does decrease in the presence of noise or DAF. Shane's (1955) early anxiety hypothesis received renewed attention. Shane argued that auditory cues from the stutterers' speech increase speech anxiety, which, in turn, elicits stuttering. When feedback is altered, the cues are less evident. Therefore, anxiety and stuttering decrease. Bloodstein's (1972) distraction hypothesis is consistent with an anxiety explanation. He stated that speakers stutter because they anticipate speech problems and struggle to avoid them. Noise and DAF distract the speaker and prevent him or her from thinking about or being anxious about speech. The speaker does not anticipate failure or struggle to avoid it, and stuttering decreases.

Adams and Moore (1972) tested the anxiety theory of stuttering by asking stutterers to read in quiet and noise. In both conditions, the authors measured palmar sweat anxiety. They found that stuttering decreased in noise, but the palmar sweat index did not change. They concluded that these data were not consistent with an anxiety explanation of stuttering reduction in noise.

Although the anxiety explanation received some attention, the most influential explanation introduced was the changed-vocalization hypothesis. Wingate (1970) noted that presentation of noise or DAF induces changes in vocalization in speakers. For example, changes in vocal intensity, rate, and fundamental frequency generally occur in the presence of noise or DAF. According to Wingate, the noise or DAF result in changes in stuttering not because they alter feedback, but because they induce changes in vocalization. This theory provided the impetus for a "new" method of attack on the stuttering problem. Now, instead of searching for a deficit in the perceptual system of the stutterer, the search was made for a deficit in the structures involved in vocalization. As the larynx seemed to be the structure most intimately involved in changes in vocal intensity or fundamental frequency, it has received the majority of attention to date. The history and current status of this research are reviewed in the next section.

MOTOR CONTROL

The search for evidence of a problem in the larynx or associated structures began with studies evaluating the relationship between changes in vocalization and changes in stuttering. If stuttering is reduced in noise or DAF because of a change in vocalization, it is important to determine whether vocalization does, indeed, change in these conditions. There is little question that stutterers increase vocal intensity in the presence of noise (Adams & Hutchinson, 1974; Adams & Moore, 1972; Brayton & Conture, 1978; Conture, 1974; Yairi, 1976). There is some indication that fundamental frequency increases as well (Brayton & Conture, 1978; Lechner, 1979). The effect of noise on temporal variables in stutterers is not as clear. Maraist and Hutton (1957), May and Hackwood (1968), and Yairi (1976) have reported an increase in rate in noise. Adams and Moore (1972) and Conture (1974) found no change in rate. Adams and Hutchinson (1974) reported that reading time decreased in noise, while Brayton and Conture (1978) found that vowel duration increased. This variability is perhaps due to the different measures used across studies and to the fact that standard rate measurements are influenced by the presence or absence of stuttering. Thus, a measure such as vowel duration may be more meaningful than the amount of time taken to read a passage.

There has been little study of the effects of DAF on the vocal intensity of stutterers. Lechner (1979) investigated the effects of DAF on fundamental frequency and found an increase in the mean and median fundamental frequency produced in DAF. In addition, the number of upward and downward inflections and upward pitch shifts increased in DAF, while the average rate of upward and downward inflections decreased. Webster, Schumaker, and Lubker (1970) found no change in rate in DAF. Logue (1962) reported that rate decreased in DAF, and Lechner (1979) found that the total time needed to read a sentence increased. Again, the interpretations of rate changes are difficult to assess because stuttering often is changing concurrently.

As singing and metronome pacing often result in increased fluency, there has been an interest in determining whether methods of vocalization change in these conditions. Healey, Mallard, and Adams (1976) and Colcord and Adams (1979) found that stuttering decreased and vocal duration increased during singing. Brayton and Conture (1978) found that vocal duration increased and fundamental frequency decreased when stutterers paced their speech with a metronome. Vocal level remained unchanged. Hutchinson and Navarre (1977) found that peak intraoral air pressure decreased and pressure duration increased during metronome pacing.

It is suggestive that noise, DAF, rhythm, and singing result in changes in vocalization as well as changes in stuttering. However, assessing the correlation between vocalization changes and stuttering is a very indirect way of determining whether these changes induce the reduction in stuttering. A much more direct approach would be to ask stutterers to alter their vocalization and to determine whether stuttering changes as a result. Given that this is a much more powerful approach, it is surprising that it has been used so seldom. Garber and Martin (1977) used this type of approach to determine whether changes in vocal intensity in noise account for the decrease in stuttering generally observed. Stutterers spoke spontaneously in quiet with a normal vocal level, in quiet with an increased vocal level, in the presence of a 90-dB noise with a normal vocal level, and in the presence of noise with an increased vocal level. If reductions in stuttering are induced by changes in vocal level, one would expect stuttering to decrease in the two increased vocal conditions. However, no decrease should be apparent in the presence of noise when the vocal level is not increased. Garber and Martin found that stuttering decreased in noise compared with quiet, but there was no change in stuttering when the vocal level was increased. In fact, the largest reduction in stuttering occurred in the condition in which the stutterers maintained a normal vocal level in the presence of noise. Interestingly, this is the condition that most reduces auditory feedback. These results do not support the theory that changes in stuttering in noise result from concomitant increases in vocal intensity. It might be argued, of course, that aspects of vocalization other than intensity did change and that these accounted for the variations in stuttering.

Ingham, Martin, and Kuhl (1974) investigated the effects of speaking rate on changes in stuttering. Three adult stutterers spoke spontaneously with a normal rate, with a minimum of a 50% increase in rate, and with a minimum decrease of 50%. The subject monitored a series of lights that provided rate information. All subjects decreased their rate in the "decrease" condition; two of the subjects increased their rate in the "increase" condition. The decrease in rate was accompanied by a reduced percentage of words stuttered for two subjects and an increase for one subject. The two subjects who increased their rate decreased the percentage of words stuttered in the "increase" condition. The results of the study provide some support for the idea that changes in rate are accompanied by decreases in stuttering. The relationship is complex, however. One subject increased the percentage of words stuttered when the rate was altered. Two subjects decreased this percentage regardless of the nature of the alteration in rate.

Adams, Lewis, and Besozzi (1973) asked stutterers to read normally and at a decreased rate. The decrease in rate was induced by allowing the subject to see and read only one word at a time. The researchers found that stuttering decreased in the reduced-rate condition and concluded that conditions that require less coordination and transition promote fluency.

The discrepancy between the Adams *et al.* and the Ingham *et al.* studies may be due to the method of reducing rate. In the Adams *et al.* study, word cards were presented at a steady rate of approximately one card/sec. Perhaps the subjects responded to this task much as they would to a metronome. The effects of rhythm on stuttering have long been recognized as dramatic and persisting. Azrin *et al.* (1968) demonstrated compellingly that when stutterers synchronize their speech with a metronome, stutterings are reduced virtually to zero, that there is no loss in effectiveness over extended trials, and that there is essentially no carryover once the metronome is removed. The effects are dramatic, immediate, and entirely tied to the external stimulus. If the subjects in the Adams *et al.* study responded to the task as they would to a metronome, the reduction in stuttering may have been due to the imposed timing regularity rather than to the reduction in rate. It should be noted that it is not clear why rhythm works so well in reducing stuttering. Is it because the metronome provides a special kind of stimulus so that it addresses the perceptual side of stuttering? Or is it because the metronome, by imposing absolute timing regularity, somehow eases the burden of motor performance or planning? The second explanation would suggest that stuttering is a disorder of timing or the initiation of speech movements. This possibility will be discussed further in the next section.

Wingate (1970) used DAF and masking studies as evidence that reductions in stuttering are related to changes in vocalization. This may be the case, but the few direct studies of this hypothesis have not totally supported the contention. Nonetheless, the idea that stuttering and vocalization are intimately tied has been embraced to such a large extent that there has been a conference totally devoted to the subject (Webster & Furst, 1975). The aspect of vocalization that has been in the forefront is phonation, with particular emphasis on the function of the larynx in stuttering. In a recent review of studies on the relationship between phonation and stuttering, Freeman (1979) concluded that abnormal laryngeal behaviors are an important part of the disrupted peripheral speech physiology that characterizes stuttering and that abnormal laryngeal behavior deserves consideration in the diagnosis and management of stuttering. She was careful to caution, however, that the research does not support claims for a laryngeal cause of stuttering.

In addition to those used in the studies cited above, two additional paradigms have been used to assess the contention that laryngeal function is an important component of stuttering. In one type of study, the stutterer's ability to initiate phonation is tested. It is assumed that difficulties in initiation will occur if phonatory disorders and stuttering are linked. In other studies, laryngeal function is observed directly, most often during the moment of stuttering, so that it can be determined whether unusual laryngeal function is present. Before reviewing these studies, it might be helpful to think about what can and cannot be gleaned from such studies.

Freeman's disclaimer concerning a laryngeal cause of stuttering is an important one. In the instance of stuttering, it is possible to become confused between the cause of the phenomenon and the phenomenon itself. Stuttering involves a disruption in the flow of speech. During the moment of stuttering, the articulators are improperly positioned or coordinated; the stutterer may be holding his or her breath or may have assumed an articulatory posture that makes it impossible for the sound to be uttered, etc. These are, of course, disturbances in motor performance, but they do not necessarily reflect an underlying physiological abnormality, any more than attempting to speak with one's teeth clenched describes a physiological disorder. Of course, for theorists of Johnson's persuasion, there is a sense in which the symptoms of the disorder are, in fact, the cause of the disorder: "Stuttering is what a speaker does trying not to stutter again" (Johnson, 1967, p. 240). Johnson would hasten to add that regardless of what the stutterer may believe about his or her problem, there is no physiological reason that compels the stutterer to perform in ways that interfere with the smooth flow of speech. For Johnson, the stutterer suffers not from a physiological disorder but from an impaired belief system.

If, however, stutterers do have an underlying physiological disturbance that precipitates motor incoordination during speech, how is this disturbance to be distinguished from the stuttering behavior itself? That is, when cause and effect intimately share the same physiological domain, how can they be separated? There is no simple solution. One approach has been to make physiological measurements during silence or the performance of nonspeech tasks. If physiological abnormalities emerge at these points, it might be argued that they represent a basic underlying condition, though even in this case, it can only be inferred that the discovered abnormality is the *cause* of the stuttering, rather than being incidental to, or even the product of, the stuttering disorder. Moreover, the failure to discover a laryngeal or other abnormality during silence or nonspeech acts does not mean that no such abnormality exists. It is feasible that the abnormality is exactly the sort that is activated only during the process of speaking. The search for the ultimate cause of stuttering is pervaded by problems of this sort, problems that are not entirely resolved, if at all, by increased technological sophistication. Studies that search for the factors that cause stuttering are typically correlational in design, and correlation provides weak inferences regarding causation. Until it is possible to deal with these physiological assumptions through more direct manipulation, correlational studies will necessarily be done, and causal inferences will be drawn.

Initiation of Voicing

When stutterers are asked to begin vocalizing as soon as some external stimulus appears, they generally perform more slowly than normal speakers in response to an auditory stimulus (Adams & Hayden, 1976) or a visual stimulus (Starkweather, Hirschman, & Tannenbaum, 1976). These results have been replicated by Cross and Luper (1979). Two studies of voice-onset time have yielded less consistent results. Agnello (1975) reported longer voice-onset and voice-termination times for stutterers than for nonstutterers. Metz, Conture, and Caruso (1979) investigated voice-onset time and duration of frication and aspiration in stutterers and control subjects. The subjects were tested on 18 phonemes and phoneme clusters. Only fluent utterances were analyzed. The stutterers differed from nonstutterers on only 6 of the 18 productions. Metz *et al.* concluded that during fluent productions, voice-onset time does not differ in stutterers and nonstutterers. The crucial difference between the Metz and Agnello studies may be the choice of only fluent utterances in the second study.

Wingate (1969) has suggested that stuttering can be characterized as a phonetic transition defect, and Adams (1978) agreed that the stutterer has difficulty making the transition from one sound to another in an articulatory sequence. Adams and Reis (1971) had stutterers read one passage that contained only voiced phonemes and a second passage containing both voiced and voiceless sounds. The stutterers had more difficulty with the mixed passage and showed less adaptation on this passage over repeated readings. Those results are predictable in that it should be more difficult to make phonetic transitions between voiced and voiceless sounds. Adams and Reis (1974) obtained mixed results when they attempted to replicate their original study, however, On this second attempt, the frequency of stuttering was higher on the all-voiced passage than on the mixed passage. Adaptation, however, was again greater on the first (voiced only) passage. In a follow-up study (Adams, Riemenschneider, Metz, & Conture, 1975), a third paragraph consisting exclusively of voiced continuant sounds was constructed. The greatest stuttering adaptation occurred on the new passage, the least on the voiced–voiceless passage. Thus, at least when adaptation is taken as the index of stuttering performance, stutterers appear to do better when the demand for phonetic transitions is at the lowest.

Whispered versus normally vocalized speech has also been studied. Perkins, Rudas, Johnson, and Bell (1976) employed three conditions: reading aloud, whispering, and nonphonated articulation. Stuttering was greatest in the first, normal-phonation condition. Bruce and Adams (1978) had stutterers read a passage five times in two conditions. In one condition, all five trials were read aloud in a normal fashion. In the second, the three middle readings were read in a whispered voice. More adaptation occurred during the normal reading of the passage than when the subjects had to switch from normal to whispered phonation. Brenner, Perkins, and Soderberg (1972) had subjects perform adaptation readings in silence and aloud. Adaptation occurred only after voiced practice.

An older study by Stromsta (1965) also suggests that phonatory transitions may play some role in stuttering. The disfluencies of 63 children who had been brought to a speech clinic because of fluency concerns were analyzed spectrographically, and the spectrograms were divided into two groups, depending on the degree to which formant transitions and terminations of phonation appeared deviant or normal. After a lapse of 10 years, questionnaires were sent to the parents asking whether the child still stuttered. The questionnaires were returned for 38 of the children, and 27 of these had been judged originally to have displayed abnormal transitions. The parents of 24 of these 27 children concurred in the judgment that their child was a stutterer. The remaining 11 children of the sample of 38 had originally been judged to have normal transitions, and for 10 of these children, the parents now believed that the child was not stuttering. Unfortunately, the study was reported incompletely, and many details of method and results were not included. Nonetheless, the idea that it may be possible to predict later stuttering from an analysis of early spectrograms is intriguing.

In summary, the reaction time studies revealed differences between stutterers and nonstutterers in vocal initiation, but the voice-onset-time studies yielded equivocal results. A problem in all of these experiments is to find speech samples that are not confounded by stuttering. Selecting out such samples is a judgmental matter and is fraught with difficulty. Any sample of speech from a stutterer may contain subtle evidences of stuttering or an anticipation of stuttering that is not immediately perceptible. Thus, even if the experimenter is entirely successful in uncovering evidence of laryngeal abnormality in the speech records of stutterers, it is difficult to establish that these patterns are the cause rather than the expression of such an abnormality. The tracking tasks used by Sussman and MacNeilage (1975) and Neilson and Neilson (1979), described earlier, are interesting in that they do not require that the stutterer vocalize and also in that they look at other aspects of the movement patterns involved in speech initiation and termination in addition to laryngeal activity.

The studies of stuttering adaptation showed that adaptation is greater when stutterers read aloud than when they whisper, and when the passage to be read contains only voiced phonemes in contrast to a mixture of voiced and voiceless sounds. These results have been cited in support of the proposal that stuttering is a defect in making phonetic transitions, but this statement seems more descriptive than explanatory. Furthermore, it is not at all clear why adaptation is facilitated by loading passages so that they contain only voiced sounds, while the actual frequency of stuttering is not necessarily reduced in such passages.

Physiological Analysis of Laryngeal Movement

The studies of vocal initiation reviewed in the last section provide indirect evidence concerning laryngeal function in that the data generated are related to patterns of vocalization, and these are the effect or outcome of laryngeal activity. Modern technology has now made it possible to observe laryngeal activity more directly, through fiberoptics and electromyography.

Conture, McCall, and Brewer (1977) had stutterers read and speak with a fiberscope in place. The output of the fiberscope (and presumably a microphone) fed a video recorder for analysis of laryngeal behavior and perceptual evaluations of stuttering. Moments of stuttering were perceptually identified, and then each moment was analyzed for whether it involved laryngeal adduction, abduction, or both. All of the broken words and 60% of the part-word repetitions involved abduction of the folds, while 72% of the prolongations involved laryngeal adduction. Laryngeal activity during fluent utterances was not described. Freeman (1975) used electromyography to study laryngeal activity during moments of stuttering and of fluency. Simultaneous recordings were made of the cricothyroid, genioglossus, inferior longitudinal, superior longitudinal, and orbicularis oris muscles for one stutterer and several control subjects. The major finding was that stuttering was accompanied by excessively high levels of muscle activity and disruption of the normal reciprocity between abductor and adductor fibers. These patterns were not evident in the speech of the nonstutterers or in the fluent speech of the stutterer. Using a combination of electromyographic, fiberoptic, and acoustic measurements with a single stutterer, Freeman, Borden, and Dorman (1976) found that the vocal folds are partially abducted during prolongations and that the laryngeal abductors and adductors are simultaneously active. When the abductor muscles cease to be active, speech proceeds fluently.

McClean and Cooper (1978) used surface electrodes to assess laryngeal activity during stuttering expectancy. Each of 19 stutterers read a series of word cards. When the card was presented, the subject read the word silently, indicated whether she or he expected to stutter the word, and then said the word aloud. The laryngeal measurement consisted of the mean microvolt value of the muscle action-potential level in the laryngeal area. The subjects were approximately 80% accurate in predicting stuttering, but the laryngeal measures were no different when stuttering was expected and when it was not, regardless of whether stuttering eventually occurred. These data provide no support for the thesis that stuttering is characterized by a breakdown in motor planning or in the ability to preset the laryngeal mechanism, but surface electrodes may be too insensitive or too noisy to pick up abnormalities.

These studies of laryngeal movement do suggest that abnormal patterns occur during moments of stuttering. A general lack of coordination is evident. The postures and patterns exhibited may vary, depending on the type of dysfluency produced. To date, there is no evidence that abnormal patterns exist during periods of fluency. If one conceives of the stuttering episode as a composite, or even a sequence, of abnormal muscular reactions, it is possible that the laryngeal activity is the trigger that sets the stuttering block in motion. It is equally possible, however, that the laryngeal abnormality is a secondary response to some other event in the behavioral sequence. While it would seem crucial to be able to choose between these possibilities, the data at this point are unfortunately uninformative.

Coordination of Speech Structures

Hutchinson and Watkin (1976) investigated the relationship between onset of phonation and jaw movement during release from stuttering. Jaw movement was measured with the aid of strain gauge transducers. Phonation was measured with a throat microphone. During the release of moments of stuttering, abnormally large opening and closing jaw velocities were frequently noted. In several cases, incoordination between jaw movement and onset of vocalization was observed, apparently reflecting a failure to initiate phonation at the proper time. Zimmerman (1980) has studied the coordination among movements of the lips, the jaw, and the tongue with the onset of phonation in the utterances of stutterers. He reported abnormal coordination among stutterers, even during fluent utterances. These studies are interesting in that they suggest that the place to look for physiological abnormalities among stutterers is not in any single muscle system but in the coordination among the systems. Zimmerman's results are, in at least one sense, rather puzzling, however. It would appear that abnormal muscular coordination does not necessarily result in abnormal speech. Is this because of a lack of perceptual acuity in judging stuttering, or is there some threshold of motoric abnormality that must be exceeded before a stuttering block occurs?

Summary of Physiological Studies

Evidence has accumulated to suggest that stuttering is characterized by deviant patterns of physiological activity among some of the speech structures and, perhaps more importantly, in the coordination among muscle systems. For the most part, these deviations have been observed during the stuttering episode, though Zimmerman's data also point to abnormal coordinations during the fluent utterances of stutterers. It is not known whether these physiological abnormalities are in any sense the cause of stuttering. They may just as likely constitute a more molecular description of what in the past has been called a moment of stuttering. In any case, this level of analysis is intriguing in that it allows for a much closer, more analytical look at the rather global concept of a stuttering moment. A number of interesting patterns might be revealed by this kind of research. It might be the case, for example, that for any particular stutterer, the judged moment of stuttering is ushered in by abnormal activity in the larynx, or the tongue, etc. If this sort of consistency can be discovered, stutterings can perhaps be averted or aborted by specific attention to the muscular event that triggers the episode. Perhaps behavior modification or biofeedback procedures are warranted. We cannot anticipate what kinds of new insights may evolve simply by developing the tools to approach the concept of the stuttering moment in a more molecular, analytical fashion.

CONCLUSION

It is instructive to compare these recent approaches to stuttering with some of the very early studies of the problem. Over a century and a half ago, Arnott, in his 1828 book on the elements of physics, described stuttering as a laryngeal problem that influences the remainder of the speech musculature. Cross (1936) provided evidence that the rates of movement of the tongue, the jaw, and the diaphragm are slower in stutterers than in nonstutterers. Shaffer (1940) concluded that the relationship between jaw movement and phonation is different in stutterers. Harms and Malone (1939) were of the opinion that a relationship exists between audition and stuttering. Of course, methodologies differ, but in other respects, some of these historical entries are indistinguishable from current research. By the same token, some of the older theories of stuttering, such as the cerebral dominance theory, long ago pronounced dead, have begun to twitch a bit in the light of the evidence on laryngeal malfunction and lack of muscular coordination in stutterers. It seems to be the fate of behavioral science that old theories neither die nor fade away. They simply retreat to the dark corners of the literature, where they lurk and wait.

The fact that some themes are so frequently revived in the study of stuttering may mean that they have captured some element of truth that is not to be denied and ultimately will out. It is also true that we yearn for simple solutions, and it has always been the case that a physiological explanation for any behavior disorder seems satisfyingly simple and direct. Perhaps the major lesson to be drawn from this review is the simple reminder that "cause," at least in the realm of behavior, is an extraordinarily complex concept that seems to slip away just as we approach it. With this in mind, there is nothing to do but to proceed with the research and theorizing, and see what new valleys it brings us to.

Finally, in this chapter, we have made an artificial separation between feedback and the motor aspects of stuttering. In fact, they are related. Feedback is the direct consequence of physiological activity in the speech mechanism. It is only in the laboratory that we tamper with nature and attempt to separate muscular activity from its proper end product. Since speakers are almost invariably also listeners, a change in one domain inevitably introduces a change in the other. Of course, integration must come in its own time. There is reason to believe, however, that our understanding of stuttering will have been significantly advanced when feedback models and physiological theory and research are more nearly integrated.

REFERENCES

Abbs, J., Folkins, J., & Sivarajan, M. Motor impairment following blockade of the infraorbital nerve: Implications for the use of anesthetization techniques in speech research. *Journal of Speech and Hearing Research*, 1976, *19*, 19–35.

Adams, M. Further analysis of stuttering as a phonetic transition defect. *Journal of Fluency Disorders*, 1978, *3*, 265–271.

Adams, M. R., & Hayden, P. The ability of stutterers and nonstutterers to initiate and terminate phonation during production of an isolated vowel. *Journal of Speech and Hearing Research*, 1976, *19*, 290–296.

Adams, M., & Hutchinson, J. The effects of three levels of auditory masking on selected vocal characteristics and the frequency of disfluency of adult stutterers. *Journal of Speech and Hearing Research*, 1974, *17*, 682–688.

Adams, M. R., & Moore, W. H., Jr. The effects of auditory masking on the anxiety level, frequency of dysfluency, and selected vocal characteristics of stutterers. *Journal of Speech and Hearing Research*, 1972, *15*, 572–578.

Adams, M. R., & Reis, R. The influence of the onset of phonation on the frequency of stuttering. *Journal of Speech and Hearing Research*, 1971, *14*, 639–644.

Adams, M. R., & Reis, R. The influence of the onset of phonation on the frequency of stuttering: A replication and reevaluation. *Journal of Speech and Hearing Research*, 1974, *17*, 752–754.

Adams, M., Lewis, J., & Besozzi, T. The effect of reduced reading rate on stuttering frequency. *Journal of Speech and Hearing Research*, 1973, *16*, 671–675.

Adams, M. R., Riemenschneider, S., Metz, D., & Conture, E. Voice onset and articulatory constriction requirements in a speech segment and their relationship to the amount of stuttering adaptation. *Journal of Fluency Disorders*, 1975, *1*, 24–31.

Agnello, J. Laryngeal and articulatory dynamics of dysfluency interpreted within a vocal tract model. In M. Webster & L. Furst (Eds.), *Vocal tract dynamics and dysfluency*. New York: Speech and Hearing Institute of New York, 1975.

Altrows, I., & Bryden, M. Temporal factors in the effects of masking noise on fluency of stutterers. *Journal of Communication Disorders*, 1977, *10*, 315–329.

Andrews, G., & Ingham, R. *The effect of alterations in auditory feedback with special reference to synchronous feedback*. Unpublished manuscript, 1971.

Asp, C. An investigation of the localization of interaural stimulation by clicks and the reading times of stutterers and non-stutterers under monaural sidetone conditions. *De Therapia Vocis et Loquellae*, 1965, *2*, 353–355.

Atkinson, C. J. Adaptation to delayed side-tone. *Journal of Speech and Hearing Disorders*, 1953, *18*, 386–391.

Azrin, N., Jones, R. J., & Flye, B. A synchronization effect and its application to stuttering by a portable apparatus. *Journal of Applied Behavior Analysis*, 1968, *1*, 283–295.

Barr, D., & Carmel, N. Stuttering inhibition with high frequency narrow-band masking noise. *Journal of Auditory Research*, 1969, *9*, 40–44.

Bloodstein, O. The anticipatory struggle hypothesis: Implications of research on the variability of stuttering. *Journal of Speech and Hearing Research*, 1972, *15*, 487–499.

Bloodstein, O. *A handbook on stuttering*. Chicago: National Easter Seal Society, 1975.

Borden, G. B., Harris, K. S., & Catena, L. Oral feedback: II. An electromyographic study of speech under nerve-block anesthesia. *Journal of Phonetics*, 1973, *1*, 297–308.

Borden, G., Dorman, M., Freeman, F., & Raphael, L. Electromyographic changes with delayed auditory feedback of speech. *Journal of Phonetics*, 1977, *5*, 1–8.

Brady, J., & Berson, J. Stuttering, dichotic listening, and cerebral dominance. *Archives of General Psychiatry*, 1975, *32*, 1449–1452.

Brandt, D., & Wilde, G. A technique for controlling speech dysfluencies induced by delayed auditory feedback. *Journal of Fluency Disorders*, 1977, *2*, 149–156.

Brayton, E., & Conture, E. Effects of noise and rhythmic stimulation on the speech of stutterers. *Journal of Speech and Hearing Research*, 1978, *21*, 285–294.

Brenner, N., Perkins, W., & Soderberg, G. The effect of rehearsal on frequency of stuttering. *Journal of Speech and Hearing Research*, 1972, *15*, 474–482.

Brown, T., Sambrooks, J., & MacCulloch, M. Auditory thresholds and the effects of reduced auditory feedback on stuttering. *Acta Psychiatrica Scandinavica*, 1975, *51*, 297–311.

Bruce, M., & Adams, M. Effects of two types of motor practice on stuttering. *Journal of Speech and Hearing Research*, 1978, *21*, 421–428.

Brutten, E. J., & Shoemaker, D. J. *The modification of stuttering*. Englewood Cliffs, N.J.: Prentice-Hall, 1967.

Burke, B. D. Reduced auditory feedback and stuttering. *Behavior Research and Therapy*, 1969, *7*, 303–308.

Burke, B. Susceptibility to delayed auditory feedback and dependence on auditory or oral sensory feedback. *Journal of Communication Disorders*, 1975, *8*, 75–96.(a)

Burke, B. Variables affecting stutterers' initial reaction to delayed auditory feedback. *Journal of Communication Disorders*, 1975, *8*, 141–155.(b)

Cerf, A., & Prins, D. Stutterers' ear preference for dichotic syllables. *Asha*, 1974, *16*, 566–567.

Chase, R. A., Rapin, I., Gilden, L., Sutton, S., & Guilfoyle, G. Studies on sensory feedback: II. Sensory feedback influences on keytapping motor tasks. *Quarterly Journal of Experimental Psychology*, 1961, *13*, 153–167.

Cherry, C., & Sayers, B. Experiments upon the total inhibition of stammering by external control and some clinical results. *Journal of Psychosomatic Research*, 1956, *1*, 233–246.

Cohen, M., & Hanson, M. Intersensory processing efficiency of fluent speakers and stutterers. *British Journal of Disorders of Communication*, 1975, *10*, 111–122.

Colcord, R., & Adams, M. Voicing duration and vocal SPL changes associated with stuttering reduction during singing. *Journal of Speech and Hearing Research*, 1979, *22*, 468–479.

Conture, E. Some effects of noise on the speaking behavior of stutterers. *Journal of Speech and Hearing Research*, 1974, *17*, 714–723.

Conture, E. G., McCall, G. N., & Brewer, D. W. Laryngeal behavior during stuttering. *Journal of Speech and Hearing Research*, 1977, *20*, 661–668.

Cross, D., & Luper, H. Voice reaction time of stuttering and non-stuttering children and adults. *Journal of Fluency Disorders*, 1979, *4*, 59–77.

Cross, H. M. The motor capacities of stutterers. *Archives of Speech*, 1936, *7*, 112–132.

Curry, F. K. W., & Gregory, H. H. The performance of stutterers on dichotic listening tasks thought to reflect cerebral dominance. *Journal of Speech and Hearing Research*, 1969, *12*, 73–82.

Curtis, W. The effects of sidetone filtering on certain speech characteristics of stutterers. *Speech Monographs*, 1961, *28*, 114–115.

Dorman, M., & Porter, R. Hemispheric lateralization for speech perception in stutterers. *Cortex*, 1975, *11*, 181–185.

Fairbanks, G. Systematic research in experimental phonetics: I. A theory of the speech mechanism as a servosystem. *Journal of Speech and Hearing Disorders*, 1954, *19*, 133–139.

Fowler, C. A., Rubin, P., Remez, R. E., & Turvey, M. T. Implications for speech productions of a general theory of action. In B. Butterworth (Ed.), *Language production*. New York: Academic Press, 1980.

Fransella, F., & Beech, H. R. An experimental analysis of the effect of rhythm on the speech of stutterers. *Behavior Research and Therapy*, 1965, *3*, 195–201.

Freeman, F. J. Fluency and phonation. In M. Webster & L. Furst (Eds.), *Vocal tract dynamics and dysfluency*. New York: Speech and Hearing Institute of New York, 1975.

Freeman, F. *The stuttering larynx: An electromyographic study of laryngeal muscle activity accompanying stuttering*. Unpublished doctoral dissertation, City Univeristy of New York, 1977.

Freeman, F. Phonation in stuttering: A review of current research. *Journal of Fluency Disorders*, 1979, *4*, 79–89.

Freeman, F. J., Borden, G., & Dorman, M. *Laryngeal stuttering: Combined physiological and acoustic studies*. Paper presented at the meeting of the American Speech and Hearing Association, Houston, Texas, November 1976.

Froeschels, E., & Rieber, R. The problem of auditory and visual imperceptivity in stutterers. *Folia Phoniatrica*, 1963, *15*, 13–20.

Fry, D. B. The development of the phonological system in the normal and the deaf child. In F. Smith & G. A. Miller (Eds.), *The genesis of language*. Cambridge, Mass.: MIT Press, 1966.

Garber, S. F., & Martin, R. R. The effects of white noise on the frequency of stuttering. *Journal of Speech and Hearing Research*, 1974, *17*, 73–79.

Garber, S., & Martin, R. Effects of noise and increased vocal intensity on stuttering. *Journal of Speech and Hearing Research*, 1977, *20*, 233–240.

Garber, S. F., & Moller, K. The effects of feedback filtering on nasalization in normal and hypernasal speakers. *Journal of Speech and Hearing Research*, 1979, *22*, 321–333.

Garber, S., Siegel, G., Pick, H., & Alcorn, S. The influence of selected masking noises on Lombard and sidetone amplification effects. *Journal of Speech and Hearing Research*, 1976, *19*, 523–535.

Glauber, I. P. The psychoanalysis of stuttering. In J. Eisenson (Ed.), *Stuttering: A symposium*. New York: Harper, 1958.

Goldiamond, I. Stuttering and fluency as manipulable operant response classes. In L. Krasner & L. P. Ullmann (Eds.), *Research in behavior modification*. New York: Holt, Rinehart & Winston, 1965.

Gregory, H. A study of the neurophysiological integrity of the auditory feedback system in stutterers. *Speech Monographs*, 1960, *27*, 243.

Gruber, L. Sensory feedback and stuttering. *Journal of Speech and Hearing Disorders*, 1965, *30*, 378–380.

Gunderson, D. Some relations between oral form discrimination and stuttering. Unpublished master's thesis, University of Minnesota, 1972.

Hall, J., & Jerger, J. Central auditory function in stutterers. *Journal of Speech and Hearing Research*, 1978, *21*, 324–337.

Ham, R., & Steer, M. D. Certain effects of alterations in auditory feedback. *Folia Phoniatrica*, 1967, *19*, 53–62.

Harms, M. A., & Malone, J. Y. The relationship of hearing acuity to stammering. *Journal of Speech Disorders*, 1939, *4*, 363–370.

Harris, R. *The effect of amplification of the stutterer's voice on the frequency of stuttering*. Unpublished M.A. thesis, Brooklyn College, 1955.

Hayden, P., Scott, D., & Addicott, J. The effects of DAF on the overt behaviors of stutterers. *Journal of Fluency Disorders*, 1977, *2*, 235–246.

Healey, E., Mallard, A., & Adams, M. Factors contributing to the reduction of stuttering during singing. *Journal of Speech and Hearing Research*, 1976, *19*, 475–480.

Held, R., & Freedman, S. J. Plasticity and sensorimotor control. *Science*, 1963, *142*, 455–462.

Horovitz, L. J., Johnson, S. B., Pearlman, R. C., Schaffer, E. J., & Hedin, A. K. Stapedial reflex and anxiety in fluent and disfluent speakers. *Journal of Speech and Hearing Research*, 1978, *21*, 762–767.

Hugo, R. 'n Kommunikatiefgefundeerde ondersoek na bepaalde waarnemingsverskynsels by disfemie. *Journal of the South African Speech and Hearing Association*, 1972, *19*, 39–51.

Hutchinson, J., & Navarre, B. The effect of metronome pacing on selected aerodynamic patterns of stuttered speech: Some preliminary observations and interpretations. *Journal of Fluency Disorders*, 1977, *2*, 189–204.

Hutchinson, J., & Norris, G. The differential effect of three auditory stimuli on the frequency of stuttering. *Journal of Fluency Disorders*, 1977, *2*, 283–293.

Hutchinson, J., & Ringel, R. The effect of oral sensory deprivation on stuttering behavior. *Journal of Communication Disorders*, 1975, *8*, 249–258.

Hutchinson, J., & Watkin, K. Jaw mechanics during release of the stuttering moment: Some initial observations and interpretations. *Journal of Communication Disorders*, 1976, *9*, 269–279.

Ingham, R., Martin, R., & Kuhl, P. Modification and control of rate of speaking by stutterers. *Journal of Speech and Hearing Research*, 1974, *17*, 489–496.

Jensen, P., Sheehan, J., Williams, W., & LaPointe, L. Oral sensory-perceptual integrity of stutterers. *Folia Phoniatrica*, 1975, *27*, 38–45.

Johnson, W. *The onset of stuttering*. Minneapolis: University of Minnesota Press, 1959.

Johnson, W. Stuttering. In W. Johnson & D. Moeller (Eds.), *Speech handicapped school children* (3rd ed.). New York: Harper & Row, 1967.

Jordan, L., Hardy, J., & Morris, H. Performances of children with good and poor articulation on tasks of tongue placement. *Journal of Speech and Hearing Research*, 1978, *21*, 429–439.

Karr, G. The performance of stutterers on selected central auditory tests. *South African Journal of Communication Disorders*, 1977, *24*, 100–109.

Kimura, D. Cerebral dominance and the perception of verbal stimuli. *Canadian Journal of Psychology*, 1961, *15*, 166–171.

Lane, H., & Tranel, B. The Lombard sign and the role of hearing in speech. *Journal of Speech and Hearing Research*, 1971, *14*, 677–709.

Lane, H., Catania, A., & Stevens, S. Voice level: Autophonic scale, perceived loudness and effects of sidetone. *Journal of the Acoustical Society of America*, 1961, *33*, 160–168.

Lechner, B. The effects of delayed auditory feedback and masking on the fundamental frequency of stutterers and non-stutterers. *Journal of Speech and Hearing Research*, 1979, *22*, 343–353.

Lee, B. S. Artificial stutter. *Journal of Speech and Hearing Disorders*, 1951, *16*, 53–55.

Locke, J. A methodological consideration in kinesthetic feedback research. *Journal of Speech and Hearing Research*, 1968, *11*, 668–669.

Logue, L. *The effects of temporal alterations in auditory feedback upon the speech output of stutterers*. Unpublished master's thesis, Purdue University, 1962.

Lotzmann, V. G. Zur Anwendung variierter Verzögerungszeiten bei Balbuties. *Folia Phoniatrica*, 1961, *13*, 276–312.

MacNeilage, P. F. Motor control of serial ordering of speech. *Psychological Review*, 1970, *77*, 182–196.

Maraist, J. A., & Hutton, C. Effects of auditory masking upon the speech of stutterers. *Journal of Speech and Hearing Disorders*, 1957, *22*, 385–389.

Martin, R., & Haroldson, S. Effects of five experimental treatments on stuttering. *Journal of Speech and Hearing Research*, 1979, *22*, 132–146.

Martin, R., & Starr, C. On the "imperceptivity" of stutterers. *Folia Phoniatrica*, 1967, *19*, 125–132.

May, A. E., & Hackwood, A. Some effects of masking and eliminating low frequency feedback on the speech of stammerers. *Behavior Research and Therapy*, 1968, *6*, 219–223.

McClean, A., & Cooper, E. Electromyographic indications of laryngeal area activity during stuttering expectancy. *Journal of Fluency Disorders*, 1978, *3*, 205–219.

McClean, M. Effects of auditory masking on lip movements during speech. *Journal of Speech and Hearing Research*, 1977, *20*, 731–741.

McCroskey, R. L., Jr. The relative contribution of auditory and tactile cues to certain aspects of speech. *Southern Speech Journal*, 1958, *24*, 84–90.

McFarlane, S., & Prins, D. Neural response time of stutterers and nonstutterers in selected oral motor tasks. *Journal of Speech and Hearing Research*, 1978, *21*, 768–778.

Metz, D., Conture, E., & Caruso, A. Voice onset time, frication and aspiration during stutterers' fluent speech. *Journal of Speech and Hearing Research*, 1979, *22*, 649–656.

Moser, H., LaGourge, J., & Class, L. Studies of oral stereognosis in normal, blind, and deaf subjects. In J. Bosma (Ed.), *Symposium on oral sensation and perception*. Springfield, Ill.: Thomas, 1967.

Murray, F. P. An investigation of variably induced white noise upon moments of stuttering. *Journal of Communication Disorders*, 1969, *2*, 109–114.

Mysak, E. D. Servo theory and stuttering. *Journal of Speech and Hearing Disorders*, 1960, *25*, 188–195.

Naylor, R. A comparative study of methods of estimating the severity of stuttering. *Journal of Speech and Hearing Disorders*, 1953, *18*, 30–37.

Neelley, J. N. A study of the speech behavior of stutterers and nonstutterers under normal and delayed auditory feedback. *Journal of Speech and Hearing Disorders, Monograph Supplement*, 1961, *7*, 63–82.

Neilson, M., & Neilson, P. *Systems analysis of tracking performance in stutterers and normals*. Paper presented at the meeting of the American Speech and Hearing Association, Atlanta, November 1979.

Novak, A. The influence of delayed auditory feedback in stutterers. *Folia Phoniatrica*, 1978, *30*, 278–285.

Perkins, W., Rudas, J., Johnson, L., & Bell, J. Stuttering discoordination of phonation with articulation and respiration. *Journal of Speech and Hearing Research*, 1976, *19*, 509–522.

Perrin, K., & Eisenson, J. *An examination of ear preference for speech and non-speech stimuli in a stuttering population*. Paper presented at the meeting of the American Speech and Hearing Association, New York, November 1970.

Peterson, G. E., & Shoup, J. E. A physiological theory of phonetics. *Journal of Speech and Hearing Research*, 1966, *9*, 5–67.

Quinn, P. Stuttering, cerebral dominance and the dichotic word test. *Medical Journal of Australia*, 1972, *2*, 639–643.

Ringel, R. L. Oral sensation and perception: A selective review. In R. Wertz (Ed.), *Speech and the dentofacial complex: The state of the art*. Washington, D.C.: American Speech and Hearing Association, 1970. (ASHA Report No. 5.)

Shaffer, G. Measures of jaw movement and phonation in non-stuttered and stuttered production of voiced and voiceless plosives. *Speech Monographs*, 1940, *7*, 85–92.

Shane, M. L. S. Effect on stuttering of alteration in auditory feedback. In W. Johnson & R. R. Leutenegger (Eds.), *Stuttering in children and adults*. Minneapolis: University of Minnesota Press, 1955.

Shearer, W. M., & Simmons, F. B. Middle ear activity during speech in normal speakers and stutterers. *Journal of Speech and Hearing Research*, 1965, *8*, 203–207.

Siegel, G. M., & Pick, H. L., Jr. Auditory feedback in the regulation of voice. *Journal of the Acoustical Society of America*, 1974, *56*, 1618–1624.

Smith, K. U. *Delayed sensory feedback.* Philadelphia: Saunders, 1962.

Soderberg, G. A. A study of the effects of delayed side-tone on four aspects of stutters' speech during oral reading and spontaneous speech. *Speech Monographs*, 1960, *27*, 252–253.

Soderberg, G. A. Delayed auditory feedback and the speech of stutterers: A review of studies. *Journal of Speech and Hearing Disorders*, 1969, *34*, 20–29.

Sommers, R., Brady, W., & Moore, W. Dichotic ear preferences of stuttering children and adults. *Perceptual and Motor Skills*, 1975, *41*, 931–938.

Speaks, C., & Niccum, N. Variability of the ear advantage in dichotic listening. *Journal of the American Audiological Society*, 1977, *3*, 52–57.

Starkweather, C. W., Hirschman, P., & Tannenbaum, R. S. Latency of vocalization onset: Stutterers versus nonstutterers. *Journal of Speech and Hearing Research*, 1976, *19*, 481–492.

Stromsta, C. Delays associated with certain side-tone pathways. *Journal of the Acoustical Society of America*, 1962, *34*, 392–396.

Stromsta, C. A spectrographic study of dysfluencies labeled as stuttering by parents. *De Therapia Vocis et Loquellae*, 1965, *1*, 317–320.

Stromsta, C. Interaural phase disparity of stutterers and nonstutterers. *Journal of Speech and Hearing Research*, 1972, *15*, 771–780.

Sussman, H., & MacNeilage, P. Hemispheric specialization for speech production and perception in stutterers. *Neuropsychologia*, 1975, *13*, 19–26.

Sutton, S., & Chase, R. A. White noise and stuttering. *Journal of Speech and Hearing Research*, 1961, *4*, 72.

Tiffany, W. R., & Hanley, C. N. Adaptation to delayed sidetone. *Journal of Speech and Hearing Disorders*, 1956, *21*, 164–172.

Timmons, B., & Boudreau, J. Delayed auditory feedback and the speech of stuttering and non-stuttering children. *Perceptual and Motor Skills*, 1978, *46*, 551–555.

Toscher, M., & Rupp, R. A study of the central auditory processes in stutterers using the synthetic sentence identification (SSI) test battery. *Journal of Speech and Hearing Research*, 1978, *21*, 779–792.

Van Riper, C. *The nature of stuttering.* Englewood Cliffs, N.J.: Prentice-Hall, 1971.

Webster, L. M., & Furst, L. (Eds.). *Vocal tract dynamics and dysfluency.* New York: Speech and Hearing Institute of New York, 1975.

Webster, L. M., & Gould, W. The effect on stuttering of selectively anesthetizing certain laryngeal nerve tracts. In L. M. Webster & L. Furst (Eds.), *Vocal tract dynamics and dysfluency.* New York: Speech and Hearing Institute of New York, 1975.

Webster, R. L., & Dorman, M. F. Decreases in stuttering frequency as a function of continuous and contingent forms of auditory masking. *Journal of Speech and Hearing Research*, 1970, *13*, 82–86.

Webster, R. L., & Lubker, B. B. Interrelationships among fluency producing variables in stuttered speech. *Journal of Speech and Hearing Research*, 1968, *11*, 754–766.

Webster, R. L., Schumacher, S. J., & Lubker, B. B. Changes in stuttering frequency as a function of various intervals of delayed auditory feedback. *Journal of Abnormal Psychology*, 1970, *75*, 45–49.

Winchester, R. A., Gibbons, E. W., & Krebs, D. F. Adaptation to sustained delayed sidetone. *Journal of Speech and Hearing Disorders*, 1959, *24*, 25–28.

Wingate, M. Stuttering as phonetic transition defect. *Journal of Speech and Hearing Disorders*, 1969, *34*, 107–108.

Wingate, M. E. Effect on stuttering of changes in audition. *Journal of Speech and Hearing Research*, 1970, *13*, 861–873.

Wischner, G. Stuttering behavior and learning: A preliminary formulation. *Journal of Speech and Hearing Disorders*, 1950, *16*, 324–335.

Wischner, G. An experimental approach to expectancy and anxiety in stuttering behavior. *Journal of Speech and Hearing Disorders*, 1952, *17*, 139–154.

Wyke, B. Phonatory reflex mechanisms and stammering. *Folia Phoniatrica*, 1974, *25*, 321–338.

Yairi, E. Effects of binaural and monaural noise on stuttering. *Journal of Auditory Research*, 1976, *16*, 114–119.

Yates, A. J. Delayed auditory feedback. *Psychlogical Bulletin*, 1963, *60*, 213–232.(a)

Yates, A. J. Recent empirical and theoretical approaches to the experimental manipulation of speech in normal subjects and in stutterers. *Behavior Research and Therapy*, 1963, *1*, 95–119.(b)

Zimmerman, G. Articulatory dynamics of fluent utterances of stutterers and nonstutterers. *Journal of Speech and Hearing Research*, 1980, *23*, 95–107.

6 Facilitating Stimulus Effects of Reward and Punishment

Discriminability as a General Principle

HARRY FOWLER

It is the presumption, if not the dictum, of investigators concerned with "basic" psychological research that relatively focused or circumscribed study of a particular problem will often uncover a general principle of behavior. This chapter seeks to illuminate such an outgrowth from the history and current extension of research on "shock-right" facilitation, one of several seemingly paradoxical effects of punishment (see Fowler, 1971b). The phenomenon in question was first detected and theoretically elaborated by Karl Muenzinger (1934). He reported that rats were facilitated in learning a visual discrimination when electric shock was administered for the correct, food-reinforced ("right") response, and virtually as well as when the same intensity of shock was administered to other animals for the incorrect, non-food-reinforced response ("shock wrong"). The generality of the shock-right facilitation effect did not go uncontested, however, and it is to George Wischner's credit that the phenomenon was first empirically delimited (Wischner, 1947) and then subsequently elaborated in a systematic program of research that he and the author conducted (e.g., Fowler & Wischner, 1969).

HARRY FOWLER ● Department of Psychology, University of Pittsburgh, Pittsburgh, Pennsylvania 15260. The research reported in this chapter was supported, in part, by Grants G-14312 and GB24119 from the National Science Foundation, and by Grants MH-08482 and MH-24115 from the National Institute of Health, United States Public Health Service. Additional support was provided by National Science Foundation Grant G-11309 and National Institute of Health Grant FR-00250 to the Computer Center, University of Pittsburgh.

In the following pages, the early history of research on shock-right facilitation is briefly reviewed, including the Muenzinger–Wischner controversy that ensued and the program of research that subsequently isolated the effect and described its mechanism of operation (for a detailed account of the early history, see Fowler & Wischner, 1969). Then, it is noted how more recent research has employed the shock-right paradigm to describe both the nature of discrimination learning and the manner in which reinforcement itself operates to facilitate performance. It is here that the phenomenon takes on particular significance, for the research indicates not only how punishment can be judiciously used to enhance performance, but also how other response-contingent events—attractive or even neutral—can similarly be employed. The final section takes stock of this generality and elaborates a simple but broad principle of behavior by which certain "well-established" phenomena and their theoretical underpinnings (e.g., the Yerkes–Dodson Law, response-mediation effects, the additivity of cues, and "predifferentiation") can be challenged and cast in an entirely different mold.

HISTORY OF RESEARCH ON SHOCK-RIGHT FACILITATION

Early studies by different investigators (e.g. Bunch, 1928; Dodson, 1917; Hoge & Stocking, 1912; Warden & Aylesworth, 1927; Yerkes & Dodson, 1908) were consistent in showing that in rodents (as well as humans), punishment in the form of electric shock for the incorrect response of a discrimination task produced a more rapid elimination of errors than in control subjects that received only reward for the correct response. Typically, this outcome was offered in support of Thorndike's (1911) *Negative Law of Effect:* responses that were accompanied or closely followed by discomfort to the animal weakened their connections with the situation, so that they would be less likely to recur. Muenzinger (1934), however, questioned the adequacy of these findings as support for the law of effect. He pointed out that only the so-called wrong response had been punished in these early studies. In order to support the generalization that punishment weakens a response, one ought also to punish a response favored by reward, the so-called right response. In this case, one could expect a conflicting tendency to manifest itself in a slowing down of learning.

Pursuing the above rationale, Muenzinger (1934) adopted the practice of administering electric shock for the correct, food-reinforced response. For rats that received correction training in a T-maze visual-discrimination task, Muenzinger found that this shock-right (SR) procedure eliminated errors more rapidly than a no-shock (NS) procedure, and almost as rapidly as the traditionally employed shock-wrong (SW) procedure. Because the difference between the SR and SW groups of his study was not statistically reliable, Muenzinger concluded that punishment had a general effect: it did not weaken or suppress the punished response; instead, it alerted the animal and made it more attentive to the relevant cues in the situation. On the basis of this interpretation, punishment anywhere in the maze could facilitate discrimination learning.

In a follow-up study that attempted to assess the proposed alerting function of punishment, Muenzinger and Wood (1935) administered shock to different groups of rats either before choice (in the stem of the T-maze) or immediately after choice (i.e., for both right and wrong responses). The latter, "shock-both" (SB), procedure also facilitated learning, and apparently as well as the SR treatment of Muenzinger's (1934) experiment (in this and most of the other early studies, the performance evaluations were largely based on the groups in the original experiment). However, the shock-before-choice condition produced an outcome comparable to that for the NS treatment of the original study and thus did not indicate a facilitating effect. These results suggested that the anticipation of shock administered after choice and the resulting cringing at the choice point were the means by which punishment of either the right or the wrong response, or both, facilitated the subject's attendance to the discriminative stimuli, and hence its discrimination performance.

The role of choice-point pausing as the basis for increased attention to the discriminative stimuli was assessed in two subsequent studies by Muenzinger. In these studies, rats were required either to jump a gap in the floor of the maze (Muenzinger & Newcomb, 1936) or, as a result of glass barriers in the maze arms, to pause at the choice point for 5 sec (Muenzinger & Fletcher, 1937). By comparison with the groups of the 1934 experiment, jumping a gap before choice (in the stem of the maze) resulted in performance comparable to that of the original NS group; however, jumping a gap at the choice point (i.e., in order to choose) produced as much facilitation as the SR treatment. Likewise, when rats were briefly delayed at the choice point by means of glass barriers, their performance was facilitated relative to the NS group of the 1934 experiment, although the magnitude of this effect, as measured by trials to a learning criterion, was reliably less than that which occurred in the original SR group.

Muenzinger and Newcomb (1936) further noted that rats of their jump-to-choice condition regularly engaged in vicarious trial-and-error (VTE) behavior just prior to making a choice jump. Because this behavior seemed to have occurred as well in previous experiments, where the rats were shocked after choice, Muenzinger and Newcomb proposed that a pause at the moment of choice was the behavioral mechanism by which punishment exerted its general alerting effect. Despite seeming corroboration of this mechanism in the Muenzinger and Fletcher (1937) study, employing the 5-sec choice-point delay, not all investigators were in agreement with Muenzinger's observations and interpretation. In a study evaluating the effect of shock locus, Drew (1938; see also Fairlie, 1937) compared SR and SW groups for which shock was administered immediately after choice with a group that received "shock in food" at the goal. Drew found that the performance of all three groups was facilitated relative to the performance of an NS group that was also included, but insofar as VTE behavior and pausing at the choice point were concerned, the three shock groups differed markedly. The SR group showed much more VTE behavior than the NS control, whereas the SW group did not, and the shock-in-food group showed none at all. In the latter, hesitation and head turning were evident only in the vicinity of the food, a finding that suggested to Drew that VTE behavior for the shocked subjects reflected an avoidance of specific cues—be they food or choice-point cues—that were associated with the shock. As Drew rightly concluded on the basis of his findings, the observations on VTE behavior did not prove or disprove the importance of factors such as increased alertness and attention.

Even the positing of a general alerting effect of punishment had to be tempered when, in a subsequent study by Muenzinger, Bernstone, and Richards (1938), the parameters of shock duration and frequency were equated for SR and SW groups. In Muenzinger's (1934) original study employing shock for either the right or the wrong response, the appropriate T-maze arm was completely electrified so that it produced shock until the subject entered the correct goal. Because of the correction procedure employed, rats in the SW condition learned quickly to turn around on entering the shocked (wrong) arm, and to enter the nonshocked (correct) arm. Consequently, "a rat of the shock-wrong group received about one fifth the amount of shock received by a rat in the shock-right group" (Muenzinger *et al.*, 1938, p. 177). To control for this difference, Muenzinger *et al.* (1938) repeated the 1934 experiment with an SR group that was yoked to the SW condition. In this study, shock was turned off in the wrong arm for the SW rat as soon as it turned around to correct; the same duration of shock was then administered to the yoked SR animal when it entered the correct arm on that trial. Consistent with the earlier findings, both the SR and the SW groups showed facilitated performance by comparison with the NS group of this study, or with the NS group in the original experiment. However, with shock duration and frequency matched, the SW group was now reliably superior to the SR group. (The fact that the NS group in this experiment was also reliably superior to the NS group in the original experiment causes some concern regarding the use of the original—presumably underestimated—control to evaluate treatment effects in the prior research.) These findings pointed to a specific avoidance-producing effect of punishment that, in the case of the SR rats, would oppose a general alerting effect of shock and, in the case of the SW rats, would complement such an effect.

The Muenzinger–Wischner Controversy

An important feature of the prior studies by Muenzinger and his colleagues, and by other investigators as well, is that they uniformly employed a correction procedure of training. Wischner (1947) questioned the adequacy of this procedure for evaluating the effects of punishment because, for all shocked groups, it generated a combination of positive and negative incentives that could favor learning of the correct response. Given that the rat was required to make a correct response on every trial, shocked subjects of either the SR or the SW groups could escape their fearful learning situation only by finally selecting the correct arm. Consequently, for these subjects, a correct response was subject to both positive and negative reinforcement: food reward and escape or avoidance of the shock (see Mowrer, 1950, for a comparable interpretation). Wischner contended that a noncorrection procedure would provide a better evaluation of the effects of punishment because, with this procedure, escape from the situation is available with, and thus equated for, correct and incorrect responses. Furthermore, with noncorrection training, the subject responds to only one discriminative stimulus on a given trial, allowing the consequences of its choice to be associated with that stimulus alone.

When Wischner (1947) evaluated the effects of SR and SW procedures by subjecting rats to noncorrection training in a "Yerkes-Wadson" discrimination box, he found that the SW treatment facilitated learning by comparison with an NS control, but that the SR treatment did not; if anything, SR subjects made more errors and were initially retarded relative to the controls. Because the performance of the SR subjects was characterized by a rise in errors early in training and then a relatively abrupt drop as they began to meet the learning criterion, the overall difference between this group and the NS control was not statistically reliable. Still, Wischner interpreted his finding as seriously challenging a general alerting hypothesis. He argued that the effect of shock was immediate and specific. It quickly led to avoidance of the cues that were associated with the shock.

In the controversy that ensued (Muenzinger, 1948; Wischner, 1948) over the interpretive significance of Wischner's (1947) findings, Muenzinger contended that correction and noncorrection procedures differed not only with respect to the consequences of an incorrect response, but also with respect to terminology and measurement. With the correction procedure that he and his colleagues used, a single error was recorded regardless of the number of times that the rat entered, or reentered, the incorrect arm before proceeding to the correct goal on that trial; however, with the noncorrection procedure used by Wischner, all such entries constituted "additional" errors (and trials). Because of this difference, as well as the fact that Wischner had used a different apparatus, Muenzinger and Powloski (1951) attempted to compare the two procedures directly. It is important to note, however, that they effected this comparison not by using the noncorrection procedure described by Wischner (1947), but by adapting the procedure to the general methodology and system of recording used with correction. Whenever their "noncorrection" animal entered the incorrect arm of the T-maze, it was permitted to return to the starting stem via an exterior gray alley, where it was detained briefly, and then, with the discriminative stimuli *in the same position* as for the preceding incorrect choice, the rat was free to choose again. Thus, their noncorrection procedure actually permitted the subject to correct, but via the gray return alley instead of the incorrect maze arm.

In view of the Muenzinger and Powloski's (1951) adaptation of the noncorrection procedure, it is not very surprising that their SR groups for both correction and noncorrection procedures showed facilitated learning in comparison with respective NS controls. Importantly, though, the SR facilitation effect with the adapted noncorrection procedure was only marginally reliable. Furthermore, the SW groups for both procedures were superior to respective SR groups, again indicating a specific avoidance-producing effect of the shock. Acknowledging this avoidance-producing effect of punishment, Muenzinger and Powloski contended that the magnitude of the SR facilitation effect depended on differences between correction and noncorrection training that allowed differential adaptation to the shock. They suggested that, with correction training, "frustration" (from nonreward) in the wrong alley and subsequent retracing toward the correct goal better counteracted the avoidance tendency to shock in the correct arm; thus, the correction procedure better allowed a general facilitating effect of punishment to manifest itself. In contrast, the noncorrection procedure enabled the animal to avoid shock by selecting the incorrect arm and therefore delayed when punishment's facilitating effect would predominate.

Couched in other terms, Muenzinger and Powloski's (1951) interpretation argued that with correction training, shock in the correct arm would be more rapidly counterconditioned by food reinforcement—a phenomenon that Pavlov (1927) had earlier documented. However, with this interpretation, it was an open question whether the facilitating effect of shock was due to some general alerting function of punishment or, in the case of SR animals, to its association with food reinforcement and hence its function as a secondary reinforcer, that is, a stimulus that could signal and therefore mediate the effect of primary reinforcement.

Offering the above interpretation as an alternative to Muenzinger's alerting hypothesis, Freeburne and Taylor (1952) investigated whether shock would facilitate learning under conditions where it could not function as a cue to the correctness of the subject's response, as when shock was administered for both right and wrong responses. This shock-both (SB) treatment had earlier been shown by Muenzinger and Wood (1935) to produce the facilitation required by the alerting hypothesis. However, because their study employed a correction procedure, the learning of the correct response by the SB subjects might well have been facilitated by escape from the fearful situation. Indeed, in the Muenzinger and Wood study (as well as in the comparable jump-to-choice study of Muenzinger & Newcomb, 1936), the correction procedure provided a 3:1 differential in the frequency of shocks experienced (or gaps to be jumped) with each incorrect as opposed to correct choice. That is, an experimental subject received shock (or encountered a gap) on selecting the incorrect arm, on retracing, and on entering the correct arm, as opposed to only one shock (or gap) in choosing the correct arm. This difference could easily have favored faster learning by the SB (or gap-both) subjects. Nevertheless, when Freeburne and Taylor (1952) eliminated this bias by using a noncorrection procedure, they found that the SB procedure facilitated learning in comparison with an NS control, and therefore they interpreted their results as supporting Muenzinger's alerting hypothesis.

Prince (1956) subsequently questioned Freeburne and Taylor's (1952) findings, however, because the difference that they reported between their SB and NS groups was only marginally reliable, and their discrimination problem so difficult that nearly one-third of their subjects failed to reach a learning criterion within 500 (as opposed to the customary 100 or so) training trials. The heightened difficulty of Freeburne and Taylor's simple black–white discrimination was apparently due to the imposition of a 5-sec delay in a gray detention chamber following choice and, likewise, the occasioning of food reinforcement in a gray goal chamber away from the positive discriminative stimulus. Prince argued that under these conditions, the observed difference might well have occurred because of the shock's effect in suppressing position habits. Furthermore, when Prince compared SB and NS groups in his own study, which also used a noncorrection procedure, he found no reliable difference between them. If anything, the difference tended toward SB retardation.

In a second noncorrection experiment, which varied the number of discrimination training trials (0, 15, or 25) prior to the introduction of shock for the correct response, Prince (1956) found improved performance for SR groups with greater amounts of shock-free training. Furthermore, by comparison with an NS control, the SR group with 0 shock-free trials was retarded (as measured by errors but not by trials to criterion), whereas the SR group with 25 shock-free trials was facilitated (as measured by trials but not by errors to criterion). Thus, Prince's second study offered evidence that SR training with a noncorrection procedure would facilitate learning, providing that a strong approach tendency was first established by sufficient shock-free training. Prince interpreted the findings of his two sudies as suppoting a secondary reinforcing effect of shock, although he indicated puzzlement over why *fewer* shock–food pairings (as for the SR group with 25 shock-free trials) would allow a stronger secondary reinforcing effect.

A final study in the series reported by Muenzinger provided a parallel to Prince's (1956) second experiment. In an attempt to manipulate the strength and type of avoidance reaction to shock, Muenzinger and Baxter (1957) gave rats food-reinforced training in a straight alley where they had either to *approach* and cross a charged grid or, being dropped directly onto the grid, to *escape* the shock by running into the goal. For subsequent adapted noncorrection training on a black–white discrimination, the brightness of the straight alley (either black or white) was used as a substitute cue for shock, so as to simulate both SR and SW treatments (in effect, generating fear-right and fear-wrong treatments). As might be expected from the presumably different reactions that were conditioned during straight alley training, Muenzinger and Baxter found that the approach group was superior to the escape group when the substitute cue designated the correct alley and simulated the SR treatment; conversely, the escape group was superior to the approach group when the substitute cue designated the incorrect alley and simulated the SW treatment. The more interesting finding, however, was that both escape- and approach-trained rats of either the simulated SR or the SW treatment were superior to control animals that had received straight-alley training without the shock. These results indicated that, apart from the type of reaction elicited by shock and conditioned to the cues in the straight alley, these (fear-producing) cues would facilitate discrimination learning when designating either a correct or an incorrect choice. Accordingly, Muenzinger and Baxter's findings argued in favor of some general facilitating factor, but to what extent this factor related to an alerting or other function of shock (or conditioned aversive stimulus) was still indeterminate.

Wischner and Fowler's Systematic Reassessment

The early research on SR training was instructive despite the varied outcomes reported by different investigators. First, it left no doubt that mild or moderate shock for the correct response would facilitate discrimination learning with correction training; and it suggested that such an effect was not merely an artifact of the correction procedure (e.g., in permitting escape from fear or punishment via the correct response). Although noncorrection training eliminated this bias and tended to preclude an SR facilitation effect, the effect could still be generated with this training procedure by ancillary manipulations that were designed to increase approach and/or reduce avoidance (Prince, 1956, Experiment 2; cf. Muenzinger & Baxter, 1957). Furthermore, the fact that noncorrection training did not usually produce a reliable retardation effect for the SR treatment (let alone a retardation effect comparable in size to the facilitation produced by SW training) indicated that some facilitating effect of punishment for the correct response (possibly, a secondary reinforcing effect of the shock) was offsetting the shock's avoidance-producing effect. In this light, the weak SR facilitation observed by Muenzinger and his colleagues with their adaptation of the noncorrection procedure (which made it similar to a correction procedure) suggested that correction and noncorrection training were related on an, as yet, unspecified dimension that regulated the facilitation effect. What was apparently needed was a more refined assessment of the differences between these procedures, one that would isolate the critical factor or dimension that determined the particular outcome of SR training.

What was also needed with equal, if not greater, priority was an assessment of the effects of the parameters of punishment. As early as his original experiment, Muenzinger (1934) had stated that only "moderate" shock-punishment would be facilitating, but systematic manipulation of the intensity of shock had never been accomplished. Furthermore, there was generally a lack of control in the early studies of the shock's duration and frequency of occurrence, and consequently its precise locus with respect to the cues and responses with which it was associated. Even in the Muenzinger et al. (1938) study, which attempted to match SR and SW groups on the amount of shock received, an experimental subject could touch a charged grid, withdraw, touch it again, and then finally attempt to run across it.

Given these shortcomings, George Wischner and I undertook a program of research that was designed to assess the functional relationships between the parameters of punishment and an assortment of nonshock methodological variables, which included manipulations of general and specific training procedures, discriminative-stimulus relations, and motivational-performance factors. These manipulations were accomplished in a series of studies using a standard apparatus and general procedure (for details, see Fowler & Wischner, 1969). In brief, our procedure merely consisted of giving male albino rats widely distributed, noncorrection training in an enclosed T-maze. The maze was constructed with opaque guillotine doors at the choice point (to prevent retracing, as well as resighting of the nonselected arm) and with translucent goalbox endwalls that were differentially illuminated from behind to provide the light–dark (or bright–dim) discriminative stimuli. With this arrangement, a discriminative stimulus was continuously visible to the subject: from the choice point, throughout the arm, and at the food cup in the goal. Depending on the subject's treatment, a single shock of a specified intensity and duration was automatically delivered to the grid when the subject interrupted an infared photoelectric beam that crossed the middle of a specified arm.

Initial Parametric Studies. In our first study (Wischner, Fowler, & Kushnick, 1963), we assessed the effect on performance of different intensities of shock for either the correct or the incorrect response in a simple, light–dark discrimination. For different SR and SW groups, the shock intensities were set slightly above the aversion threshold (30 V AC, in series with .3 megohms; cf. Campbell & Teghtsoonian, 1958) at 45, 60, and 75 V, with shock duration held constant at .2 sec. These intensities constituted an effective range of .15–.25 mA and encompassed the intensities employed in the earlier research by both Muenzinger and Wischner. In this first study, an effort was also made to evaluate the effects of the number and order of shock (and food) experiences received by the SR and SW subjects. To this end, half of the subjects in each group, including an NS group, were trained with the typically utilized free-choice procedure, and half with a quasi-forced-choice procedure. With the latter, the first trial of every four was a free choice, and the remaining trials were forced choices, so that occasions of food (and of shock for SR and SW subjects) were equated for the groups and were balanced over left and right maze arms.

Error scores based on the comparable free-choice trials of the free- and forced-choice training procedures indicated that there was no overall difference between the two procedures. With respect to the effects of shock, the findings of the two procedures showed that the SW treatment facilitated and the SR treatment retarded performance relative to that of the NS controls, and that these effects were greater with stronger intensities of shock. However, the retarding effect of the SR treatment was less pronounced than the facilitating effect of the SW treatment, particularly with the free-choice procedure. These findings were consistent with Wischner's (1947) earlier results highlighting the absence of SR facilitation with noncorrection training. Like his results, ours argued for a specific avoidance-producing effect of the shock.

In our second study (Wischner & Fowler, 1964), which also used a simple light–dark discrimination, we investigated the effect of shock duration. For different SR and SW groups, shock duration was set at .1, .2, and .4 sec, with shock intensity held constant at the intermediate value (60 V) employed in the prior intensity study. Because of the absence of any overall difference between the free- and forced-choice training procedures in the preceding study, only a free-choice procedure was used in the present experiment.

The findings of the present study (see Figure 1), comparable to the results of our prior study, showed that errors to criterion for the SW animals were increasingly reduced by longer durations of shock. However, for the SR animals, errors remained relatively constant across increasing shock durations and did not depart significantly from the performance level of the NS (i.e., 0-second shock) controls. To evaluate whether this effect was a sampling artifact, we trained additional animals under the NS condition and each of the three SR duration conditions. Viewed separately, or in conjunction with the data for the subjects previously run under these conditions (cf. the broad-line function in Figure 1), the data for the additional subjects also failed to demonstrate significant retardation with increasing shock durations for the correct response. In light of the pronounced SW effect, indicating avoidance of the punished (incorrect) re-

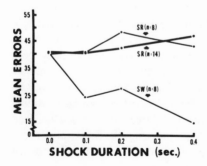

FIGURE 1. Mean errors to criterion as a function of shock duration for shock-right (SR) and shock-wrong (SW) groups. (From "Discrimination Performance as Affected by Duration of Shock for Either the Correct or Incorrect Response" by G. J. Wischner and H. Fowler, *Psychonomic Science*, 1964, *1*, 239–240. Reprinted by permission.)

sponse, the findings for the SR subjects (and, to some extent, those of the prior study) suggested that an additional factor was operating to offset an avoidance-producing effect of punishment for the correct response.

Assessment of a Secondary Reinforcing Effect. Given the outcome of earlier research on SR training (e.g., Prince, 1956), it seemed reasonable that an avoidance-producing effect of punishment for the correct response might be offset by a secondary reinforcing effect of the shock, that is, as a consequence of the shock's association with food reinforcement. To assess this possibility, we conducted a study (Fowler & Wischner, 1965b) in which the potential secondary reinforcing effect of shock for the correct response during discrimination training was evaluated by the shock's effect during extinction (e.g., in maintaining the response previously reinforced by food). In this study, different groups of rats first received NS- or SR-acquisition training on a light–dark discrimination where, through use of the previously described forced-choice procedure, occasions of reinforcement were equated for the two training conditions and were balanced over left and right maze arms. Then, the subjects received free-choice extinction training in which the NS-acquisition group (NS-A) was continued as before without shock. However, the SR-acquisition subjects (SR-A) were subdivided into three extinction groups, which received the following treatments: SR-E, shock for the previously reinforced response; SW-E, shock for the previously nonreinforced response; and NS-E, a no-shock extinction treatment controlling for the SR experiences of acquisition training. In this experiment and in all subsequent research (except where otherwise noted), shock was set and maintained at an intermediate intensity and duration (60 V, .2 sec).

The results of our extinction study showed that on the free-choice trials of the quasi-forced-choice procedure used in discrimination acquisition, the performances of the NS-A and SR-A subjects were virtually identical. These results matched the findings of our prior duration study (Wischner & Fowler, 1964). However, the extinction data did not provide any evidence that shock for the correct response had acquired a secondary reinforcing property via its association with food reinforcement, or even that its aversiveness had been attenuated. Relative to the extinction performances generated by both control treatments (NS-E and NS-A), the SR-E treatment facilitated extinction by rapidly increasing responses to the nonshocked (incorrect) arm, rather than as a secondary reinforcer protracting responses to the previously reinforced arm. Furthermore, as the SW-E subjects extinguished their correct response tendency, thereby making more "errors" and hence increasing their receipt of shock, their responses to the previously reinforced arm were abruptly augmented. For both the SR-E and SW-E subjects, then, the only apparent effect of shock during extinction was to suppress those responses with which the shock was associated.

There was, however, an ancillary finding to the extinction results. Despite the apparent avoidance-producing effect of shock during extinction, prior SR-acquisition training tended to facilitate extinction in that the NS-E group (or the three SR-A subgroups taken collectively) showed a more rapid rate of extinction than did the NS-A control. Although the difference between the NS-E and NS-A groups was not statistically reliable and might well have been due to a generalization decrement (since the change from acquisition to extinction for the NS-E group entailed the omission of both shock and food, as opposed to only food for the NS-A group), this trend pointed up the need for a more sensitive assessment of the effect of SR-acquisition training on subsequent performance. To that end, we initiated a follow-up study employing a reversal paradigm.

In this unpublished "reversal" study, different groups of rats again received NS- or SR-acquisition training (NS-A and SR-A) on a light–dark discrimination via the quasi-forced-choice training procedure. Then, for reversal training, where the correct response of acquisition training was incorrect and vice versa, the subjects in both the NS-A and the SR-A conditions were subdivided into NS, SR, and SW reversal groups, which received, respectively, no shock and shock for either the correct or the incorrect response on the *reversal* problem. During reversal training, all subjects received free-choice trials, with food reinforcement for the correct response being continued as before at two pellets.

Like the findings of our prior investigations, the results of this reversal study showed that there was no difference in error performance between the NS-A and SR-A groups during acquisition training. Similarly, during reversal training, there was no difference between the NS and SR reversal subjects in either errors or trials to a reversal criterion. By comparison, however, the SW reversal subjects were superior on both measures (p's $<.025$). Figure 2 shows that these effects of shock during reversal training did not interact with the subject's treatment during acquisition training (i.e., NS-A or SR-A). Hence, with respect to the shock's association with food reinforcement in acquisition training, the reversal data provided no evidence of an acquired reinforcing property of the shock. Indeed, the SW reversal group in the SR-A condition (which received shock for the incorrect response of reversal training and therefore should have been slowed in learning) showed the fastest reversal learning. A related finding was that the SR reversal group in the SR-A condition (which received shock for the correct

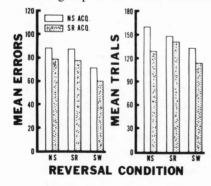

FIGURE 2. Mean errors and trials to a reversal criterion for NS, SR, and SW reversal groups that received either NS- or SR-acquisition training.

response of reversal training and therefore should have been facilitated in learning) showed reversal performance that was not different from the performance of its respective NS reversal control.

As in the results of our extinction study, though, the present findings did show that SR-acquisition training exerted a general facilitating effect on reversal performance in terms of trials to the reversal criterion ($p < .025$), and marginally so in terms of errors to criterion ($p < .07$). But unlike our extinction results, the difference in reversal learning between the SR-A and NS-A subjects could not be ascribed to a generalization decrement. In the case of the SW reversal condition, for example, there was less of a change from acquisition to reversal training for the SR-A than for the NS-A subjects, since the former subjects continued to receive shock (but not food) for the previously correct response, whereas the latter subjects were confronted for the first time with shock (and no food) for the previously correct response. This general facilitating effect of SR-acquisition training on subsequent reversal learning was similar to Muenzinger and Baxter's (1957) finding showing that prior shock–food pairings in a straight alley would facilitate subsequent discrimination learning when the straight-alley brightness was used as a substitute cue for shock. Both sets of findings suggested what seemed to be a general alerting or "sensitizing" function of shock that was mediated by fear. Operating in conjunction with the shock's avoidance-producing effect, this sensitizing effect could account for the absence in our research of a performance difference between NS and SR groups in acquisition training or, as shown by the present study, in reversal training as well.

Isolation of a "Distinctive-Cue" Effect. Along with the prior studies assessing a secondary reinforcing effect of shock, we considered an alternative interpretation which focused on the likelihood that not only shock but *all* of the stimuli associated with food reinforcement in the correct arm (i.e., physical features, feedback from the running response, interoceptive or "drive" stimuli, and, of course, the discriminative stimulus) would, at least initially, develop secondary reinforcing properties. (Readers familiar with contemporary learning theory will recognize that this interpretation posits conditioning to background stimuli, X, as well as to the positive discriminative stimulus, A, with the reinforcement of an AX compound; cf. Rescorla & Wagner, 1972.) So viewed, the operation of secondary reinforcing effects or, in more cognitive terms, a reward expectancy would not be restricted to correct-arm cues alone but would be mediated by all such similar stimuli (X) in the incorrect arm (i.e., the nonreinforced BX compound). In other words, a reward expectancy would generalize from the correct-arm to the similar incorrect-arm cues with the result that discrimination learning would initially be impeded. However, by introducing shock into one maze arm (say, the correct arm), the configuration of stimuli comprising that arm would be altered so that the arm is more readily perceived by the subject as different from a similar, alternative arm that is without shock (cf.

ASX and *BS*). Operating in this fashion as a "distinctive" cue that can increase the discriminability of the stimulus alternatives, shock should delimit the generalization of a reward expectancy from the food-associated correct-arm cues to those in the incorrect arm. And, in comparison with no-shock animals, this restriction of a reward expectancy to the correct-arm cues for the shocked subjects should lead (other things being equal) to facilitated discrimination learning.

Because of its emphasis on discriminability of the stimulus alternatives, the above interpretation suggested that a distinctive-cue effect of the shock would not be readily apparent in the customarily employed light–dark discrimination, where the alternatives, as served by the discriminative stimuli (cf. *A* and *B*), are highly discriminable. Here, the generalization of a reward expectancy from the correct- to the incorrect-arm cues would already be restricted. Given this consideration, we conducted a study (Fowler & Wischner, 1965a) in which respective groups of rats received NS, SR, or SW training on a scaled set of more difficult (bright–dim) discriminations, that is, where problem difficulty was systematically increased by reducing the difference in relative brightness of the discriminative stimuli (cf. *AX* and *A'X*). As expected, the results of this study showed that the performance of both shocked and nonshocked animals was progressively retarded across increasing levels of problem difficulty. More importantly, though, the SR group at every problem level was now reliably *facilitated* by comparison with its respective NS group—and the respective SW group even more so. Here, then, were findings that indicated both a distinctive-cue and an avoidance-producing effect of shock, the former as reflected in the superior performance of SR over NS subjects, and the latter as indicated by the superior performance of SW over SR subjects.

Because our prior reversal study had suggested a possible sensitizing or alerting function of the shock, we could not be certain whether the SR facilitation observed in our problem-difficulty study (Fowler & Wischner, 1965a) was due to this factor rather than to a distinctive-cue effect of the shock. Quite possibly, a sensitizing effect of the shock might also be potentiated in a more difficult discrimination. To compare these two interpretations, we conducted a follow-up study in which rats were trained on a moderately difficult (bright–dim) discrimination under one of the following treatments: NS, SR, SB (shock-both), and SP (shock-paired). As in earlier research (e.g., Freeburne & Taylor, 1952; Muenzinger & Wood, 1935; Prince, 1956), the subjects of the SB treatment received shock contingent on both correct and incorrect responses; similarly, in the SP treatment, the subjects received shock for both correct and incorrect responses, but only when a paired running mate in the SR condition had made a correct response and had received the shock. All three shock treatments (SR, SB, and SP) permitted a sensitizing effect of the shock to operate, but both the SB and the SP conditions precluded a distinctive-cue effect of the shock because, in these conditions, the shock was not selectively associated with one alternative. (In addition, the SP condition controlled for the number and order of shocks received by the SR subjects.) Inasmuch as our prior problem-difficulty study had not included an easy (light–dark) discrimination and thus had precluded a direct comparison of performance on easy and difficult discriminations, we ran comparable groups of shocked and nonshocked rats on both an easy (light–dark) and a moderately difficult (bright–dim) discrimination.

The results of this unpublished "shock-both" study are presented in Figure 3. As shown, errors and trials to criterion for all of the groups were greater on the difficult (D) as compared with the easy (E) discrimination ($p < .001$). However, at either problem level, there was no difference between the SB and SP groups, and although Figure 3 suggests that these two groups exhibited fewer errors and trials to criterion than the NS group, the between-groups difference for both measures was unreliable. Indeed, the only reliable difference was that between the NS and SR groups on the difficult discrimination ($p < .025$ for both errors and trials). This outcome not only replicated the SR facilitation effect observed in our problem-difficulty study (Fowler & Wischner, 1965a) but showed clearly that the effect was restricted to a more difficult (bright–dim) discrimination. In addition, the absence of a facilitating effect for the SB and SP treatments indicated that the SR facilitation effect could not be ascribed to a sensitizing or alerting function of the shock. Likewise, it could not be attributed to a secondary reinforcing effect of the shock in that such an effect would also be expected to facilitate performance in an easy discrimination; but clearly, this was not the case.

By establishing a distinctive-cue effect of shock for the correct response, the results of the above study afforded a basis for reinterpreting the findings of our earlier reversal study. That study had shown that prior SR-acquisition training facilitated reversal learning, presumably through a sensitizing or alerting function of the shock, as mediated via the fear conditioned to the correct-arm cues in acquisition training. But, if this were so, the facilitating effect of SR-acquisition training on subsequent reversal performance could be ascribed to the increased

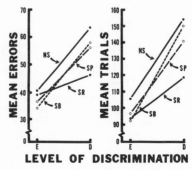

FIGURE 3. Mean errors and trials to criterion for NS, SR, SB (shock-both), and SP (shock-paired) groups trained on either an easy (E) or a difficult (D) discrimination.

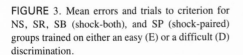

(i.e., acquired) distinctiveness of the alternatives that fear itself provided. The fact that our more recent research (e.g., Fowler & Wischner, 1965a) had shown that a distinctive-cue effect was manifest only in relatively difficult discriminations was not inconsistent with the conditions of training characterizing our reversal study. By our interpretation, increased problem difficulty was the result of a generalized reward expectancy for the incorrect alternative. However, in our reversal paradigm, a reward expectancy had actually been conditioned to the incorrect alternative through prior reinforcement of that alternative in acquisition training. This circumstance, in conjunction with reinforcement of the correct response in reversal training, could well have produced a relatively difficult discrimination, as indeed the frequency of errors and trials to reversal learning (cf. Figures 2 and 3) readily suggests.[1]

Motivational-Performance Manipulations. Muenzinger (1934) had early acknowledged that shock for the correct response would generate a conflict between the tendency to approach food and the tendency to avoid shock, and that the particular outcome would depend on the relative strengths of the two tendencies. The interplay of these tendencies in modulating the SR facilitation effect was evident in the findings of Prince's (1956) study, which had used initial shock-free training trials to increase the subject's approach tendency, and in the results of Muenzinger and Baxter's (1957) study, which had employed initial shock–food pairings in a straight alley, and then the brightness of the straight alley as a substitute cue for shock in discrimination training, in order to lessen the subject's avoidance tendency (see Muenzinger, Brown, Crow, & Powloski, 1952, for a similar manipulation entailing shock–food pairings in a straight alley prior to SR-discrimination training). We, too, felt that the subject's approach and avoidance tendencies would be important determinants of a facilitating cue effect of the shock, and therefore, in two subsequent studies, we separately varied the strength of each.

The first of these studies, a Ph.D. dissertation by R. P. Hawkins (1965), focused on the approach variables of drive (extent of food deprivation) and incentive (magnitude of food reward). Because our prior research had uniformly employed moderate levels of drive and incentive (12-g daily ration and two 45-

---

[1] For convenience of exposition, we have emphasized the operation of a reward expectancy for both the correct and the incorrect response of reversal training. However, it is more likely that the increased difficulty of a reversal problem is due to the operation of a nonreward expectancy for both responses because, in reversal training, subjects do not begin responding to the previously incorrect arm (for which a nonreward expectancy is developed in acquisition training) until they have extinguished responding (and thus have presumably developed a nonreward expectancy) to the previously reinforced arm. While this interpretation is more in keeping with the extended chance performance that usually occurs in reversal learning between the extinction of the previously reinforced response and the acquisition of the currently reinforced response (cf. Mackintosh, 1974), it does not vitiate the suggested interpretation of acquired distinctiveness of the alternatives as a consequence of prior SR-acquisition training.

mg pellets of food reward), Hawkins factorially manipulated high and low drive (10-g and 15-g daily ration) and high and low incentive (4 and 1 pellets of food reward) in conjunction with NS and SR training on both an easy (light–dark) and a moderately difficult (bright–dim) discrimination. The results of Hawkins's study indicated that higher amounts of drive and incentive facilitated the learning of both the easy and the moderately difficult discriminations and, like the results of our prior research, that SR training facilitated learning, but only in the difficult discrimination. The more interesting aspect of Hawkins's data, however, related to the interaction of drive and incentive with SR training: whereas high incentive reduced the SR facilitation effect (evidently because the facilitating effect of a large reward magnitude was itself so pronounced as to produce a "floor" effect and negate the effects of all other variables), high drive actually amplified the facilitating effect of SR training but, again, only in the difficult discrimination. These findings were amenable to the interpretation that a distinctive-cue effect of shock, in restricting the generalization of a reward expectancy from the correct to the similar incorrect alternative in a difficult discrimination, operated essentially through the development of differential associative strengths for correct and incorrect responses (i.e., a "habit" difference), which could be amplified by high drive.

In our second study (Fowler, Goldman, & Wischner, 1968), which focused on the subject's avoidance tendency, we attempted to reduce the aversive component of punishment without affecting its facilitating cue or stimulus component. To accomplish this, we trained different groups of rats on a moderately difficult (bright–dim) discrimination under the influence of either sodium amytal or no drug (both placebo and no-injection controls) and different intensities of shock for the correct response. Earlier research (e.g., Miller, 1961) had shown that sodium amytal would reduce the fear or anxiety motivating avoidance in conflict situations, and therefore, it was used in the present study to separate a facilitating cue effect of shock from its avoidance-producing effect. The results of this study

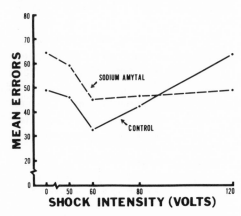

FIGURE 4. Mean errors to criterion as a function of shock intensity for the sodium-amytal and combined placebo and no-injection control subjects. (From "Sodium Amytal and the Shock-Right Intensity Function for Visual Discrimination Learning" by H. Fowler, L. Goldman, and G. J. Wischner, *Journal of Comparative and Physiological Psychology,* 1968, *65,* 155–159. Copyright 1968 by the American Psychological Association. Reprinted by permission.)

are shown in Figure 4. As indicated, the performance of the control, no-drug subjects was initially facilitated and then retarded across increasing intensities of shock for the correct response by comparison with their NS (0-V) control. This outcome suggested that the facilitating cue effect of shock in a difficult discrimination predominated at the weaker intensities but then gave way to an avoidance-producing effect at the stronger intensities. In contrast, SR facilitation for the sodium-amytal subjects increased with stronger shock intensities by comparison with their NS control and did not give way to retardation at the strongest intensities.[2]

The findings for the sodium-amytal subjects were particularly important because they showed that with the avoidance-producing component of punishment considerably reduced, the facilitating cue effect of shock for the correct response was an increasing S-shaped function (or, beyond the near threshold value of 50 V, an exponential function) of shock intensity. These results strongly supported a distinctive-cue effect of the shock because they modeled Weber's Law (cf. Crozier, 1940) describing the psychophysical relationship between performance and the discriminable cue properties of a stimulus (in this case, the intensity of the shock). In short, our research indicated that, once an aversive stimulus like shock had its aversiveness attenuated, it acted like any other stimulus in providing a basis for detecting a difference between similar stimulus compounds in which the (shock) stimulus was selectively embedded.

Resolution of the Correction–Noncorrection Controversy

In the course of our research, we had made a complete turnabout: our initial parametric study on shock intensity (Wischner et al. 1963) had shown that increasing intensities of shock for the correct response tended to increase avoidance and to retard discrimination learning. However, in our "sodium-amytal" study (Fowler et al. 1968), increasing intensities of shock over a comparable range (45–75 V; see Figure 4) increased SR facilitation, even for the control (no-drug) subjects. The key to the difference in outcomes, of course, rested in the use of an easy (light–dark) discrimination in our earlier research and a moderately difficult (bright–dim) discrimination in our more recent work. Like Muenzinger, we now had the means to produce consistent SR facilitation, but only with noncorrection training in a moderately difficult (bright–dim) discrimination. In contrast, Muenzinger's research had consistently shown SR facilitation with correction training in an easy, black–white (or light–dark), discrimination. This disparity in methodologies suggested that the earlier discrepant findings for

---

[2] The observed difference between the NS (0-V) groups in the drug and control conditions of this study is in line with evidence (e.g., Miller, 1961) suggesting that, in addition to reducing the fear motivating avoidance, sodium amytal also reduces frustrative inhibition from nonreinforcement of the incorrect response and, for this reason, tends to retard discrimination performance.

correction and noncorrection training might relate to an inherently greater difficulty of the correction task as a whole. In line with this supposition, the findings of studies comparing the two procedures had shown that correction training produced significantly more errors in both discrimination acquisition and discrimination extinction (e.g., Kalish, 1946; Seward, 1943). The question we considered, though, was not merely whether the two procedures generated different levels of task difficulty, as evidently they did, but whether such differences related to a common, underlying dimension that determined the magnitude of the SR facilitation effect.

To answer this question, we undertook a study (Fowler, Spelt, & Wischner, 1967) that addressed the relationship between problem difficulty (as we had manipulated it, through similarity of the discriminative stimuli) and the type of training procedure (correction or noncorrection) that was characteristic of our work and of Muenzinger's. Thus, different groups of rats in this study were given NS or SR training via a correction or noncorrection procedure on either an easy (light–dark) or a moderately difficult (bright–dim) discrimination. Our correction and noncorrection procedures were identical insofar as a correct choice was concerned: the subjects were prevented from retracing when in the correct (food-reinforced) arm, and after 10 sec in the correct goal, they were removed to await the next trial some 15 min later. Insofar as an incorrect choice was concerned, correction subjects were required to retrace and enter the correct (food-reinforced) arm, whereas noncorrection subjects were directly removed from the incorrect goal to await the 15-min interval to the next trial. For both procedures, an error was recorded whenever the subject's initial choice on a trial was the incorrect arm. In addition, further retracing by a correction subject (i.e., prior to the subject's entering the correct arm) was scored for entries into the stem and reentries into the incorrect arm.

The results of this study are presented in Figure 5. Like our prior findings, the results of the present study showed SR facilitation with noncorrection train-

FIGURE 5. Mean errors to criterion for NS and SR subjects receiving noncorrection or correction training on either an easy (E) or a difficult (D) discrimination. (From "Discrimination Performance as Affected by Training Procedure, Problem Difficulty, and Shock for the Correct Response" by H. Fowler, P. F. Spelt, and G. J. Wischner, *Journal of Experimental Psychology*, 1967, *75*, 432–436. Copyright 1967 by the American Psychological Association. Reprinted by permission.)

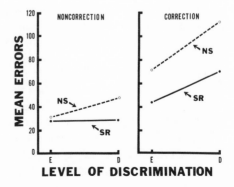

LEVEL OF DISCRIMINATION

ing, but only in the difficult discrimination. And like Muenzinger's findings, the present results showed SR facilitation with correction training in the easy discrimination, although more so in the difficult discrimination. A particularly important aspect of these data related to the performances of the NS controls for the two problem levels within each training procedure: for these NS subjects, errors increased progressively from the easy to the difficult noncorrection problem (and continuing across the panels of Figure 5) on through the easy to the difficult correction problem. Thus, the data for the NS subjects pointed to a composite dimension of task difficulty based on the interaction of problem level and training procedure. Furthermore, as Figure 5 indicates and as was confirmed statistically, this composite dimension bore a direct relationship to the magnitude of the SR facilitation effect. Not only did correction training produce a more difficult task, but greater SR facilitation was associated with this increased difficulty.

These findings now made possible an interpretation of the results of experiments using either a correction or a noncorrection procedure. With correction training, there is, in addition to any generalized reward expectancy in the incorrect arm (due to the physical similarity of the discriminative stimuli), a related secondary reinforcing effect that derives from the short delay of primary reinforcement that follows each incorrect response, that is, as a consequence of the correction subject's retracing toward the positive discriminative stimulus and then, on correcting, obtaining the food reward. Hence, in correction training, a reward expectancy would actually develop to the incorrect-arm cues via their sequential association with food reward in the correct arm. By comparison with noncorrection training, wherein an "infinite" delay of reinforcement (i.e., no reinforcement) follows each incorrect response, correction training should therefore generate slower learning. And with the increased problem difficulty effected by a correction procedure, SR training should produce greater facilitation for two reasons. First, as a distinctive cue, shock should increase discriminability of the *sequential* stimulus–response components involved in correcting, and in this manner, it should restrict the mediation of reward from late to early components of the chain (as well as delimit any generalized reward expectancy based on physical similarity of the discriminative stimuli). Second, as a fear-producing stimulus, shock should cause the subject to slow down in the course of correcting (and even to enter the stem of the T-maze, as was observed), and therefore, it should increase the delay of reward contingent on the incorrect response.

In sum, our findings suggested that with correction training, both the cue and the aversive components of punishment operated to facilitate discrimination learning for the SR subjects. However, of greater significance was the fact that we had apparently uncovered a factor that controlled SR facilitation generally, for our findings indicated that as a distinctive cue, shock for the correct response would facilitate learning to the extent that *conditioned reward* for the incorrect response was augmented either by increasing the similarity of the discriminative stimuli or by using correction instead of noncorrection training.

THE SHOCK-RIGHT PARADIGM AS AN EXPERIMENTAL ASSAY

In offering the above interpretation as a resolution of the Muenzinger–Wischner controversy on correction and noncorrection training, we actually broadened the scope of our research because we were now confronted with an additional set of questions concerning the nature of discrimination difficulty and the interactive effects of SR training. For example, if correction training provided a more difficult discrimination because of delayed reward for the incorrect response, should it not be possible to make correction training on a light–dark discrimination an *easier* task (comparable to noncorrection training) by extending the delay between the subject's incorrect response and its attempt at correcting? And in this manner, would we not reduce conditioned reward for the incorrect response and therefore the magnitude of the SR facilitation effect? On the other hand, should it not be possible to make noncorrection training on a light–dark discrimination a more *difficult* task (comparable to correction training) by reducing the "infinite" delay of reward that follows each incorrect response with this procedure? In this way, we should be able to augment conditioned reward for the incorrect response and thereby potentiate an SR facilitation effect in this "easy" (i.e., light–dark) discrimination, where the effect had always eluded us.

If our analysis of discrimination difficulty were correct, there would be still other ways in which conditioned reward for the incorrect response could be augmented with noncorrection training in an "easy" discrimination, that is, so as to generate an SR facilitation effect. Conceivably, the effect should be produced by using a simple black–white discrimination in which the goalboxes of both the correct and incorrect arms are of the same intermediate (e.g., gray) brightness; or by using a conditional discrimination in which the subject must go, say, right for reinforcement in the presence of two lighted arms, but left for reinforcement in the presence of two dark arms. With both these procedures, there are similar stimulus elements in the compounds comprising the correct and incorrect alternatives that can mediate reward for the incorrect response. Therefore, these manipulations should also generate a more difficult task, and hence, they should potentiate a facilitating effect of shock for the correct response. Note, however, that with these manipulations, our focus was not so much on SR facilitation *per se* as on the variables controlling discrimination difficulty and the extent to which SR facilitation, as an indicator of that control, could be made manifest. In effect, our research was entering a transitional stage: we were beginning to use the SR paradigm as an experimental assay to evaluate the nature of difficulty of a discrimination task, as well as the extent to which such difficulty was attributable to mediated reward for the incorrect response.

Variables Affecting Discrimination Difficulty

As indicated in our analysis of the differences between correction and noncorrection training, mediated reward for the incorrect response can be accomplished in basically two ways: (a) by employing a short delay of primary reinforcement for the incorrect response, the logical end-point of which is no delay or immediate reinforcement for that response; and (b) by increasing the physical similarity of the stimulus compounds constituting the correct and incorrect alternatives. In the following, findings on both of these manipulations are examined, with the dual aim of relating their significance to earlier research on SR facilitation and of describing the nature of discrimination difficulty. Unlike our previous research, though, which manipulated the discriminative stimuli in order to vary problem difficulty, the following research deals with "ancillary" manipulations that were designed to vary problem difficulty in training contexts where the discriminative stimuli were already highly discriminable.

Delayed Reward for the Incorrect Response. As a logical follow-up to our comparison of correction and noncorrection training (Fowler *et al.*, 1967), a study was conducted (Spelt & Fowler, 1969) that attempted both to eliminate the SR facilitation effect that was typically present with correction training in an easy (light–dark) discrimination and to produce the effect, typically absent, with noncorrection training in the same discrimination. To this end, different groups of rats were given NS or SR training on a light–dark discrimination with either a correction or a noncorrection procedure, and with a delay of reward for the incorrect response systematically varied across groups.

For correction subjects of this experiment, the delay was accomplished by allowing the rat to retrace to the choice point following an incorrect choice, and by then detaining the rat in the choice-point and stem region for either 0, 15, 30, or 60 sec before permitting it to enter the correct (food-reinforced) arm. (Detention of the subject was effected by first closing the guillotine door to the correct arm during the subject's incorrect choice, and then closing the incorrect-arm door after the subject had retraced to the choice point. With the 0-sec delay, the guillotine doors were not employed.) In contrast, noncorrection subjects received the standard treatment of being removed from the goalbox following an incorrect choice, but whereas half of the subjects had to await the next trial for some 11 min, half were immediately returned to the start box for a forced run to the correct (food-rewarded) arm. (Forcing was accomplished by lowering the guillotine door to the incorrect arm.) Accordingly, noncorrection subjects received either an "infinite" delay of reward (as determined by the intertrial interval and a subsequent correct choice) or a "0-sec" delay of reward following each incorrect response (actually, about 8 sec, the time required to remove the rat from the goalbox and place it back in the start box).

The results of this study showed that, by comparison with the standard correction treatment involving no delay in correcting, a 15-sec or longer delay significantly reduced both errors and trials to criterion, as well as the magnitude of the SR facilitation effect. Conversely, by comparison with the standard noncorrection treatment involving an "infinite" delay of reward following each incorrect response, a "0-sec" delay tended to increase errors and trials to criterion and to promote an SR facilitation effect. These effects for the correction and noncorrection subjects were systematically related, as is indicated by Figure 6. In this figure, mean trials to criterion for NS and SR groups are presented as a function of the log delay of reward following an incorrect response, and hence *independently* of training procedure. The left panel shows the data for the "short"-delay groups of the two procedures, that is, those receiving the standard 0-sec delay correction treatment and the "0-sec" (actually 8-sec) delay noncorrection treatment; the right panel shows the data for the "long"-delay groups, that is, those receiving the 60-sec delay correction treatment and the standard "infinite"-delay noncorrection treatment. Inspection of the data across the two panels shows that trials to criterion were increasingly reduced with increasing delays of reward for the incorrect response and that, associated with this outcome, the SR faciliation effect was progressively weakened. These findings left no doubt that a short delay of reward following the incorrect response in correction training was a major controlling factor of the SR facilitation effect. (For an analysis of the role of the positive discriminitive stimulus in mediating reward for the incorrect response during correction, see Domber, Fowler, & Wischner, 1971.)

The above findings were significant not only to our prior research on correction and noncorrection training (Fowler *et al.*, 1967), but also to the earlier research by Muenzinger, which had employed an "adapted" noncorrection procedure (e.g., Muenzinger & Powloski, 1951). Because Muenzinger's

FIGURE 6. Mean trials to criterion for NS and SR groups of the correction (C) and noncorrection (NC) short- and long-delay conditions as a function of log delay of reward for the incorrect response. (From "Effects of Shock-Right Discrimination Training Using a Correction Procedure with an Enforced Delay Following an Incorrect Choice" by Philip F. Spelt, Unpublished doctoral dissertation, University of Pittsburgh, 1967. Reprinted by permission.)

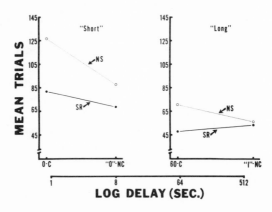

"adapted" procedure allowed the subject to correct via an exterior gray alley that connected the incorrect goal to the start box (or via direct replacement in the start box; cf. Muenzinger & Baxter, 1957), it was similar to our "0-sec" delay noncorrection procedure. Like our procedure, it, too, produced a marginal SR facilitation effect. We were pleased with the comparable outcomes, but we were somewhat disappointed that we had not been able to generate more substantial SR facilitation with our short-delay noncorrection treatment. However, there was no way in which we could additionally shorten the actual delay of about 8 sec required to remove the subject from the incorrect goal and place it back in the start box for a forced run to the correct arm; the methodology was simply too cumbersome. For this reason, we considered alternative ways in which we could provide a more immediate reward for the incorrect response with noncorrection training in a light–dark discrimination.

Prior Reward for the Incorrect Response. The logical extension of our short-delay manipulation was to provide an immediate reward for the incorrect response, but in a way that would allow differential responding in subsequent training. To a certain extent, we had already accomplished this manipulation in our "reversal" study. In that study, the incorrect response of reversal training had been directly reinforced by food in prior acquisition, with the result that SR training during acquisition facilitated subsequent reversal learning (see Figure 2). This manipulation suggested still another: simply reinforcing *both* correct and incorrect responses in a pretraining phase, and then reinforcing just the correct response during discrimination training. Such "nondifferential" pretraining should also retard the learning of an easy (i.e., light–dark) discrimination, as indeed had been shown by other investigators (e.g., Bitterman & Elam, 1954; Crawford, Mayes, & Bitterman, 1954).

We, too, had observed a retarding effect of nondifferential pretraining on subsequent discrimination performance in an earlier, unpublished study that was prompted by our demonstration of SR facilitation with noncorrection training in a difficult (bright–dim) discrimination (Fowler & Wischner, 1965a). Because our general training procedure included 16 forced-choice, food-reinforced pretraining trials that were evenly distributed over discriminative stimuli and left and right maze arms (so as to reduce both brightness and position preferences in discrimination learning), we had conducted a study to determine whether that amount of pretraining contributed to the absence of SR *retardation* in an easy (light–dark) discrimination, or indeed whether greater amounts of pretraining might even potentiate an SR-facilitation effect in this context. The results of that study showed the expected retarding effect of nondifferential pretraining (cf. Fowler & Wischner, 1969), but there was no evidence of a facilitating effect of SR training in discrimination learning. At best, there was only a suggestion of this effect for subjects that had received the maximum amount of pretraining (i.e., 64 trials). Given the interpretive significance of this manipulation in relation to the effect of a short delay of reward for the incorrect response (Spelt & Fowler,

1969), we repeated the study but extended the amount of nondifferential pretraining from 0 through 64 to 128 trials.

In this unpublished follow-up study, different groups of rats were again given NS or SR noncorrection training in an easy (light–dark) discrimination following their designated amounts of nondifferential pretraining. Like our prior results, the findings of this study (see Figure 7) showed that greater amounts of pretraining increased errors and trials to criterion in discrimination learning ($p <$ .025), but now the findings also allowed an overall facilitation effect of SR training with the trial measure ($p < $ .025), and marginally so with the error measure ($p = $ .08). Nevertheless, in agreement with our earlier results, separate comparisons showed that the difference between respective NS and SR groups was reliable only for the 128-trial pretraining condition ($p < $ .025 for both measures).

These results complemented our other findings in showing that prior reward (like delayed reward) for the incorrect response would impede discrimination learning and thereby promote a facilitating effect of SR training. However, with nondifferential pretraining, the particular basis for such an effect was somewhat different: specifically, extensive pretraining would cause the light–dark discriminative stimuli to become functionally equivalent (i.e., they would *acquire* equivalence) through the pronounced reward expectancy that was conditioned to each alternative; and, in turn, the stimulus features of these common reward expectancies would provide the basis for *mediated* generalization effects. Hence, frustrative inhibition from nonreinforcement of the incorrect response in discrimination training would generalize to the correct alternative to impede learning of the discrimination. But with SR training, the cue effect of shock could increase the discriminability of the alternatives and thereby restrict the effects of frustrative nonreward to the incorrect alternative. In this fashion, nondifferential pretraining would promote relatively rapid learning for the SR subjects despite prior reinforcement of the incorrect response.

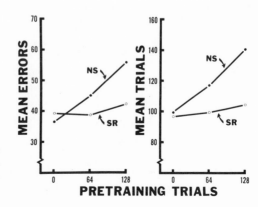

FIGURE 7. Mean errors and trials to criterion for NS and SR groups as a function of the amount of nondifferential pretraining.

Generalized Reward for the Incorrect Response. Through its emphasis on mediated generalization effects, the preceding study provides a link with other kinds of manipulations that can be used to promote a reward expectancy for the incorrect response, not by prior reward, or by a short delay of reward for the incorrect response, but instead via the generalization of a reward expectancy that is conditioned to "background" stimuli in the correct alternative. One very straightforward manipulation of this type that we attempted was to reinforce rats for a correct response in a simple (black–white) discrimination where the discriminative stimuli were movable wall inserts. To provide varying amounts of background-mediated generalization for different groups, the black and white wall inserts covered (in 30.5-cm units) the first third, the first two-thirds, or all three-thirds of the *gray* T-maze arms (Conditions I, II, and III, respectively), or all three-thirds of the arms, with the goalbox endwalls and food cups of a corresponding brightness as well (Condition IV). Under these training conditions, all groups had the same opportunity to discriminate between black and white arms at the choice point. The question, of course, was whether increasing extents of a common gray brightness *beyond* the choice point would mediate a reward expectancy for the incorrect response and, in this manner, retard discrimination learning. If so, shock for the correct response should function as a distinctive cue to restrict such generalization effects and thereby facilitate performance relative to that of NS controls.

The results of this unpublished "insert" study are shown in Figure 8. As indicated, errors and trials to criterion markedly increased when dissimilarity of the alternatives was reduced by greater extents of a common gray brightness in the T-maze arms (p's $< .001$). Furthermore, the SR facilitation effect was not only pronounced ($p < .001$ for both measures), but increasingly so with greater extents of the common background brightness (interaction $p < .025$ for both measures). Indeed, a facilitating effect of SR training was absent only when the arms, including the goalbox endwalls and food cups, were completely dissimilar in brightness, as in Condition IV.

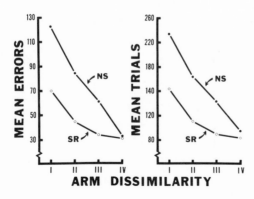

FIGURE 8. Mean errors and trials to criterion for NS and SR groups as a function of increasing arm dissimilarity. Black and white wall inserts covered either the first third, the first two-thirds, or all three-thirds of the gray arms (Conditions I, II, and III, respectively), or all three-thirds of the arms, with the goalbox endwalls and food cups of a corresponding brightness as well (Condition IV).

These findings are instructive in two major respects. First, they indicate that the difficulty of a discrimination is regulated, not merely by similarity of the discriminative stimuli (since all of the above training conditions entailed black–white choice stimuli), but also by "irrelevant" stimuli that are common to the alternatives. Second, they suggest that most if not all of the early SR research, which used a simple black–white discrimination, generated increased task difficulty by employing common background elements in the alternatives. For example, Muenzinger's research with correction training on a black–white discrimination generally employed a T-maze in which both the correct and the incorrect goal compartments were gray (cf. Condition II of Figure 8). Similarly, the "adapted" noncorrection procedure of Muenzinger and Powloski's (1951) study made use of a gray chamber by which noncorrection subjects were permitted to return to the start box following an incorrect response, and also an identical gray goal chamber in which the subjects were reinforced by food following a correct response. Prince's (1956) study, which utilized a standard noncorrection procedure, employed movable white wallboards that covered the entire length of one of the black T-maze arms, but apparently not the goalbox endwall or the food cup (cf. Condition III of Figure 8). With all of these arrangements, the basis exists for background mediation of a reward expectancy to the incorrect alternative, and hence a facilitating effect of shock for the correct response.

To demonstrate further the role of "irrelevant" stimuli in modulating discrimination difficulty and the magnitude of the SR facilitation effect, we conducted a study in which rats were subjected to a conditional discrimination. In this study, both arms of the T-maze were either lighted or dark over random trials. The task for the rat was to go, say, right (R) for reinforcement when in the bright (B) maze and left (L) for reinforcement when in the dark (D) maze. This problem can be especially difficult because the brightness and position elements constituting the stimulus compounds that are associated with reinforcement (BR and DL) also constitute the stimulus compounds that are associated with nonreinforcement (BL and DR), and therefore the elements of both dimensions can mediate a reward expectancy for incorrect responses. However, shock can be used as a distinctive cue to delimit the generalization effects based on one or the other or both of these dimensions; that is, shock can be associated with one brightness element (B or D), or with one direction element (L or R), or with one type of the several combinations of elements, such as the correct (+) or incorrect (−) stimulus compounds. In the present study, these conditions were arranged for six different groups of rats so that the subjects received shock for a choice response in either the B or D maze, for an R or L position response in both mazes, or for a correct (+) or an incorrect (−) response in both mazes. In addition, a seventh group, serving as a control, received no shock (N) for any response.

The results of this unpublished study are presented in Figure 9, which shows mean errors to criterion for the different shock-contingency groups. As indicated, the collective performance of the six shock groups was facilitated relative

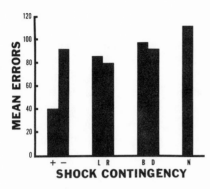

FIGURE 9. Mean errors to criterion in a conditional discrimination for subjects receiving shock contingent on either correct (+) or incorrect (−) responses, left (L) or right (R) position responses, or responses in the bright (B) or dark (D) maze; or no shock (N).

to that of the N group ($p < .05$). Furthermore, for the six shock groups, there was no difference between the B and D groups, nor between the L and R groups, nor between these two sets of groups. However, these two sets of groups differed reliably from the combined + and − groups ($p < .05$), which themselves were different ($p < .005$; comment on this difference is offered below). Accordingly, a trend analysis of the data, including those for the N group, showed that the magnitude of facilitation was scaled according to the number of dimensions involved in the shock contingency ($p < .005$); that is, there was less facilitation when shock was administered for the single dimension of either brightness (B or D) or position (L or R) than when it was administered for the composite stimulus dimension of correctness (+ or −). Hence, to the extent that a distinctive-cue effect of shock rendered the elements of one or both of the dimensions more discriminable, it also facilitated discrimination learning.

The observed difference between the + and − groups is not surprising if it is taken into consideration that these groups differed with respect to the percentage of trials on which shock was followed by food reward (100% or 0%, respectively), and thus the extent to which the aversive component of punishment would be attenuated. (In contrast, shock for the single-dimension groups was associated with food reward on 50% of the trials—a procedure that obviates a potential confounding in the comparison of these groups with the combined + and − groups.) The difference between the + and the − groups suggests, therefore, that the heightened discriminability provided by the shock for the + group was complemented by an attenuation of the shock's aversiveness, whereas that for the − group was opposed by the shock's aversiveness, with a consequent loss in performance.[3] This difference points up another aspect of punishment training that is relevant to the early research on SR facilitation, that is, the extent

---

[3] In a conditional discrimination of the present type, punishment-produced avoidance of the incorrect stimulus compounds (BL and DR) does not necessarily facilitate the learning of a response to the

to which prior shock–food pairings in preliminary training attenuated shock's aversive effect and thereby allowed its cue effect to predominate (cf. Muenzinger *et al.*, 1952; Muenzinger & Baxter, 1957).

Overview. Although the studies reviewed in this section differ markedly in their designs, their findings are consistent in supporting two general statements on the nature of discrimination learning. First, it is eminently clear that discrimination difficulty is not dependent merely on the animal's failure to detect or perceive a physical difference between the discriminative stimuli, as all of the manipulations of problem difficulty in the preceding studies were accomplished with a simple, or a conditional, light–dark discrimination. Rather, the difficulty of a discrimination lies in the similarity of all of the elements, *relevant and irrelevant,* that constitute the stimulus alternatives and/or the extent to which these elements are common to the alternatives. Second, these common or similar stimulus elements apparently heighten the difficulty of a discrimination by means of their mediation of a reward expectancy for the incorrect response (and/or a nonreward expectancy for the correct response). Such mediation can also be accomplished through the close temporal association of the incorrect response with a primary reward (as in correction training where a short delay of reward follows the incorrect response) and through prior reward for the incorrect response, and hence the learned equivalence that results with the conditioning of a common reward expectancy.

Food Reward as a Distinctive Cue

The foregoing description of discrimination difficulty is, of course, complementary to a distinctive-cue effect of shock for the correct response: just as elements that are common to the stimulus alternatives can increase discrimination difficulty, so conversely can an element that is unique to one alternative (e.g., shock) facilitate discrimination learning. To this point, our focus on stimuli that are unique to one alternative has concerned only selective punishment. However, there is another unique stimulus element in discrimination learning that we have tended to ignore: food reward for the correct response. From our interpretation of a facilitating cue effect of selective punishment, it follows unequivocally that selective reward will also exert a facilitating *cue* effect. In other words, the reinforcing effect of food reward on discrimination performance is due not

---

correct stimulus compounds (BR and DL). This is so because the animal cannot avoid the brightness of the maze (B or D) but only the position of the arm (R or L) in which it is punished. However, being punished for *both* positions, the animal quickly adopts a single, dominant position response in both mazes and therefore is subject to 50% reinforcement. In turn, this maintains the position response and interferes with the learning of the correct responses, as indeed was observed for the – group in the present experiment.

merely to its incentive property, but also to its property as a distinctive stimulus that is uniquely associated with the correct response. Furthermore, like shock, the magnitude of a facilitating cue effect of food reward should be a positive function of the magnitude or "intensity" of reward (cf. shock intensity as a distinctive cue; Figure 4).

In earlier research addressing the interaction of approach variables (drive and reward) with punishment for the correct response (Hawkins, 1965), it was found that SR facilitation in a difficult (bright–dim) discrimination was maximal under high drive and *low* (1-pellet) reward for the correct response. At the time, the absence of comparable SR facilitation under high (4-pellet) reward had been viewed as due to a "floor" effect, that is, a physical limit to discrimination performance. However, with our recognition of the potential cue effect of reward, particularly a large magnitude of reward, it became evident that the high-reward condition could have precluded SR facilitation not because of a physical limit to learning, but because high reward as a particularly distinctive stimulus condition could itself increase the discriminability of the alternatives and thereby obviate the cue effect of another stimulus like shock. Given this possibility, we conducted a follow-up study in which rats received NS or SR noncorrection training on a moderately difficult (bright–dim) discrimination with food reinforcement for the correct response set for different groups at a 1-, 2-, 4-, or 8-pellet reward. To allow full expression of any difference between respective NS and SR groups, the subjects of this study were maintained on a 12-g daily diet (moderate drive), which was corrected for the amount of food received in discrimination training.

The results of this unpublished study are presented in Figure 10. As shown, larger magnitudes of food reward facilitated discrimination learning ($p < .001$ for errors and trials to criterion), and so similarly did shock for the correct response (p's $< .001$). Aside from the effects for the 1-pellet condition, which were constrained because of a training cutoff of 300 trials (or, by chance, 150 errors), Figure 10 also indicates that the magnitude of the SR facilitation effect diminished with larger magnitudes of reward. Although the overall interaction of these variables was not significant, separate comparisons showed that the differences between respective NS and SR groups in the 4- and 8-pellet conditions were

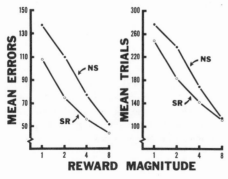

FIGURE 10. Mean errors and trials to criterion for NS and SR groups as a function of magnitude of reward for the correct response of a difficult discrimination.

unreliable for both the error and the trial measures. Furthermore, when the reward magnitude by shock interaction was assessed for just the 2-, 4-, and 8-pellet conditions (to avoid the measurement constraint in the 1-pellet condition), it was found to be reliable for the trial measure ($p < .05$), and marginally so for the error measure ($p < .10$). This reduction in SR facilitation with increasing magnitudes of reward would not seem to be due to any floor effect, since an extrapolation of the error and trial functions for the NS subjects indicates that there is ample room for further improvement in performance. In this light, the virtual absence of SR facilitation for the 8-pellet condition ($F < 1$ for both errors and trials) suggests that a large reward itself functioned as a distinctive cue to preclude a comparable cue effect of the shock.

Some comment on the means of operation of food reward as both a distinctive cue and an incentive would seem profitable at this point. In the above discussion, it is not being denied that larger magnitudes of reward provide greater incentive and that this aids in the learning of a discrimination. Rather, it is being argued that in the context of a difficult discrimination (as provided by similar discriminative stimuli in the present study), the stimulus characteristics of large amounts of reward and the feedback from associated consumatory activity in the correct goal (by contrast with the absence of such stimulation in the incorrect goal) increase discriminability of the alternatives and thereby delimit the generalization of a (large) reward expectancy from the correct to the incorrect alternative. To put it another way, one can draw a parallel between the reward-magnitude manipulation of the present study and the arm-dissimilarity manipulation of our prior "insert" study (cf. Figure 8). As in that manipulation, increasing magnitudes of food reward for the correct response should also generate greater arm dissimilarity and, in this fashion, facilitate discrimination performance.

To be sure, support for the above argument is not accomplished in a convincing way by a comparison based on the similar effects of another variable, or by the extrapolation of data functions. But the problem is that it is difficult to obtain support for the argument when the proposed cue effect of reward is confounded with its well-documented incentive effect (unlike the opposed cue and aversive functions of shock for the correct response). What was needed, therefore, was a manipulation by which the cue effects of reward could be demonstrated in a counterintuitive way. To this end, we undertook several studies that were designed to show that only reduced or *poorer* conditions of reward would potentiate a facilitating effect of punishment for the correct response.

Discriminability Modulated by Reward

Basically, our approach to demonstrating a distinctive-cue effect of food reward was the same as that earlier employed in assessing the role of common background cues: we would manipulate the parameters of the reward in such a way as to *increase* the similarity of the stimulus alternatives in an easy (light

–dark) discrimination, where the SR facilitation effect was typically absent. In this manner, we would hope to produce SR facilitation as evidence of the loss of control exerted by food reward as a distinctive cue.

Delayed Reward for the Correct Response. By our interpretation, the cue or stimulus effects of reward should be determined not only by the magnitude of reward, but also by the frequency or percentage of reward over trials, and by the temporal locus or point of occurrence of reward within a trial. In an initial study designed to illustrate these cue effects of reward, we focused on the latter variable: rats were given NS or SR noncorrection training in an easy (light–dark) discrimination, with a 2-pellet reward for the correct response being administered in the goal, but after a delay of 0, 8, 16, or 24 sec for different groups (detention time in the incorrect goal matched time in the correct goal). The rationale for this study was straightforward. If immediate food reward in the correct goal provided a distinctive-cue effect that increased the discriminability of the alternatives, then a delay of reward for the correct response would, by comparison with the "infinite" delay of reward for the incorrect response, increase the *similarity* of the alternatives and thereby potentiate a facilitating cue effect of shock for the correct response. To ensure that shock would "capture" the distinctive-cue effect that was presumably provided by immediate food reward, shock punishment in this study (unlike in our earlier studies) was administered in the goal immediately adjacent to the food cup.

The results of this study (Fowler, Fago, & Wischner, 1971) are shown in Figure 11. As indicated, there was no SR facilitation with a short (0- or 8-sec) delay of reward for the correct response; if anything, immediate shock in the goal under these conditions tended to retard discrimination learning, although not reliably so. However, with a relatively long (16- or 24-sec) delay of reward, immediate goal-shock exerted a pronounced facilitating effect relative to the retarded performances exhibited by the NS controls. Here, then, were our counterintuitive findings: shock punishment for the correct response produced a facilitating effect *only* when the food reward for that response was considerably

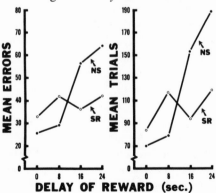

FIGURE 11. Mean errors and trials to criterion for NS and SR groups as a function of delay of reward for the correct responses of an easy discrimination. (From "Shock-Right Facilitation in an Easy, Noncorrection Problem as Effected by Delay of Reward" by H. Fowler, G. C. Fago, and G. J. Wischner, *Learning and Motivation*, 1971, 2, 235–245. Reprinted by permission.)

delayed. Consequently, a more immediate reward, in precluding a facilitating effect of the shock, must have generated *its own* cue effect.

The above results also complemented earlier findings (Spelt & Fowler, 1969) on the effect of a delay of reward for the incorrect response (cf. Figure 6). With correction training on an easy (light–dark) discrimination, where the SR facilitation effect was typically present, a long delay of reward for the incorrect response reduced the shock's facilitating effect. Now, with noncorrection training on the same light–dark discrimination, where the effect was typically absent, a long delay of reward for the correct response produced the SR facilitation effect. These results were theoretically symmetric: in the former (i.e., correction) case, the delay would reduce mediated reward for the incorrect response, whereas in the latter (i.e., noncorrection) case, the delay would induce, through generalization, a reward expectancy for the incorrect response (or a nonreward expectancy for the correct response).

Differential Magnitudes of Reward for Correct and Incorrect Responses. Although the results of the preceding study were consistent with our interpretation of a facilitating cue effect of immediate reward for the correct response, the findings were not without an alternative interpretation. One could argue, for example, that with a long delay of reward for the correct response, immediate shock in the goal produced stereotyped reactions, such as cringing, which mediated the effect of reward across the delay and, in this manner, facilitated performance. In other words, the shock had functioned as a secondary reinforcer. Even though our earlier findings (e.g., Fowler & Wischner, 1965b) argued against this interpretation, it behooved us to consider an alternative manipulation of food reward by which a secondary reinforcing effect of the shock would not be possible. For this purpose, we resorted to the use of differential magnitudes of reward for the correct and incorrect response.

In this study, different groups of rats received NS or SR noncorrection training on an easy (light–dark) discrimination with reward magnitude for the correct and incorrect response set, respectively, at 3 and 1 and at 5 and 1 pellets for some subgroups, and for comparison purposes, at 1 and 0 and at 2 and 0 pellets for other subgroups. According to our interpretation, relatively similar reward magnitudes for the correct and incorrect response (i.e., 3–1 and 1–0) would enhance the generalization of a reward expectancy between the alternatives and thereby promote a facilitating cue effect of immediate shock in the correct (i.e., large-reward) goal. Furthermore, this effect should be especially pronounced in the 3–1 condition because this condition affords greater similarity of the alternatives through feedback from consumatory activity in both the correct and incorrect goals. In contrast, relatively dissimilar magnitudes of reward for the correct and incorrect response (i.e., 5–1 and 2–0) would, via the discriminable cue properties of reward, reduce the similarity of the alternatives and therefore preclude a facilitating effect of SR training.

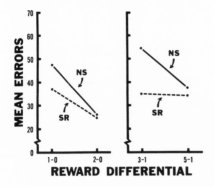

FIGURE 12. Mean errors to criterion for NS and SR groups receiving different magnitudes of reward for correct and incorrect responses in an easy discrimination. (From "Facilitating Stimulus Effects of Reward and Punishment in Discrimination Learning" by H. Fowler, M. Hochhauser, and G. J. Wischner, *Animal Learning and Behavior*, 1981, *9*, 16–20. Reprinted by permission.)

As shown in Figure 12, the findings of this recently published study (Fowler, Hochhauser, & Wischner, 1981) were entirely consistent with our interpretation. The SR facilitation effect was pronounced for the 3–1 condition, marginally reliable for the 1–0 condition ($p < .10$), and unreliable for the 5–1 and 2–0 conditions. These findings could not be ascribed to a secondary reinforcing effect of shock in the correct goal because the temporal relationship of shock to food was the same for all groups. Furthermore, shock's facilitating effect occurred with a relatively small magnitude of reward for the correct response (as in the 3–1 and 1–0 conditions) but not with a relatively large magnitude of reward for the correct response (as in the 5–1 and 2–0 comparison conditions). Such findings could hardly be taken as evidence for a secondary-reinforcing effect of the shock—unless one wanted to argue that stronger secondary reinforcers were established by smaller magnitudes of reward!

Partial Reward for the Correct Response. As part of our assessment of the cue properties of reward, we also investigated whether a reduced percentage of reward for the correct response would attenuate discriminability of the alternatives and thereby promote an SR-facilitation effect. In an early initial experiment on this topic, a Ph.D. dissertation by M. L. Ascher (1968), different groups of rats were given noncorrection training on an easy (light–dark) discrimination with the percentage of reward (two pellets) for the correct response set at 50 or 100%, and with the percentage of shock for the correct response factorially varied at 0% (no shock) and 50%.

In this experiment, it was not expected that shock for the correct response (even on a 50% basis) would facilitate learning with 100% reward for the correct response, because the stimulus alternatives would be highly discriminable as a consequence of consistent versus no reward for the correct and incorrect response. However, with 50% reward for the correct response SR training could *conceivably* facilitate learning because the similarity of the alternatives would be enhanced by occasions of nonreward for both correct and incorrect responses. With this arrangement, though, the facilitation effect would depend on whether the shock, administered on a 50% basis, occurred on correct trials that were either rewarded or nonrewarded. If the shock was positively correlated with food and occurred on rewarded trials, there would be little, if any, SR facilitation relative to the performance of the NS (50% food-alone) control because the food reward itself would function as a distinctive cue and would therefore preclude a cue effect of the shock. Conversely, if the shock was negatively correlated with food and occurred on nonrewarded correct trials, SR facilitation would be maximal because the cue effect of shock would not be obviated by the cue effect of food. Based on these considerations, Ascher (1968) divided his 50% food-and-shock subjects into three groups, which received a positive, a zero, or a negative correlation of food and shock on correct trials.

To a large extent, Ascher's (1968) findings confirmed the expectations outlined above: for the 50% food-and-shock subjects, a negative correlation of food and shock led to more rapid learning than the zero correlation, and, in turn, the zero correlation produced more rapid learning than the positive correlation of food and shock. This outcome clearly supported a cue effect of food, since only the absence of food (as on nonrewarded correct trials) provided the basis for an increased similarity of the alternatives and hence a facilitating cue effect of the shock. The problem was, however, that none of the 50% food-and-shock groups showed facilitated learning relative to their NS (50% food-alone) control. Evidently, the facilitating cue effect of shock was relatively weak by comparison with its avoidance-producing effect. Ascher's results also showed that there was no SR facilitation with 100% reward for the correct response, but this finding was expected.

The basis for Ascher's (1968) finding of differences among his 50% food-and-shock correlation groups, but not facilitated performance relative to their NS control, appears to lie in two considerations. First, the use of a reduced (50%) schedule of food reward for the correct response probably did not attenuate the shock's aversiveness as well as the customary 100% schedule of food reward. Second, Ascher administered his shock at an intermediate locus in the T-maze arm, in contrast to the goal shock used in the other studies reported in this section. Ascher's selection of an intermediate shock locus was based on our prior unpublished findings, which showed that in a difficult (bright–dim) discrimination, shock at an intermediate locus produced greater facilitation relative to an NS control than did shock at the goal, or just after choice. At the time, our interpretation of this effect was that rats, after choosing an arm, typically run with their heads down and thus without attending to the discriminative stimulus. Consequently, the maximum similarity between the alternatives would occur at an intermediate locus in the arms, with shock's function as a distinctive cue being best served by its administration in this position.

With further understanding of the cue effects of food reward, however, it became apparent to us that food, as a cue, would augment discriminability of the alternatives *primarily at the goal*. Hence, when the parameters of reward were manipulated so as to reduce the discriminability of the alternatives (e.g., through the use of a smaller magnitude, a delay, or a reduced percentage of reward), then shock as a distinctive cue would best facilitate performance when administered at the goal, that is, so as to capitalize on the reduced cue effect of food. Indeed, pilot investigations for the studies reported earlier in this section showed that with increased goal similarity effected by a delay or a small magnitude of reward for the correct response, shock at the goal produced appreciably greater facilitation than did shock at an intermediate locus in the arm.

"Reinforcement" by a Neutral Cue

With the foregoing information at hand, Ascher's (1968) study was eventually repeated, but with several important modifications. First, a nonaversive, 85-dB white-noise stimulus was substituted for shock, and the noise was administered at the food cup in the correct goal (thereby generating a "noise-right" condition). Second, Ascher's design was extended so that, basically, it constituted a 2 × 2 factorial of 50% and 100% food reward for the correct response, and 0% and 100% noise for the correct response. In addition, three other noise-right groups received 50% noise in conjunction with 50% food for the correct response, but with the correlation of noise and food over trials being either positive, zero, or negative. Again, all animals received noncorrection training on an easy (light–dark) discrimination, with the magnitude of food reward being set, as usual, at 2 pellets.

The results of this study (Zanich & Fowler, 1975) are presented in Figure 13, which shows mean trials, errors, and correct responses to criterion for groups that received different percentages of noise (designated by the numerical values within each panel) in conjunction with either 50% or 100% food reinforcement for the correct response. Focusing on the trial measure, which is a composite of the error and correct-response measures, we may first note that the 0% noise

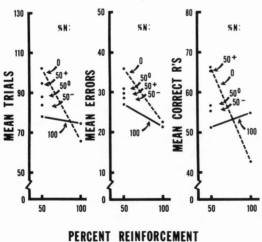

PERCENT REINFORCEMENT

FIGURE 13. Mean trials, errors, and correct responses to criterion in an easy discrimination as a function of percentage of food reinforcement for subjects receiving a 0%, a 50%, or a 100% schedule of noise for the correct response. For the 50% noise and 50% food groups, the correlation between noise and food on correct trials was either positive (+), zero (0), or negative (−). (From "Primary and Secondary Reinforces as Distinctive Cues which Acquire Information Value in Partial-Reinforcement Discrimination Training" by M. L. Zanich and H. Fowler, *Learning and Motivation,* 1975, *6,* 299–313. Reprinted by permission.)

subjects (see the dashed function in Figure 13) showed appreciably retarded discrimination performance with 50% reward relative to 100% reward. By comparison, the 100% noise subjects (see the solid-line function) showed marked facilitation under 50% reward and a slight, although nonsignificant, retardation effect under 100% reward. Note also that the addition of 100% noise to 50% food almost completely recovered the loss in performance occasioned by 50% food alone. The question at issue is whether the facilitating effect of 100% noise was due to the addition of noise primarily on rewarded or on nonrewarded correct trials; and the answer, of course, lies in the performance of the 50% food-and-noise correlation groups. As indicated, the positive correlation group (50 +) showed little improvement in performance relative to the 0% noise group, whereas the negative correlation group (50 −) showed improved performance that was almost as good as the performance of the 100% noise group. In that the difference between (but not within) these two sets of groups was reliable ($p <$ .005), the answer is clear: The observed facilitating effect of noise was primarily due to the presence of noise on the nonrewarded trials.

The above findings are particularly important because they show that a neutral stimulus, which is negatively correlated with food and thus cannot itself function as a conditioned reinforcer, nonetheless produces better discrimination performance than either a 50% food-alone condition or a condition in which the noise and the food are positively correlated (and hence the noise is *operationally* equivalent to a secondary reinforcer). Given that the facilitating effect of noise occurred on nonrewarded correct trials, one is tempted to conclude that the noise effectively functioned as a primary reinforcer. But, of course, this outcome can be meaningfully attributed only to a distinctive cue effect of the noise. Still, it indicates quite clearly that the retarded performance of a 50% food-alone group, by comparison with a 100% food-alone group, is due not merely to the reduced occasions of food as an incentive, but to the reduced occasions of food as a cue which can heighten the discriminability of the alternatives and, in this manner, facilitate performance.

ELABORATION OF THE DISCRIMINABILITY PROCESS

From a total perspective of our findings on both the facilitating cue effects of selective reward and punishment and the retarding effects of cues that are common to the discrimination alternatives, it is evident that we have been dealing generally with the process of discriminability, and that our diverse investigations have merely touched on different aspects and expressions of this process. In the following discussion, this process is elaborated by first empirically documenting the generality of a distinctive-cue (or discriminability) effect of stimuli, and then, on the basis of our findings, by formulating a succinct theoretical statement that describes the workings of this process. In this context, several subpropositions of the principle that is offered are examined, with the intent of delineating those that are supported by both our findings and the findings of others and those that are in need of further assessment. Having accomplished that, we examine how the principle can be applied to some other, seemingly unrelated phenomena, with a consequent reinterpretation of those phenomena or a challenge to their generality. In the process, we hope to accomplish a description of the nature of discrimination learning will be accomplished.

Generality of a Distinctive-Cue Effect

In our prior research assessing whether a partial schedule of food reward for the correct response in a light–dark discrimination would reduce the discriminability of the alternatives and thereby promote an SR-faciliation effect (Ascher, 1968; Zanich & Fowler, 1975), it was necessary to use a neutral white-noise stimulus in place of shock because of the apparent lack of attenuation of shock's aversiveness in the presence of a reduced schedule of reward. That substitution was not made without foreknowledge, for we had earlier established that a neutral stimulus could function as a distinctive cue to facilitate discrimination learning. Our research on this subject had been prompted by our initial demonstration of an SR-facilitation effect and by our desire to separate the cue and the aversive components of punishment. One approach to effecting this separation, as previously indicated, was to use a drug like sodium amytal, which could attenuate the shock's aversive effect by reducing the fear motivating avoidance (Fowler *et al.*, 1968). However, another approach was to replace the shock with a neutral stimulus, such as white noise, which could be varied in intensity from a low, nonaversive value to a high, aversive value.[4] In this manner, the cue effect could be studied alone at low intensities, and an interaction of the cue and averisve effects of the stimulus could be studied at the high, aversive intensity.

For this manipulation, equal-aversion scales for white noise and shock (cf. Campbell & Bloom, 1965) were used to select three intensities of noise so that the highest intensity (105 dB) corresponded in aversiveness to the shock intensity (60 V, .3 megohms) that was customarily employed in our SR research. The other intensities were scaled in equal steps downward so that the moderate intensity (87.5 dB) approached an aversion-threshold value, and the lower intensity (70 dB) corresponded to a value slightly above the detection threshold for noise (i.e., relative to an ambient level of 65 dB). These three intensities of noise were administered to subgroups of each of three different squads of rats, which received either noise-right (NR), noise-wrong (NW), or noise-paired (NP) noncorrection training on a moderately difficult (bright–dim) discrimination entailing a 2-pellet food reward for the correct response. For all groups, the noise was

---

[4] This manipulation was not possible with shock because other research (e.g., Campbell & Masterson, 1969) had shown that the detection and aversion thresholds for shock were virtually the same.

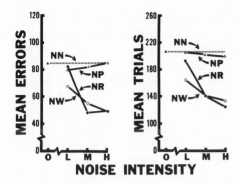

NOISE INTENSITY

FIGURE 14. Mean errors and trials to criterion for noise-right (NR), noise-wrong (NW), noise-paired (NP), and no-noise (NN) groups receiving zero (0), low (L), moderate (M), or high (H) intensities of noise in a difficult discrimination. (From "Facilitated Discrimination Learning as Effected by Response-Contingent Neutral and Aversive Stimuli" by G. Fago and H. Fowler, *Learning and Motivation*, 1972, *3*, 20–30. Reprinted by permission.)

administered for .2 sec at a midposition in the T-maze arms. Whereas the NR and NW subjects received the noise contingent, respectively, on a correct or an incorrect response, the NP subjects were yoked in equal number to the NR and NW subjects and received the noise only on those trials on which their paired running mates received the noise. Hence, the NP subjects received comparable frequencies and schedules of noise throughout training, but contingent on *both* correct and incorrect responses. An additional group, serving as a control, received no noise (NN) during discrimination training.

The results of this study (Fago & Fowler, 1972) are presented in Figure 14. As shown, increasing intensities of noise produced increasing facilitation for both the NR and the NW groups relative to the NN control. Furthermore, the noise-intensity functions for the NR and NW subjects were virtually coincidental and indicated that a particular intensity of noise for either the correct or the incorrect response generated a comparable facilitation effect. In contrast, the performance of the NP subjects was not affected by noise intensity and thus did not differ from that of the NN control. Like our prior findings for shock (cf. Figure 3), this outcome argued against any sensitizing or alerting function of noise and established that its facilitating effect for the NR and NW subjects was a consequence of its unique association with either the correct or the incorrect response. These findings were, of course, open to an alternative interpretation, namely, that noise selectively associated with one response, and occurring midway in the T-maze arm, mediated the effect of reward (or of nonreward) and in this manner facilitated performance. However, this secondary reinforcement (or nonreinforcement) interpretation can now be dismissed on the basis of our more recent findings (Zanich & Fowler, 1975) showing that in a partial-reinforcement context, the facilitating effect of noise is produced not by its positive correlation with food, but by its negative correlation with food on correct trials.

There was one surprising aspect of the present findings. We had expected that the noise-intensity functions for the NR and NW subjects would separate at the highest (aversive) intensity in evidence of an avoidance-producing effect of the noise. However, as Figure 14 shows, this did not occur. Observations of the subjects indicated that unlike a comparable intensity of shock, which tended to elicit stopping or withdrawal, the high-intensity noise tended to produce a forward movement. Operating anticipatorily (i.e., at the choice point), this forward movement would mitigate avoidance based on conditioned fear and would therefore obscure a potential difference between the NR and NW subjects (cf. Fowler, 1963; Fowler & Miller, 1963). Thus, the findings for the high-intensity noise, like those for the lesser intensities of noise, reflected primarily a cue effect of the noise. Indeed, taken singly or in combination, the intensity functions for the NR and NW subjects matched the intensity function earlier obtained for SR subjects that had received sodium amytal to attenuate the aversiveness of shock (cf. Figure 4). Both sets of findings indicated that the facilitating effect of a stimulus was an increasing S-shaped function of the intensity of that stimulus, consistent with Weber's Law relating performance to the discriminable cue properties (e.g., the intensity) of the stimulus.

Viewed in conjunction with our other findings for both shock and food, the present findings for noise clearly established the generality of a distinctive-cue effect, for collectively, our findings indicated that any stimulus—aversive, appetitive, or neutral—that was uniquely associated with one discrimination alternative could increase the discriminability of the alternatives and thereby facilitate performance. In this light, the SR and SW acronyms earlier coined for shock-right and shock-wrong facilitation effects could now be meaningfully extended to designate *stimulus*-right and *stimulus*-wrong effects.

Formalization of the Discriminability Principle

Taken *in toto,* our findings also provided an extensive empirical base for inferring a general rule, or principle, on the discriminability function of a stimulus. In its simplest form of qualitative expression, this principle can be cast as follows: To the extent that the stimulus compounds constituting the alternatives of a discrimination task are *similar*, a stimulus *uniquely* associated with one alternative functions as a "distinctive" cue" to increase the discriminability of the alternatives and thereby facilitate learning; conversely, to the extent that the stimulus compounds constituting the alternatives are *dissimilar,* a stimulus that is *commonly* associated with both alternatives decreases the discriminability of the alternatives and thereby retards discrimination learning. (As indicated throughout this paper, the action of a unique or common cue in facilitating or retarding discrimination learning is regarded as occurring by means of the reduced or increased mediation of a reward, or a nonreward, expectancy between the alternatives.) It should be apparent, in this statement of the principle, that the original and converse propositions on the respective effects of unique and common cues are complementary; they merely reflect two sides of the same coin. However, for purposes of exposition, these propositions are treated separately here, so that the parameters and variables that influence the effects of each type of cue, and the extent to which such effects are supported by both our findings and those of others, can be examined fully.

Increased Discriminability by a Unique Cue. It is clear that the facilitating effect of a unique cue is dependent on its "impact" as a stimulus (i.e., its magnitude or intensity and duration), and that the size of its effect follows the familiar Weber–Fechner Law, $\Delta S = c \log S$.[5] This proposition is amply supported by our findings on the distinctive-cue effects of different intensities of shock and noise for the correct response, and of noise for the incorrect response (cf. Figures 4 and 14), and also by our findings on the effects of different magnitudes of food reward. The latter is evident when one acknowledges that food reward has both cue and incentive functions, and that the facilitating effect of reward on discrimination performance is linearly related to the logarithm of reward magnitude (cf. the NS function in Figure 10). It would also seem likely that the impact of a unique cue, in generating a facilitating effect, is a function of other parameters, such as the novelty or the complexity of the cue and its form or configuration. Although our findings do not speak to the effects of these parameters (at least not independently of magnitude and intensity manipulations), it is noteworthy that other investigators have reported better performance with several pieces of food reward as opposed to a single chunk of the same volume (e.g., Wolfe & Kaplan, 1941).

The facilitating effect of a unique cue is also dependent on its frequency and distribution across trials, as well as its locus or position within a trial, that is, within the stimulus–response chain constituting the discrimination alternative. Support for the effects of the first two parameters derives from our findings on partial schedules of noise and food reward for the correct response in a light–dark discrimination (Zanich & Fowler, 1975). In that research, increasing percentages (or frequencies) of noise from 0% through 50% to 100% for a 50% food-rewarded response increased facilitation (cf. Figure 13). Also, the facilitating effect of 50% noise was greater when the noise was administered on non-rewarded, as opposed to rewarded, correct trials. This finding highlights the import of the cue's distribution across different trials. That the locus of a unique cue within a trial is also important is indicated by some of our unpublished findings. Typically, a facilitating effect of shock for the correct response is greatest when the shock is administered in the middle of the T-maze arm, rather than just after choice or contiguously with an immediate and relatively large food reward in the correct goal. However, when the cue effect of the food reward is itself reduced, either by delaying the reward or by using a small magnitude of reward or even slightly different magnitudes of reward for the correct and

---

[5] This equation indicates, of course, that the increment in (say, the intensity of) stimulation, ΔS, required for a discriminable difference is equal to a constant, c, times the logarithm of the present (intensity of) stimulation, S. For a more contemporary version of the law, stressing a sigmoidal rather than a linear relationship of ΔS to $\log S$, see Crozier (1940).

incorrect response, then the facilitating effect of SR training is more pronounced with shock administered immediately in the goal rather than midway in the arm (cf. Fago, 1967; Hochhauser, 1970).

As implied in the preceding, and as explicitly recognized in the stated principle, the facilitating effect of a unique cue is determined not merely by its own properties, but by the properties of the stimulus compounds constituting the discrimination alternatives. It is here that the Weber ratio, $\Delta S/\log S = c$, takes on particular force, for it prescribes that the discriminability provided by a unique cue of a *particular* intensity, etc., increases as the discriminability of the alternatives decreases (or, conversely, as the *similarity of the alternatives* increases). This proposition is supported in at least two of the several ways in which similarity of the alternatives can be accomplished: by rendering the discriminative stimuli of a single dimension similar, and by increasing the amount or extent of the common background cues. In agreement with the proposition, our findings show that shock of a particular intensity, etc., for the correct response facilitates learning in a difficult (bright–dim) discrimination, but not in an easy (light–dark) discrimination (cf. Figure 3). Likewise, a facilitating effect of SR training is present, and increasingly pronounced, in a black–white discrimination when a common gray background cue is extended backward from the goal toward the choice point, but not when the arms are uniformly black and white (cf. Figure 8).

It is noteworthy in the above regard that an effective manipulation of "background" cues, which can also heighten the similarity of the alternatives in a light–dark discrimination, is that accomplished by manipulations of the reward itself, for example, by delaying the reward for the correct response (so as to approximate the "infinite" delay of reward for the incorrect response), or by using slightly different magnitudes of reward for correct and incorrect responses. A facilitating cue effect of SR training is also observed under these circumstances, but not when the reward is immediate, or when the magnitude of the reward or the reward differential between the alternatives is large (cf. Figures 11 and 12). On the other hand, SR training facilitates learning with an immediate and moderate (e.g., 2-pellet) reward for the correct response if the similarity of the alternatives is augmented by employing similar compounds of elements from two dimensions, as in a conditional discrimination (cf. Figure 9).

In a light–dark discrimination, increased similarity of the alternatives can also be accomplished by conditioning a common reward expectancy to the alternatives, that is, by generating a *learned-equivalence* effect (cf. Goss, 1955). When this is done, as in nondifferential pretraining, shock for the correct response in discrimination learning also facilitates learning (cf. Figure 7). A variant of this learned-equivalence effect can also be obtained with reversal learning, where a reward expectancy for the correct response is opposed by a previously established reward expectancy for the incorrect response, that is, the reinforced response of acquisition training (but see footnote 1). In this context, it is noteworthy that through the selective conditioning of fear, SR-acquisition training produces a learned-distinctiveness effect by which reversal performance is facilitated (cf. the NS reversal groups of Figure 2). Note, though, that with SR-acquisition training a facilitating effect of shock for the correct response in reversal training would not be expected (relative to its respective NS reversal control) because fear is conditioned to both alternatives and therefore generates a learned-equivalence effect.

The above elaboration of discriminability focuses on the effect of a single unique cue. However, there is no reason that *two or more unique cues* (e.g., shock and noise) could not be employed for the same response or, better yet, for different responses, so as to increase discriminability even more. Although our research does not speak to this issue,[6] the findings of other investigators do. For example, Trapold (1970) has reported that in a conditional discrimination involving two stimulus–response (S–R) links of the type, if S1 then R1, and if S2 then R2, rats learn faster if different reinforcers (e.g., food and sucrose) are employed for the two links than if one or the other reinforcer is used for both. Furthermore, this facilitating effect of different reinforcers is augmented when prior Pavlovian conditioning is given involving the same relationships of S1 and S2 and the different reinforcers (as are employed in instrumental conditioning) but is reduced if the relationships are reversed. This finding suggests that the reward expectancies for the different reinforcers are themselves discriminably different and, when consistently applied in conditional discrimination training, also benefit learning (see Miller, 1961, for similar evidence).

Results comparable to Trapold's findings on conditional discrimination learning without prior Pavlovian conditioning have also been reported for pigeons when food and water are used as the different reinforcers (e.g., Brodigan & Peterson, 1976; Peterson, Wheeler, & Armstrong, 1978). Importantly, for our purposes, these studies have also shown that the facilitating effect of different reinforcers is much more pronounced if a delay is inserted between the presentation of the conditional cue, S1 or S2, and the opportunity to choose between R1 and R2. Indeed, under these conditions of increased problem difficulty as effected by a common delay, the subsequent use of only one reinforcer for both S–R links produces a marked deterioration of performance.

Decreased Discriminability by a Common Cue. Although empirically less well documented, the decreased discriminability produced by common or similar cues in the discrimination alternatives would also appear to be a function of the cue's impact (i.e., its intensity, duration, etc.) Most directly on this point, our results show increasingly retarded learning in a black–white choice discrimination when a common gray brightness is progressively extended from the goalbox endwalls to the first third of each arm (cf. the NS functions in Figure 8). In like

---

[6] Even though, in our research, the use of a food reward in conjunction with, say, shock for the correct response constitutes an effective use of two cues, it is the basis by which a conclusion is drawn about an added *single* cue for the SR group, relative to its NS (food-alone) control.

fashion, the learning of a light–dark discrimination is retarded when relatively similar reward magnitudes are used for the correct and incorrect response, or when a long delay of reward is employed for the correct response, thereby approximating the "infinite" delay of reward for the incorrect response (cf. Figures 11 and 12). Normally, these reward effects would be ascribed to a reduction of the incentive difference in favor of the correct response. However, given a discriminability effect of reward itself, it is evident that such effects are also due to a reduction of the reward's unique cue effect (or, conversely, an increment in its common cue effect). In this regard, one can also reference the retarded learning that prevails in a light–dark discrimination when the magnitude of reward for the correct response is reduced to the point of approximating the zero value employed for the incorrect response (cf. Figures 10 and 12).

As implied in the above, reduced discriminability by a common cue is also dependent on the cue's *frequency, percentage,* or *proportion* of occurrence in each alternative. In this context, it should first be pointed out that the practice of increasing the similarity of the discriminative stimuli of a single dimension to generate a more difficult discrimination is essentially a common-cue manipulation entailing different proportions of the same cue. Likewise, increasing the similarity of discriminative-stimulus *compounds* by employing similar combinations of cues from two or more dimensions, as in a conditional discrimination, also reduces discriminability and retards learning—and, as noted, especially so if the same reinforcer is used for both of the correct compounds (e.g., Brodigan & Peterson, 1976; Peterson *et al.,* 1978; Trapold, 1970). No less different conceptually is the reduced discriminability of a light–dark discrimination that prevails with a greater percentage of nonreward for the correct response, as with a partial schedule of reward for the correct response (cf. Figure 13); or with more time in the correct goal without reward, that is, as a result of a long delay of reward for the correct response (cf. Figure 11). In similar but reverse fashion, a short delay of reward for the incorrect response, as with correction training on a light–dark discrimination, also reduces the discriminability of the alternatives and thereby retards learning by comparison with noncorrection training (cf. Figures 5 and 6).

It should also be reiterated in this context that *learned-equivalence* or reduced-discriminability effects are produced by the conditioning of a common reward expectancy to the alternatives: greater amounts of nondifferential pretraining to the correct and incorrect alternatives of a light–dark discrimination increasingly retard subsequent learning when only the correct response is reinforced (cf. the NS function in Figure 7; see also Bitterman & Elam, 1954; Crawford *et al.,* 1954). Similarly, acquisition training on a light–dark discrimination can retard subsequent reversal performance on the same dimension because of the equivalence effect that is promoted by reinforcement of the incorrect response for reversal training (and/or by nonreinforcement of the correct response for reversal training). An interesting parallel to this effect is that produced by the use of both SR acquisition and SR reversal training. Because of the fear that is common to both of the alternatives in reversal training, this combination should generate an equivalence effect and should therefore retard learning. And, to some extent, our data suggest that it does: following SR acquisition training, NS reversal subjects show better reversal performance than SR reversal subjects (cf. the trial measure for Figure 2).

There is, of course, a more direct manipulation of common cues than that noted above involving fear for both correct and incorrect responses of a reversal problem: that of presenting shock or noise for both responses in discrimination acquisition. To this point, we have avoided mentioning these procedures, or their counterparts (shock and noise paired, i.e., yoked to, say, an SR or NR subject), because our results have uniformly shown that although these procedures do not facilitate learning, they also do not retard learning (cf. Figures 3 and 14). In part, the absence of a retardation effect for these procedures (as well as the marginal effect for the "fear-both" reversal condition noted above) can be attributed to our assessment of their effects primarily in difficult discriminations. Indeed, both the Weber Law and our statement of the discriminability principle stress that an equivalence effect will predominate only to the extent the stimulus alternatives are *dissimilar*. One should therefore not expect a common cue (particularly one of exceedingly brief duration, i.e., .2 sec, as the noise and shock were) to reduce discriminability much more than that already provided by far more pervasive stimulus elements, such as the similar discriminative stimuli and the complex of common background cues.

The above explanation is quite reasonable, particularly when it is recognized that all of the evidence cited in support of a common-cue effect derives from training contexts in which, in the absence of that cue, the response alternatives were highly dissimilar. (Conversely, the evidence in support of a distinctive-cue effect derives solely from training contexts in which, in the absence of the cue, the response alternatives were highly similar.) However, a problem still remains in accounting for the absence of a retardation effect with shock-both and shock-paired training in an easy (light–dark) discrimination where the alternatives are highly discriminable (cf. Figure 3). This outcome appears to represent a true anomaly—at least insofar as a common *shock* cue is concerned, and this may well be the telltale clue. Aversive stimuli have many functions: they elicit motor reactions, generate fear, and potentiate reinforcement (through their termination or omission), and, as cues, they function as discriminative stimuli, as possible secondary reinforcers, and even as distinctive events. Furthermore, any one of these functions can oppose another, with a consequent obscuring of each (see Fowler, 1971b). Thus, it may well be the case that shock also serves a sensitizing or alerting function that can offset any equivalence effect produced by its common occurrence in the discrimination alternatives. Perhaps Muenzinger (1934) was not so wrong after all.

Some Applications to Related Phenomena

With a fuller understanding of the factors and conditions that influence the discriminability effects of unique and common cues, it would seem fitting to conclude this chapter by illustrating how a discriminability principle can be applied to some other, seemingly unrelated phenomena. In considering this application, we shall refrain from concentrating on the more obvious effects of unique cues, such as selective reward and punishment, and instead focus on those cues that, as typified by our research paradigm, are usually common to the alternatives: the interoceptive or "drive" stimuli that the animal carries with it into the alternatives, apparatus cues such as the physical features of the T-maze arms, and proprioceptive or feedback cues stemming from the subject's instrumental response in both alternatives. With this assortment, we can better appreciate how the discriminability functions of stimuli can influence the outcome, and interpretation, of certain "well-established" phenomena.

The Yerkes–Dodson Law. A phenomenon of long standing in the annals of learning research is that described by the Yerkes–Dodson Law (Yerkes & Dodson, 1908). In essence, this law posits that heightened drive retards performance in a difficult discrimination task. At first glance, such a law appears to be very consistent with our findings, for it suggests that an intensification of the animal's interoceptive or "drive" stimuli will function as a common cue to reduce the discriminability of the alternatives and thereby to retard discrimination learning. There are, however, two good reasons that heightened drive should *not* work this way. First, our statement of the discriminability principle posits that a common cue will reduce discriminability only to the extent that the stimulus alternatives are *dissimilar;* this means that as a common cue, high drive should retard performance more in an easy than in a difficult discrimination! Second, there is ample reason to believe that drive manipulations, such as food deprivation, do not act merely on their own to produce interoceptive stimuli and generally to energize behavior, but that they act primarily through the reinforcer. In particular, deprivation drives can be viewed as "setting" conditions that regulate the impact of a reinforcer (cf. Fowler, 1971a). According to this view, heightened drive effectively augments the consummatory reaction to food and thereby amplifies the stimulus consequences of food (e.g., through intensified consummatory feedback). From this perspective, high drive should work more as a strong *unique* cue (cf. large reward) to facilitate the discrimination performance, and more so in a difficult discrimination task!

We had some reservations about this interpretation when we first realized that it predicted an outcome exactly opposite to the longstanding Yerkes–Dodson Law—but then, Weber's Law had an even longer standing. Furthermore, we were aware of evidence (e.g., Hawkins, 1965) indicating that high drive would amplify an SR-facilitation effect in a difficult discrimination; so why not the facilitating cue effect of food reward as well? What was needed, particularly in the absence of any clear evidence on the Yerkes–Dodson Law in the context of appetitive motivation, was an extensive parametric study investigating the functional relationships of different levels of drive (food deprivation), different levels of reward magnitude, and different levels of problem difficulty. To that end, we conducted a study (Hochhauser & Fowler, 1975) in which different groups of rats received noncorrection training on an easy light–dark discrimination, a moderately difficult bright–dim discrimination, or an even more difficult bright–dim discrimination, with the food reward for the correct response factorially varied at a 1-, 2- and 4-pellet reward and the drive factorially varied at moderate and high levels of food deprivation (daily diets of 13.5 g and 10.5 g, respectively). By comparison with the weights of nonexperimental *ad lib* animals, these deprivation conditions produced a weight loss over the course of training of 75%–65% for the moderate-drive subjects and of 65%–50% for the high-drive subjects. Thus, the high-drive condition represented a "near to fatal" diet (cf. Moskowitz, 1959).

The results of this study are presented in Figure 15. As expected, performance was increasingly retarded with more difficult problems and with smaller magnitudes of reward for the correct response; and as predicted, high drive facilitated learning but only in the more difficult discriminations. Furthermore, this facilitating effect of high drive was more pronounced with smaller rewards, indicating that the facilitating cue effect of a *large* reward was itself sufficiently pronounced to preclude any intensification of its effects by high drive. These results duplicated the findings that we had obtained earlier for SR training with various magnitudes of reward for the correct response in a difficult discrimination (cf. Figure 10). Like shock, high drive also generated a facilitating effect, but through the action of a small reward that, by itself (i.e., in conjunction with moderate drive), provided relatively little impact as a unique cue for the correct response.

The above findings are important in two major respects. First, they indicate that the facilitating cue effect of a food reward is amplified with greater magnitudes of reward, but only to the extent that the alternatives are similar, as in more difficult discrimination tasks. This finding is exactly as the discriminability

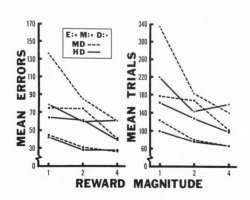

FIGURE 15. Mean errors and trials to criterion as a function of reward magnitude for moderate-drive (MD) and high-drive (HD) subjects trained on an easy (E), a moderate (M), or a difficult (D) discrimination. (From "Cue Effects of Drive and Reward as a Function of Discrimination Difficulty: Evidence against the Yerkes-Dodson Law" by M. Hochhauser and H. Fowler, *Journal of Experimental Psychology: Animal Behavior Processes*, 1975, *104*, 261–269. Copyright 1975 by the American Psychological Association. Reprinted by permission.)

principle would have it, and it explains why other investigators using an *easy* discrimination have often failed to obtain a reward-magnitude effect (for a review of this research, see Hochhauser & Fowler, 1975). Second, and more importantly, by demonstrating that high drive can augment the cue effect of a (small) reward in a difficult discrimination and thereby facilitate learning, the present findings severely challenge the Yerkes–Dodson Law. Apparently, this law is not a general law encompassing all drives; rather its operation is limited to aversive motivational states. Indeed, the little research that actually supports this law (and there is some question about that support; see, e.g., Brown, 1965) derives entirely from manipulations of aversive stimuli in escape and avoidance tasks.

Response Mediation of Secondary Reinforcement. Within the history of research on secondary reinforcement (cf. Hendry, 1969), one of the more classic investigations of this phenomenon has been that of Grice (1948). The primary purpose of Grice's research was to determine the temporal gradient of primary reinforcement, that is, the length of delay over which a stimulus–response association would be formed by primary reinforcement alone. For this purpose, Grice employed a procedure whereby mediated or secondary reinforcement of that association would be neutralized. Rats were trained on a visual discrimination in which choice of either a black or a white arm was followed by a delay (varied across groups) in a neutral gray arm, and then, depending on the subject's choice, food reinforcement or no reinforcement in a gray goalbox. In comparison with the results of earlier studies (e.g., Perkins, 1947; Wolfe, 1934), which had employed a spatial discrimination and therefore had not neutralized the differential secondary reinforcing effects of position cues, Grice's results showed an extremely steep gradient of primary reinforcement. At delays of only a few seconds, learning was virtually eliminated.

Grice (1948) went on to assess the role of secondary reinforcement by comparing the effect of a 5-sec delay in the above ("primary-reinforcement") procedure with the same delay in two other procedures: one in which the subject had to make different responses in the black and white choice arms (traverse an inclined plane or run through a baffle of blocks); and another in which the brightness of the goal compartments matched the black and white brightnesses of their respective choice arms. Because the latter two procedures produced performance superior to that in the primary reinforcement procedure, Grice interpreted his results as reflecting the operation of secondary reinforcing effects. In the procedure entailing identical choice and goal brightnesses within each arm, the development of secondary reinforcement to the goal brightness associated with food reward would generalize to the choice brightness and thereby facilitate learning. For the different-response procedure, Grice argued that proprioceptive traces of the distinctive response in the correct arm would become associated with food reinforcement in the goal and would therefore mediate reinforcement for the correct choice. Thus, Grice's results provided the foundation of support for a response-mediation interpretation of secondary reinforcement.

Let us now compare Grice's (1948) procedures with those employed in our "insert" study (see Figure 8). Condition I of that study was virtually identical to Grice's primary reinforcement procedure in that it required the rat to choose between black and white alternatives, then run through a comparable arm-segment of gray, and then run into a gray goal, where it was reinforced if it had made the correct choice. Under these conditions, where the delay of primary reinforcement was about 1 sec (the time required by the rat to run to the goal), the performance of a NS group was appreciably retarded, like that of Grice's group with approximately the same delay. By comparison, however, the performance of the SR group for this treatment was very much facilitated. Why, because of the secondary reinforcement? Conceptually, there is no difference between the SR group of this treatment and Grice's different-response group; and yet, in our research, there is no independent evidence that supports a secondary reinforcing effect of the shock. Our findings suggest that the facilitating effect of Grice's different-response procedure was due not necessarily to the mediating effect of a distinctive response in the correct-choice alley, but to the increased discriminability of the alternatives occasioned by the different responses. Also, climbing an inclined plane and jumping off it in the presence of one brightness, as well as twisting through a series of baffles of another brightness, can well augment the impact (cf. salience) of the discriminative stimuli, with the result that *their* traces better perseverated over the delay and thus better differentiated the common gray goalboxes. In this light, there is no compelling reason to assume, as Grice did, that proprioceptive traces of the different responses were more effective in bridging the delay.

The significance of the increased discriminability of the alternatives in facilitating discrimination performance is even better illustrated in the outcome that obtained for another condition in our "insert" study (not shown in Figure 8). This condition matched Grice's secondary reinforcement procedure in that the goalbox of an arm was the same brightness as the initial choice segment, with the intervening arm segment being gray. Like Grice's secondary reinforcement procedure, this condition markedly improved the performance of an NS group (by comparison with the effect of the primary reinforcement procedure: Condition I), presumably because conditioned reinforcement to the brightness in the correct goal generalized directly to the corresponding brightness of the choice segment. However, the imposition of shock for the correct response in the intervening gray segment facilitated learning even more! This outcome indicates that even with direct (as opposed to response-mediated) generalization of secondary reinforcement *within* the response chain, the presence of a unique stimulus like shock (or a distinctive response, as in Grice's different-response procedure) can delimit the generalization of reward and nonreward expectancies *between* the alternatives and, in this manner, facilitate performance.

Additivity of Cues and the "Easy-to-Hard" Effect. Throughout this paper, our focus has been primarily on the function of a unique cue that is *contingent* on a response to the discriminative stimulus (e.g., as with selective reward and punishment). It is fitting, therefore, to end this treatise by "taking a small step" and adding the unique cue directly to the discriminative stimulus. When this is done—that is, when dissimilar elements from one dimension are added to those of another dimension to form compound discriminative stimuli—discrimination learning is improved by comparison with performance based on either dimension alone. This "additivity-of-cues" (AC) effect has been demonstrated with a variety of stimuli, for a comparable variety of organisms (e.g., Eninger, 1952; Miles & Jenkins, 1973; Sutherland & Holgate, 1966; Warren, 1953). Furthermore, it is entirely consistent with the discriminability principle, and it attests to the fact that in addition to providing the basis for choice, discriminative stimuli function in the same manner as response-contingent events in modulating the discriminability of the alternatives.

The broader significance of the AC effect is that, conceptually, it represents a focal point of differences between theories of selective attention (e.g., Lovejoy, 1968; Sutherland & Mackintosh, 1971; Zeaman & House, 1963) and those like conditioning-extinction theory (e.g., Hull, 1952; Rescorla & Wagner, 1972; Spence, 1936), which are devoid of an attentional construct. According to selective-attention theory (e.g., Sutherland & Mackintosh, 1971), organisms have a limited capacity for processing information, and therefore, they attend to only one dimension at any one time, or on any one trial, in contrast to the multidimensional processing assumed by conditioning-extinction theory—and indeed required by the discriminability principle. The AC effect is therefore a problem for attention theories because it indicates that organisms can and do process more than one dimension at a time. In fact, when test assessments are made separately for each dimension of the discriminative-stimulus compound, it is generally found that learning has occurred to both dimensions (providing, of course, that the salience of one dimension is not so weak that it is completely "overshadowed" by the other, more salient dimension). Moreover, the conditioning that occurs to both dimensions cannot be ascribed to selective attention to one dimension on one trial and to the other dimension on another trial. Even when a single conditioning trial is employed, so that sufficient conditioning occurs to the compound, conditioning is also evident for the individual dimensions (e.g., Mackintosh, 1971).

Selective-attention theory fares much better (and conditioning-extinction theory worse), however, when other seemingly unrelated phenomena are considered, such as the "easy-to-hard" effect. This term refers to the well-documented fact (cf. Mackintosh, 1974) that the learning of a difficult discrimination entailing similar elements (say, S2 and S3) of one dimension is facilitated by prior training on an easy discrimination entailing dissimilar elements of the same dimension (say, S1 and S4). According to selective-attention theory, training on the easy problem better enables the organism to learn to attend to the relevant dimension, to the detriment of irrelevant background cues, and this selective attention then facilitates the learning of the difficult discrimination. By comparison, subjects originally trained on the difficult problem are still struggling to differentiate the relevant from the irrelevant cues. Conditioning-extinction theory, on the other hand, seems to be at a loss in handling this problem, unless it assumes that the excitatory and inhibitory generalization gradients resulting from reinforcement and nonreinforcement are of such a shape (i.e., concave downward) that they produce *poorer* differentiation of the S2 and S3 elements with direct training on these elements in the difficult problem than with training on dissimilar elements (S1 and S4) in the easy problem (cf. Lawrence, 1955; Logan, 1966). When one has to assume specifically shaped generalization gradients to explain an effect, the explanation is, by its assumption, restricted and therefore far less convincing. But does one have to make such an assumption?

Both the discriminability principle and the AC effect indicate that whenever dissimilar elements of a dimension are added to the discriminative-stimulus elements of another dimension, learning is facilitated. The principle expressed, however, does not require that the added elements be of any particular dimension or characteristic other than dissimilar and uniquely associated with one or the other of the discriminative stimuli. Consider, in this light, the effects of initial training on easy and difficult discrimination problems. In a difficult problem, where the discriminative stimuli (S2 and S3) are similar, there will be a generalization of both reward and nonreward expectancies between the alternatives, with the result that the alternatives are not well differentiated and learning is impeded. However, in an easy problem, where the discriminative stimuli (S1 and S4) are dissimilar, an AC effect should occur as a result of the reward and nonreward expectancies that come to be *uniquely* associated with the discriminative stimuli, and thus the alternatives should become even better differentiated. In turn, this better differentiation should further restrict the generalization effects between S1 and S4 so that when the easy-problem subjects are transferred to the difficult problem, the similar discriminative stimuli of that problem (S2 and S3) will be better differentiated for these subjects than for the difficult-problem subjects. Accordingly, with further training on the difficult problem, the added and selective expectancy cues for the easy-problem subjects should maintain discriminability and should therefore promote rapid learning.

I believe that the foregoing account essentially describes the nature of discrimination learning: just as the primary reinforcer itself can function both as an incentive and as a distinctive cue, so can the reward and nonreward expectancies associated with the discriminative stimuli serve similarly both to motivate behavior differentially and to increase the discriminability of the alternatives.

Acknowledgments

The author wishes to express his gratitude to the many students, both graduate and undergraduate, who were involved in the research effort. Although their names are, for the most part, duly noted in the publications cited, a special note of appreciation is owing to Stephen A. Kushnick, Philip F. Spelt, George C. Fago, Edward A. Domber, Mark Hochhauser, and Mary Lou Zanich; and lest the undergraduates be forgotten, Martin Samuels, Douglas A. Bernstein, Ronald Gandelman, Kenneth Hoffman, and Paul L. DeVito.

REFERENCES

Ascher, L. M. *The effects on shock-right discrimination training of various schedules of food and shock in a partial reinforcement situation.* Unpublished doctoral dissertation, University of Pittsburgh, 1968.

Bitterman, M. E., & Elam, C. B. Discrimination following varying amounts of nondifferential reinforcement. *American Journal of Psychology,* 1954, *67,* 133–137.

Brodigan, D. L., & Peterson, G. B. Two-choice conditional discrimination performance of pigeons as a function of reward expectancy, prechoice delay, and domesticity. *Animal Learning and Behavior,* 1976, *4,* 121–124.

Brown, W. P. The Yerkes-Dodson law repealed. *Psychological Reports,* 1965, *17,* 663–666.

Bunch, M. E. The effect of electric shock as punishment for errors in human maze-learning. *Journal of Comparative Psychology,* 1928, *8,* 343–359.

Campbell, B. A., & Bloom, J. M. Relative aversiveness of noise and shock. *Journal of Comparative and Physiological Psychology,* 1965, *60,* 440–442.

Campbell, B. A., & Masterson, F. A. Psychophysics of punishment. In B. A. Campbell & R. M. Church (Eds.), *Punishment and aversive behavior.* New York: Appleton-Century-Crofts, 1969.

Campbell, B. A., & Teghtsoonian, R. Electrical and behavioral effects of different types of shock stimuli on the rat. *Journal of Comparative and Physiological Psychology,* 1958, *51,* 185–192.

Crawford, F. T., Mayes, G. L., & Bitterman, M. E. A further study of differential afferent consequences in nondifferential reinforcement. *American Journal of Psychology,* 1954, *67,* 717–719.

Crozier, W. J. On the law for minimal discrimination of intensities: IV. ΔI as a function of intensity. *Proceedings of the National Academy of Sciences,* 1940, *26,* 382–389.

Dodson, J. D. Relative values of reward and punishment in habit formation. *Psychobiology,* 1917, *1,* 231–276.

Domber, E. A., Fowler, H., & Wischner, G. J. Shock-right facilitation: Correction training with differential S^D availability during an enforced delay following an error. *Journal of Experimental Psychology,* 1971, *89,* 329–334.

Drew, G. C. The function of punishment in learning. *Journal of Genetic Psychology,* 1938, *52,* 257–267.

Eninger, M. V. Habit summation in a selective learning problem. *Journal of Comparative and Physiological Psychology,* 1952, *45,* 604–608.

Fago, G. C. *Shock-right facilitation in an easy problem, noncorrection context as effected by a delay of primary reinforcement.* Unpublished master's thesis, University of Pittsburgh, 1967.

Fago, G., & Fowler, H. Facilitated discrimination learning as effected by response-contingent neutral and aversive stimuli. *Learning and Motivation,* 1972, *3,* 20–30.

Fairlie, C. W. The effect of shock at the "moment of choice" on the formation of a visual discrimination habit. *Journal of Experimental Psychology,* 1937, *21,* 662–669.

Fowler, H. Facilitation and inhibition of performance by punishment: The effects of shock intensity and distribution of trials. *Journal of Comparative and Physiological Psychology,* 1963, *56,* 531–538.

Fowler, H. Implications of sensory reinforcement. In R. Glaser (Ed.), *The nature of reinforcement.* New York: Academic Press, 1971.(a)

Fowler, H. Suppression and facilitation by response contingent shock. In F. R. Brush (Ed.), *Aversive conditioning and learning*. New York: Academic Press, 1971.(b)

Fowler, H., & Miller, N. E. Facilitation and inhibition of runway performance by hind- and forepaw shock of various intensities. *Journal of Comparative and Physiological Psychology*, 1963, *56*, 801–805.

Fowler, H., & Wischner, G. J. Discrimination performance as affected by problem difficulty and shock for either the correct or incorrect response. *Journal of Experimental Psychology*, 1965, *69*, 413–418.(a)

Fowler, H., & Wischner, G. J. On the "secondary reinforcing" effect of shock for the correct response in visual discrimination learning. *Psychonomic Science*, 1965, *3*, 209–210.(b)

Fowler, H., & Wischner, G. J. The varied functions of punishment in discrimination learning. In B. A. Campbell & R. M. Church (Eds.), *Punishment and aversive behavior*. New York: Appleton-Century-Crofts, 1969.

Fowler, H., Spelt, P. F., & Wischner, G. J. Discrimination performance as affected by training procedure, problem difficulty, and shock for the correct response. *Journal of Experimental Psychology*, 1967, *75*, 432–436.

Fowler, H., Goldman, L., & Wischner, G. J. Sodium amytal and the shock-right intensity function for visual discrimination learning. *Journal of Comparative and Physiological Psychology*, 1968, *65*, 155–159.

Fowler, H., Fago, G. C., & Wischner, G. J. Shock-right facilitation in an easy, noncorrection problem as effected by delay of reward. *Learning and Motivation*, 1971, *2*, 235–245.

Fowler, H., Hochhauser, M., & Wischner, G. J. Facilitating stimulus effects of reward and punishment in discrimination learning. *Animal Learning and Behavior*, 1981, *9*, 16–20.

Freeburne, C. M., & Taylor, J. E. Discrimination learning with shock for right and wrong responses in the same subjects. *Journal of Comparative and Physiological Psychology*, 1952, *45*, 264–268.

Goss, A. E. A stimulus-response analysis of the interaction of cue-producing and instrumental responses. *Psychological Review*, 1955, *62*, 20–31.

Grice, G. R. The relation of secondary reinforcement to delayed reward in visual discrimination learning. *Journal of Experimental Psychology*, 1948, *38*, 1–16.

Hawkins, R. P. *Effects of drive, incentive and problem difficulty on the facilitation of discrimination performance by punishment of correct responses*. Unpublished doctoral dissertation, University of Pittsburgh, 1965.

Hendry, D. P. (Ed.). *Conditioned reinforcement*. Homewood, Ill.: Dorsey Press, 1969.

Hochhauser, M. *The effect of shock for the correct response on performance in an easy visual discrimination task entailing differential reinforcement*. Unpublished master's thesis, University of Pittsburgh, 1970.

Hochhauser, M., & Fowler, H. Cue effects of drive and reward as a function of discrimination difficulty: Evidence against the Yerkes–Dodson law. *Journal of Experimental Psychology: Animal Behavior Processes*, 1975, *104*, 261–269.

Hoge, M. A., & Stocking, R. J. A note on the relative value of punishment and reward as motives. *Journal of Animal Behavior*, 1912, *2*, 43–50.

Hull, C. L. *A behavior system*. New Haven, Conn.: Yale University Press, 1952.

Kalish, D. The non-correction method and the delayed response problem of Blodgett and McCutchan. *Journal of Comparative Psychology*, 1946, *39*, 91–107.

Lawrence, D. H. The applicability of generalization gradients to the transfer of a discrimination along a continuum. *Journal of General Psychology*, 1955, *52*, 37–48.

Logan, F. A. Transfer of discrimination. *Journal of Experimental Psychology*, 1966, *71*, 616–618.

Lovejoy, E. *Attention in discrimination learning*. San Francisco: Holden-Day, 1968.

Mackintosh, N. J. An analysis of overshadowing and blocking. *Quarterly Journal of Experimental Psychology*, 1971, *23*, 118–125.

Mackintosh, N. J. *The psychology of animal learning*. London: Academic Press, 1974.

Miles, C. G., & Jenkins, H. M. Overshadowing in operant conditioning as a function of discriminability. *Learning and Motivation*, 1973, *4*, 11–27.

Miller, N. E. Some recent studies of conflict behavior and drugs. *American Psychologist*, 1961, *16*, 12–24.

Moskowitz, M. J. Running-wheel activity in the white rat as a function of combined food and water deprivation. *Journal of Comparative and Physiological Psychology*, 1959, *52*, 621–625.

Mowrer, O. H. *Learning theory and personality dynamics*. New York: Ronald Press, 1950.

Muenzinger, K. F. Motivation in learning: I. Electric shock for correct responses in the visual discrimination habit. *Journal of Comparative Psychology*, 1934, *17*, 267–277.

Muenzinger, K. F. Concerning the effect of shock for right responses in visual discrimination learning. *Journal of Experimental Psychology*, 1948, *38*, 201–203.

Muenzinger, K. F., & Baxter, L. F. The effects of training to approach vs. to escape from electric shock upon subsequent discrimination learning. *Journal of Comparative and Physiological Psychology*, 1957, *50*, 252–257.

Muenzinger, K. F., & Fletcher, F. M. Motivation in learning: VII. The effect of an enforced delay at the point of choice in the visual discrimination habit. *Journal of Comparative Psychology*, 1937, *23*, 383–392.

Muenzinger, K. F., & Newcomb, H. Motivation in learning: V. The relative effectiveness of jumping a gap and crossing an electric grid in a visual discrimination habit. *Journal of Comparative Psychology*, 1936, *21*, 95–104.

Muenzinger, K. F., & Powloski, R. F. Motivation in learning: X. Comparison of electric shock for correct turns in a corrective and non-corrective situation. *Journal of Experimental Psychology*, 1951, *42*, 118–124.

Muenzinger, K. F., & Wood, A. Motivation in learning: IV. The function of punishment as determined by its temporal relation to the act of choice in the visual discrimination habit. *Journal of Comparative Psychology*, 1935, 20, 95–106.

Muenzinger, K. F., Bernstone, A. H., & Richards, L. Motivation in learning: VIII. Equivalent amounts of electric shock for right and wrong responses in a visual discrimination habit. *Journal of Comparative Psychology*, 1938, *26*, 177–186.

Muenzinger, K. F., Brown, W. O., Crow, W. J., & Powloski, R. F. Motivation in learning: XI. An analysis of electric shock for correct responses into its avoidance and accelerating components. *Journal of Experimental Psychology*, 1952, *43*, 115–119.

Pavlov, I. P. *Conditioned reflexes* (translation by G. V. Anrep). London and New York: Oxford University Press, 1927.

Perkins, C. C., Jr. The relation of secondary reward to gradients of reinforcement. *Journal of Experimental Psychology*, 1947, *37*, 377–392.

Peterson, G. B., Wheeler, R. L., & Armstrong, G. D. Expectancies as mediators in the differential-reward conditional discrimination performance of pigeons. *Animal Learning and Behavior*, 1978, *6*, 279–285.

Prince, A. L., Jr. Effect of punishment on visual discrimination learning. *Journal of Experimental Psychology*, 1956, *52*, 381–385.

Rescorla, R. A., & Wagner, A. R. A theory of Pavlovian conditioning: Variations in the effectiveness of reinforcement and nonreinforcement. In A. H. Black & W. F. Prokasy (Eds.), *Classical conditioning: II. Current research and theory*. New York: Appleton-Century-Crofts, 1972.

Seward, J. P. An experimental analysis of maze discrimination. *Journal of Comparative Psychology*, 1943, *35*, 17–27.

Spelt, P. F. *Effect of shock-right discrimination training using a correction procedure with an enforced delay following an incorrect choice*. Unpublished doctoral dissertation, University of Pittsburgh, 1967.

Spelt, P. F., & Fowler, H. Shock-right discrimination training: The effect of correction training with an enforced delay following an incorrect choice. *Journal of Experimental Psychology,* 1969, *79,* 504–508.

Spence, K. W. The nature of discrimination learning in animals. *Psychological Review,* 1936, *43,* 427–449.

Sutherland, N. S., & Holgate, V. Two cue discrimination learning in rats. *Journal of Comparative and Physiological Psychology,* 1966, *61,* 198–207.

Sutherland, N. S., & Mackintosh, N. J. *Mechanisms of animal discrimination learning.* New York: Academic Press, 1971.

Thorndike, E. L. *Animal intelligence.* New York: Macmillan, 1911.

Trapold, M. A. Are expectancies based upon different positive reinforcing events discriminably different? *Learning and Motivation,* 1970, *1,* 129–140.

Warden, C. J., & Aylesworth, M. The relative value of reward and punishment in the formation of a visual discrimination habit in the white rat. *Journal of Comparative Psychology,* 1927, *7,* 117–127.

Warren, J. M. Additivity of cues in visual pattern discriminations by monkeys. *Journal of Comparative and Physiological Psychology,* 1953, *46,* 484–486.

Wischner, G. J. The effect of punishment on discrimination learning in a noncorrection situation. *Journal of Experimental Psychology,* 1947, *37,* 271–284.

Wischner, G. J. A reply to Dr. Muenzinger on the effect of punishment on discrimination learning in a non-correction situation. *Journal of Experimental Psychology,* 1948, *38,* 203–204.

Wischner, G. J., & Fowler, H. Discrimination performance as affected by duration of shock for either the correct or incorrect response. *Psychonomic Science,* 1964, *1,* 239–240.

Wischner, G. J., Fowler, H., & Kushnick, S. A. Effect of strength of punishment for "correct" or "incorrect" responses on visual discrimination performance. *Journal of Experimental Psychology,* 1963, *65,* 131–138.

Wolfe, J. B. The effect of delayed reward upon learning in the white rat. *Journal of Comparative Psychology,* 1934, *17,* 1–21.

Wolfe, J. B., & Kaplan, M. D. Effect of amount of reward and consummative activity on learning in chickens. *Journal of Comparative Psychology,* 1941, *31,* 353–361.

Yerkes, R. M., & Dodson, J. D. The relation of strength of stimulus to rapidity of habit formation. *Journal of Comparative Neurology and Psychology,* 1908, *18,* 459-482.

Zanich, M. L., & Fowler, H. Primary and secondary reinforcers as distinctive cues which acquire information value in partial-reinforcement discrimination training. *Learning and Motivation,* 1975, *6,* 299–313.

Zeaman, D., & House, B. J. The role of attention in retardate discrimination learning. In N. R. Ellis (Ed.), *Handbook of mental deficiency: Psychological theory and research.* New York: McGraw-Hill, 1963.

7 The Clinical Uses of Punishment

Bane or Boon?

DONALD K. ROUTH AND JUDY LYNNE PERLMAN

Psychologists, including clinical psychologists, have traditionally felt that the use of punishment should be discouraged. This opinion was fostered on the basis of three professional beliefs about punishment. In the first place, punishment was thought to have only a temporary suppressive effect on behavior and could thus be considered of little use to parents or therapists who wished to make a lasting impact. Second, punishment was thought to provide a model for future aggressive behavior by the recipient. Finally, as detailed later in this chapter, punishment was regarded as the source of many problems brought to the clinician, including (according to some theoretical accounts) stuttering, impulsive behavior, and even schizophrenia.

Like others trained in the same era, the first author absorbed these beliefs in graduate school and went forth into the world assuming that effective treatment, like effective parenting, should be based on the exclusive use of reward. However, in his own research, carried out with students and colleagues over the past several years, he repeatedly encountered findings that contradicted these simple assumptions about punishment. Research suggested that punishment might be quite an effective strategy for changing behavior, more so than reward in some cases, and that it might sometimes ameliorate psychopathology, rather than causing the difficulty. These research findings provided a reason to take another look at the literature on punishment and other aversive stimulation, in order to

DONALD K. ROUTH AND JUDY LYNNE PERLMAN • Department of Psychology, University of Iowa, Iowa City, Iowa 52242.

reevaluate these beliefs. The opportunity to write the present chapter thus came at a very useful time. Preparing this review of the literature also provided an opportunity to learn more about the work of Wischner, Fowler, and their colleagues on the facilitating effects of punishment for the correct response in discrimination learning (this work is reviewed in depth in Fowler's chapter in the present volume). This is an important and, we believe, clinically relevant area of research with which the present authors previously had insufficient familiarity.

In this chapter, we focus first on the traditional attitudes of psychology toward punishment and then on the research findings that spurred the present reevaluation. Thereafter, we review some important discoveries and theoretical advances in the field of punishment and aversive stimulation, the abuses and uses of punishment with children, some clinical uses of punishment with adults, and the use of punishment as a facilitator in the learning of difficult tasks. To save the reader any suspense, the conclusions of the chapter may be stated at the outset. Punishment and other aversive stimulation do indeed seem to have a grave potential for misuse. But under carefully chosen circumstances and in modulated amounts, punishment is an effective tool for the clinician.

PUNISHMENT AS A TECHNIQUE TO BE AVOIDED

At one time or another, punishment has been rejected as an approach to changing behavior by some of the most eminent names in psychology including Freud, Thorndike, and Skinner. Freud regarded emotional traumas, including those connected with parental punishment, as among the most important causes of neurosis (Freud, 1909/1953–1974). Thorndike had, of course, originally stated his law of effect in symmetrical form: satisfying consequences were said to strengthen the behaviors they followed, and annoying consequences were said to weaken the behaviors they followed (Thorndike, 1911). Later, however, he withdrew the second part of the statement, viewed punishment as generally ineffective, and preferred to explain the effects it did have in terms of the elicitation of competing responses (Thorndike, 1932). Skinner (1938, 1953) stated that punishment causes only a temporary suppression of behavior and regarded its assumed side effects, such as neurotic and other behavior disorders, as too severe to justify using punishment as a method of behavior change with humans.

SOME PERSONALLY UNSETTLING RESEARCH FINDINGS

Within the field of clinical psychology, there are many theoretical approaches imputing a negative role to punishment. For example, Garmezy (1952) hypothesized that schizophrenic individuals were particularly adversely affected by social censure. In the original version of the theory, it was predicted that any type of social censure would have an adverse effect; the revised model (Garmezy, 1966) stated that censure would adversely affect schizophrenics' performance only if it were unrelated to the task and not contingent on erroneous response. An attempt by Van Dyke and Routh (1973) to test this theory led to one of those unexpected research findings that was mentioned above as contradicting the traditional assumptions about the effects of punishment. In the Van Dyke and Routh study, schizophrenic and normal subjects performed a reaction-time task. On some trials, after the subject reacted, a tone sounded. Some subjects were told that the tone was a signal that their response had been slower than average, while others were told that the tone was a meaningless noise sometimes made by the apparatus. For half the subjects, the tone was, in fact, contingent on slow responding, while for the rest, it was presented after randomly selected trials. Contrary to theoretical predictions, the censure instructions *improved* the reaction times of all subjects, including schizophrenics, regardless of whether the tone was contingent on poor performance.

Another phenomenon theoretically expected to be made worse by punishment is children's "impulsivity," operationalized by Kagan as fast, inaccurate responding on tasks with high response uncertainty, such as the Matching Familiar Figures Test (Kagan, Rosman, Day, Albert, & Phillips, 1964). Kagan originally formulated the hypothesis that because of anxiety over failure, the impulsive child responded rapidly, in order to avoid the discomfort that would otherwise be felt during the period of delay. It seemed to Kagan that if the child was doing poorly because of anxiety, punishment could only make things worse. The first author's attempt to test this implication of Kagan's position, however, resulted in findings in flat contradiction to it. Errickson, Wyne, and Routh (1973) found that a "negative" punishment procedure (response cost) in which tokens were taken away for errors improved the performance of academically handicapped children on the Matching Familiar Figures Test relative to their performance on the standard (nonpunishment) version of the task. A subsequent study by Brent and Routh (1978) extended these findings to another task, oral reading, hypothesized by Kagan (1965) to be sensitive to an impulsive as opposed to a reflective cognitive style. In the Brent and Routh study, fourth-grade children with reading disability were first given a list of 40 words to read as a pretest. Then the children were given a second list under one of three different experimental conditions: control, positive reinforcement (one nickel for each word read correctly), and response cost (one of 40 nickels taken back for each word read incorrectly). Positive reinforcement led to no change in error scores, while punishment led to a decrease in errors by every subject assigned to that experimental condition. Once more, research findings suggested that punishment was an effective way of changing behavior. One should note, in justice to Kagan, that he formulated a revised fear-of-failure hypothesis (Kagan, 1966), which unlike his original theory, correctly accounted for the above research results.

NEW DISCOVERIES AND THEORETICAL ADVANCES CONCERNING PUNISHMENT AND AVERSIVE STIMULATION

Psychology seems to have moved beyond some of the views of punishment ascribed to our eminent forbears, partly because of new research findings, and partly through a reevaluation of old ones. In fact, a review of the studies on which Thorndike (1949) based his conclusions about punishment suggests that he may have been misled by his results in this respect. These studies, carried out with both animal and human subjects, were unfortunately ones in which there were three to five choice alternatives, only one of which was "correct." Under these circumstances, punishment for an incorrect choice simply does not convey as much information to the subject as can reward for the correct choice. Most subsequent research with both animals and humans has used two-choice problems in which this confounding between the motivational and the informational aspects of punishment is absent.

One important milestone in the psychological literature on punishment was the Church (1963) review. Among other contributions, Church clarified the distinction between the definition of punishment as a procedure ("One in which a noxious stimulus is contingent upon the occurrence of a response," p. 370) and as an effect (a reduction in the frequency of the behavior that preceded the punishment event). The present chapter is organized mainly in terms of the procedural definition of punishment, since it allows consideration of circumstances under which the presentation of contingent "noxious" stimulation can facilitate responding. (The chapter also deals with some types of aversive stimulation not contingent on the subject's response and thus not meeting any strict, technical definition of punishment.) Church (1963) argued that facilitative effects might be regarded as occurring in spite of, rather than because of, this primary effect. Solomon (1964) took the opportunity of a presidential address to the Eastern Psychological Association to "decry some unscientific legends" (p. 239) about punishment and to rehabilitate it as a significant area of study for psychologists. Among the important findings Solomon discussed was that the general paradigm of avoidance learning (e.g., Solomon, Kamin, & Wynne, 1953) was a powerful means of suppressing behaviors—in some cases, permanently.

A more recent example of a striking finding in the area of aversive stimulation is the discovery of the special characteristics of taste aversion learning (Garcia, MacGowan, Ervin, & Koelling, 1968). Animals were found to be able to acquire an association between a novel flavor and X-ray–induced illness hours later; however, such an association was not acquired concerning the *size* of food pellet and subsequent illness. These findings, which seem to be generalizable to humans (Garb & Stunkard, 1974), were clearly an exception to the Pavlovian concept that conditioning is possible only with a very brief conditioned stimulus–unconditioned stimulus (CS–US) interval. The findings of Garcia *et al.* seemed very applicable to clinical problems, for example, the aversive conditioning of alcoholics.

ABUSES AND USES OF PUNISHMENT WITH CHILDREN

First, we wish to discuss the use of punishment as a child-rearing technique, in relation to various alternatives. Then, we consider a clinical phenomenon of the 1960s, the use of electric shock and other such severe aversive methods with autistic and retarded children, and the public reactions it generated. Having dealt with the possible abuses of punishment with children, we discuss some instances in which the uses of milder forms of punishment for clinical purposes seem well accepted by professionals and laypersons, namely, in the treatment of self-injurious behavior and of ruminative vomiting. Then, we discuss some developments in behavior modification such as the use of timeout and "overcorrection."

Punishment as a Child-Rearing Technique

Doubtless the most extreme example of the inappropriate use of aversive stimulation is the phenomenon of child abuse, which is responsible for the death or maiming of many children, and which is unfortunately quite prevalent (Helfer & Kempe, 1974). A detailed consideration of child abuse is beyond the scope of this chapter, but reviews of the problem are available elsewhere (e.g., Parke & Collmer, 1975). One relevant finding in this area has been that parents who abuse their children frequently give a history of having been abused as children by their own parents (Spinetta & Rigler, 1972).

Of course, almost all parents use punishment techniques of a less intense variety in dealing with their children. Developmental research suggests that by the child's second year, and certainly in the third, the parent–child relationship involves many attempts by the parent to correct the child's behavior. For example, Minton *et al.* (1971) observing 2-year-olds at home, found that, on the average, mothers interrupted children every 6–8 minutes to remind them of a behavior they should stop or a command they should heed. Undoubtedly, many of these interruptions, being somewhat noxious to the child and contingent on certain child behaviors, would fall under the technical definition of punishment cited above. Nevertheless, some families are demonstrably more punitive than others in their approach to child rearing. Lefkowitz *et al.* (1978) presented data from a longitudinal study suggesting that parents who reported the use of physical methods of punishment with their children had children (particularly boys) who were more aggressive with their third-grade classmates, who were more aggressive 10 years later by self-report and peer ratings, and who were themselves more punitive when they came to be parents. Findings that punishment effective in the immediate situation may backfire in the long run are not confined to children. In a study of crime and punishment in the army, Hart (1978) presented evidence that soldiers who were punished by their superiors responded in the following months with a sense of injustice and increased lawlessness.

Another possible adverse effect of the use of punishment by parents or other adults on children is that it may influence the child's attitudes toward the punishing agents. Morris and Redd (1975) set up an experiment in which one adult dispensed positive comments for task responding by the child, a second reprimanded off-task behavior, a third used both contingencies, and a fourth remained silent. Although the punitive adult was the most effective in controlling a child's behavior, this adult was shortly afterward rated as less preferred by the child than the rewarding adult.

The major alternatives to physical punishment that have been suggested for use by parents for correcting their children's behavior are love withdrawal and reasoning with the child, including "inductive" methods. Love withdrawal, as described by DePalma (1974) and Hoffman (1970), is a procedure at least superficially resembling "time-out" in which after the child misbehaves, the parent refuses to provide attention and care until the child shows some evidence of guilt and attempts to make amends. Hoffman (1975) used the term *induction* to refer to "techniques which point up the consequences of the child's behavior for others," and he thought that it produced in the child "a moral orientation characterized by independence of external sanctions and high guilt." If parental physical punishment has long-term effects as unfavorable as current evidence seems to suggest, alternatives such as these need to be explored in further developmental research. For the present, psychologists need to continue their traditional discouragement of parents from the excessive use of such "power-assertive" methods of raising their children.

Though there is considerable evidence of an association between parental punishment and antisocial behavior, it is interesting that there is remarkably little evidence linking punishment and the types of neurotic difficulty with which Freudian theory has occupied itself.

Controversy over the Use of Electric Shock with Children

Lovaas, Schaeffer, and Simmons (1965) reported experiments in which electric shock was used with autistic children. Their work (which was also featured in a 1964 issue of *Life* magazine) showed that the children learned to approach an adult in order to escape or avoid shock to their bare feet from metal tapes on the floor of the room, and that shock (from a stock prod) could be used to eliminate stereotyped behaviors and tantrums. Since that study appeared, numerous other single-subject studies have been reported in which the contingent presentation of electric shock was used to control self-injurious behavior in autistic or retarded children (Tate & Baroff, 1966) and to decrease the rate of a child's self-induced seizures (Wright, 1973) or suppress stereotyped behaviors (Koegel, Firestone, Kramme, & Dunlap, 1974).

The response of critics to the use of shock with children was immediate (Breger, 1965) and has continued over the past decade and a half (e.g., Akerley, 1976). The controversy has not been confined to the professional literature but has spilled out into newspapers and popular magazines and has been a factor in court decisions and in the emergence of administrative guidelines restricting the use of such procedures or requiring prior review and monitoring of their use by committees. Breger (1965), the discussant of the original Lovaas *et al.* report, said that he thought there *was* a real ethical problem "when pain is deliberately inflicted on subjects, without their consent, in an attempt to 'control' their behavior" (p. 111). Of course, many of the same criticisms apply to other common (and not very satisfactory) means of dealing with, for example, self-injurious behavior, such as the use of tranquilizing medications or physical restraint. Nevertheless, many persons find the use of cattle prods with human beings to be, in the words of the U.S. Constitution, a "cruel and unusual punishment," and clinicians have actively searched for alternative approaches to the severe behavioral problems manifested by some autistic and retarded children.

Treatment of Self-Injurious Behavior

Children who repeatedly bang their heads against hard surfaces, slap their own faces, bite themselves, or engage in other self-injurious and sometimes life-threatening behaviors present a problem that simply cannot be ignored by parents or by institutional personnel. There has been no consensus about how to deal with these behaviors, and thus, they have been a prime target for the use of electric shock. However, besides being considered cruel, electric shock has often not proved to be a very reliable technique with these children. Subjects have usually been able to develop a discrimination as to whether the cattle prod and someone authorized to use it are nearby, and they inhibit their self-injurious behaviors only under these circumstances. This effect presents a real dilemma if restrictive regulations limit the number of persons permitted to administer shock.

From a theoretical standpoint, the problem here resides in the fact that a discriminated (or signaled) punishment procedure is, in effect, being used instead of a nonsignaled procedure.

One alternative to electric shock that has been demonstrated as being effective in suppressing self-injurious behaviors is aromatic ammonia (Tanner & Zeiler, 1975). Ammonia fumes are very unpleasant, yet produce no lasting ill effect when inhaled in dilute form. Ammonia capsules are inexpensive (2.5–15 cents each) and can thus be distributed to all staff of an institution who come in contact with the self-injurious individual. In addition, it is difficult for the child to discriminate whether people in the immediate environment are carrying ammonia capsules, whereas the presence of a cattle prod is more obvious. Ammonia has also been demonstrated as being effective in suppressing the self-injurious behavior of children in varied natural settings, including the home, the grandparents' home, and the school (Altman, Haavik, & Cook, 1978) when family members and school personnel carry ammonia capsules around with them for this purpose. Another alternative treatment for self-injurious behavior is overcorrection (Harris & Romanczyk, 1976; Measel & Alfieri, 1976), which is discussed in more detail below. One single-subject study (Lutzker, 1978) demonstrated the effectiveness of simply screening a child's face with a terry-cloth bib to suppress self-injurious behavior across three different settings.

Perhaps it is a mistake to regard all self-injurious behavior as a homogeneous class of responses. The inherited disorder known as Lesch–Nyhan syndrome is characterized by a typical form of self-injurious behavior, the biting of the child's own fingers and lips. Anderson, Dancis, and Alpert (1978) found that this self-injurious behavior of Lesch–Nyhan children (unlike that of other handicapped children we have discussed) was not suppressed by contingent electric shock. For these children, only the positive reinforcement of non-self-injurious behavior and time-out from social reinforcement for self-injury were consistently and rapidly effective.

Treatment of Ruminative Vomiting

Sometimes an infant or an older mentally retarded individual develops the habit of regurgitating food after meals, often with accompanying rumination or rechewing of the vomitus. Like self-injurious behavior, ruminative vomiting can be a life-threatening condition and has thus seemed to justify extreme therapeutic measures, including the presentation of electric shock contingent on vomiting or its identifiable precursors. Although most of the literature on the use of shock to suppress ruminative vomiting consists of single-subject case reports, the findings seem quite consistent. The usual result reported is that shock completely suppresses such vomiting, with a consequent weight gain by the infant or child, and often with favorable side effects, such as greater social responsiveness (Cunningham & Linscheid, 1976; Galbraith, Byrick, & Rutledge, 1970; Kohlenberg, 1970; Lang & Melamed, 1969; Luckey, Watson, & Musick, 1968; Toister, Condron, Worley, & Arthur, 1975). The above studies presented only baseline and conditioning data, with no rigorous attempt to demonstrate experimental control. One recent study (Linscheid & Cunningham, 1977) did include a three-day reversal of treatment and it was found that when the shock source was discontinued, rumination increased from 4 instances on the first reversal day to 10 instances on the third day and then was suppressed when shock began again. Several of the above case reports included follow-up data for periods of from 3 to 12 months posttreatment; in five out of six cases, the rumination and vomiting remained suppressed at follow-up. In the remaining case (reported by Kohlenberg, 1970), in the initial training many shocks were needed before any substantial effect was seen, and at follow-up one year later, the child's vomiting had again become a problem. Overall, the use of electric shock seems to be more effective in producing a generalized, long-term suppression of ruminative vomiting than in eliminating self-injurious behavior. Perhaps one reason is that children treated for rumination are so young (or so mentally impaired) that they are less able to discriminate the conditions under which punishment is or is not potentially present.

Although shock seems to be more effective in treating ruminative vomiting than in treating self-injurious behavior, the use of shock on infants and children is offensive to the ethical and aesthetic sensibilities of many people, and thus, the search continues for more acceptable, milder approaches. One such method involves squirting a small amount of lemon juice into the mouth of an infant whenever rumination or its precursors are detected. Sajwaj, Libet, and Agras (1974) reported the successful treatment of a 6-month-old infant ruminator with this procedure, using an ABAB reversal design. Cook, Altman, Shaw, and Blaylock (1978) reported that the use of contingent lemon juice in the mouth eliminated the public masturbation of a severely retarded boy. Lemon juice, like ammonia (but unlike electric shock), can be effectively administered by many individuals in such a child's environment, including parents, teachers, and paraprofessionals.

Use of Time-Out

Time-out from positive reinforcement seems to be an aversive event (Leitenberg, 1965) and can therefore be used to suppress unwanted behaviors. Since it does not involve actual physical punishment, time-out may be viewed as a more humane approach to correcting children's misbehaviors than some of the methods discussed above. In a pioneering study of the effects of time-out on children, Baer (1962) demonstrated that turning off television cartoons when a child was sucking his or her thumb and re-presentation of the cartoons when the thumb was removed from the mouth quickly suppressed the behavior, while yoked withdrawal and re-presentation did not produce suppression.

Barton, Guess, Garcia, and Baer (1970) showed how time-out procedures could be used to suppress a number of undesirable mealtime behaviors in institutionalized retarded individuals. The behaviors were suppressed one at a time in a multiple-baseline experimental design. Although it was a very convincing demonstration, with no ill effects on its subjects' health, this study did derive its effects from withholding food, a practice that, like the use of electric shock, has been the subject of public controversy, litigation, and administrative regulation.

Two versions of the time-out procedure seem to be in common use: exclusionary and nonexclusionary. In the former procedure, the child is briefly isolated in a time-out room or cubicle. White, Nielsen, and Johnson (1972) studied the relative effects of 1, 15, and 30 min in the time-out room on the aggression, tantrums, and self-injurious behavior of retarded subjects and found 15 min more effective than 1 min, but they found little difference in effectiveness between 15 and 30 min. The briefness of the exclusion intervals is an important way in which modern time-out procedures differ from the traditional, and less humane, use of solitary confinement.

In nonexclusionary time-out, a parent or teacher simply withdraws attention, play materials, etc., from the child for the duration of the time-out interval. Foxx and Shapiro (1978) have recently developed a novel variation on time-out procedures: the time-out ribbon. Each child in a special-education class was given a distinctive ribbon to wear and received edibles and praise every few minutes while wearing it. When a child misbehaved, that child's ribbon was taken away for 3 min, or until the misbehavior stopped, as a signal that no reinforcement would be forthcoming during that time. The children rapidly learned the significance of the ribbons, and the procedure was demonstrated as being effective in suppressing disruptive behavior. There was, however, a problem with children trying to steal each other's ribbons once they learned their "value."

Overcorrection

Foxx and his colleagues (Azrin, Kaplan, & Foxx, 1973; Foxx & Azrin, 1972, 1973) developed a rather elaborate set of procedures, collectively known as *overcorrection*, which they have demonstrated as being effective in suppressing a number of problem behaviors. All overcorrection procedures involve inducing the individual to go through some standard set of actions contingent on misbehavior. If necessary, the person is physically guided through the overcorrective behaviors, with this manual guidance being withdrawn gradually as the individual begins to perform the overcorrection voluntarily. Overcorrection often involves a "restitution" component (Foxx & Azrin, 1972), in which the individual is required to assume the responsibility for the disturbed situation and restore it to a "greatly improved state" (p. 16). The restitution is to be directly related to the misbehavior, not for any empirically validated reason but "lest it become arbitrary and punitive" (p. 16). For example, a person who throws a chair or turns over a table or bed is required not only to restore these objects to their correct position but also to straighten out all other chairs, tables, and beds on the ward. Or a person who injures others is required to help in providing medical assistance for the victim and perhaps others as well. (Actually, by our definition, overcorrection, including its restitution component, is in fact punitive in the sense of being a response-contingent aversive event.) The other major component of overcorrection is "positive practice," in which the individual is required to engage intensely in "overly correct forms of relevant behavior" (Foxx & Azrin, 1973, p. 2). Like restitution, positive practice is tailored to the particular misbehavior of the individual. For example, each time a child engaged in stereotyped hand movements, the child might be required to go through a positive-practice sequence involving putting the hands up, the hands out, and the hands down in response to commands (Arzin *et al.*, 1973). A resident of an institution who engaged in loud, disruptive behavior might be required to spend a fixed period of time in a relaxed posture in bed each time a disruptive incident occurred. This procedure differs from time-out in that some particular behavior (in this case "relaxation") is required of the individual (Webster & Azrin, 1973).

A recent review (Harris & Ersner-Hershfield, 1978) concluded that overcorrection procedures had proved "markedly effective in reducing such aggressive behaviors as hitting, biting, and throwing of objects" (p. 1362) but were less broadly effective in suppressing stereotyped behaviors. A study by Matson, Ollendick, and Martin (1979) found that of eight chronically institutionalized subjects successfully treated by overcorrection for stereotyped behaviors, only two were maintaining the response suppression a year later. In the other six, the stereotyped behaviors a year later approximated the pretreatment rates. Harris and Ersner-Hershfield (1978) also stated that overcorrection had been found to be effective in the treatment of enuresis, recurrent vomiting, nocturnal head-banging, recurrent floor-sprawling, public disrobing, disruptive behavior, and noncompliance.

Epstein, Doke, Sajwaj, Sorrell, and Rimmer (1974) studied the issue of whether there was a specific relationship between the type of overcorrection prescribed and the type of behavior to be suppressed and concluded that there probably was not. Rather, "overcorrection procedures that are effective for one behavior can be used to reduce the frequency of topographically different behaviors" (p. 385). Likewise, Roberts, Iwata, McSween, and Desmond (1979) concluded that an effective overcorrection procedure need not be incompatible with the response to be suppressed.

Treatment of Bed-Wetting

In 1904, the German pediatrician Pfaundler (as cited in Mowrer & Mowrer, 1938), somewhat serendipitously, developed the bell-and-pad method of treating children's bed-wetting. The device was originally used simply to signal the institutional staff that a child had wet the bed, but it was found that over time, the device decreased the frequency of bed-wetting. In an influential and much cited article, Mowrer and Mowrer (1938) explained the effectiveness of the device in terms of the principles of Pavlovian conditioning. Awakening the child contingent on bed-wetting also, of course, fits a procedural definition of punishment. The Mowrers' explanation in Pavlovian terms has always been somewhat difficult to assess, for example, because of the difficulty in specifying exactly what the CS and the unconditioned response (UR) are. The US, of course, was regarded as being the bell, which wakes the child contingent on the electronic detection that urination has occurred. The CS is usually regarded as being bladder tension, but that is inferred rather than measured. The UR may also involve a number of components of an internal somatic nature that are difficult to measure directly. At any rate, the bell-and-pad device has been widely used to treat bed-wetting and has been repeatedly subjected to controlled experimental study. In a review of this research, Doleys (1977) estimated that the use of the device is effective in about 75% of the cases. The relapse rate is estimated at 41%, mostly within six months after treatment. The retreatment of relapsed subjects has been successful about 68% of the time.

Azrin and Foxx (1971) developed a method of toilet training institutional retarded persons that they reported to be effective immediately about 90% of the time, with incontinence eventually reaching near zero rates. This method involved a number of elements resembling overcorrection, including requiring the resident to clean himself or herself, his or her clothing, and the general area after a toilet accident. A time-out contingency was also involved. Azrin, Sneed, and Foxx (1974) then reported a procedure called *dry-bed training,* which they found to be 100% effective in eliminating the bed-wetting of nonretarded children living at home. This procedure included the use of the bell-and-pad device and also many elements reminiscent of overcorrection, for example, "cleanliness training" and also "positive practice," a procedure in which the child repeats 20 times the following sequence: (a) child lies down in bed; (b) child counts to 50; (c) child arises and attempts to urinate in toilet; and (d) child returns to bed (Azrin *et al.,* 1974). In his review, Doleys (1977) found Azrin and Foxx's dry-bed training program to be "the most promising" of the new treatment procedures for bed-wetting.

Azrin and his colleagues have argued that the Pavlovian explanation of the way that the bell-and-pad device works may not be sufficient. They pointed out that the procedure is still effective if the alarm is delayed (Collins, 1973; Peterson, Wright, & Hanlon, 1969) or if the alarm goes off in the parents' room rather than in the child's. In other words, a brief CS–US interval is not necessary, though it admittedly facilitates training. Azrin and Thienes (1978) have demonstrated the effectiveness of a version of the dry-bed procedure that eliminates the use of the bell-and-pad apparatus. Presumably, the principles underlying the success of this new approach involve the suppression of nocturnal urination by contingent presentation of noxious "overcorrection" procedures, that is, punishment. Of course, there are also elements of positive reinforcement involved, and further research is necessary to elucidate the relative contribution of the separate elements of the treatment package.

SOME CLINICAL USES OF PUNISHMENT WITH ADULTS

In adults, as in children, aversive techniques have been used most often to suppress unwanted or socially deviant behaviors. One major difference is that the adults usually voluntarily present themselves for treatment. They are also intellectually able to understand the procedures to be used and legally capable of giving their informed consent. Since the adult client can serve as an advocate of his or her own rights, the therapist operates under fewer legal and administrative constraints than, for example, a therapist working with children in a residential setting.

Alcoholism

Long before Garcia *et al.*'s (1968) demonstration of the special properties of taste aversion learning, those doing aversive conditioning with alcoholics had an intuitive realization that gastrointestinal illness might be a powerful unconditioned stimulus. In giving a rationale for conditioning alcoholics to associate the taste of alcohol with the nausea produced by an emetic, Thimann (1943) made the following statement: "Everyone is familiar with the fact that the ingestion of tainted food causes sickness, disgust and abhorrence for this kind of food for a long time" (p. 333). The earliest known aversive conditioning of alcoholics was used by two Russians, Sluchevsky and Friken in 1933 (cited in Thimann, 1943). A similar approach to treating alcoholics was begun at the Shadel hospital in Seattle, Washington in 1935 and continues up to the present time. Voegtlin and Broz (1949) summarized the results of their conditioned-reflex treatment of 2,323 alcoholics at Shadel as follows: "Conditioning procedures, when used alone, will cause 85% of all chronic alcoholics to remain abstinent for six months or longer" (p. 596). It was said that 70% would remain abstinent for a year or longer and 60% for two years or longer. Although this was an uncontrolled treatment study, its results remain impressive today.

The particular chemical substance used to produce the physical illness to be associated with the taste of alcoholic beverages has varied over the years. For example, apomorphine has been gradually replaced by emetine. A related treatment approach involves the use of disulfram (Antabuse) to cause the individual to associate drinking alcohol with sickness. Disulfram, discovered by Hald and Jacobsen (1948), alters the metabolism of alcohol, resulting in an accumulation of toxic acetaldehyde in the body and causing blurred vision, chest pains, difficulty in respiration, flushing, malaise, headache, low blood pressure, nausea and vomiting, and other markedly unpleasant symptoms. As Wilson (1975) pointed out, the main limitation of disulfram treatment has been the ease with which the alcoholic can discontinue taking it on return to an environment offering temptations to resume drinking.

Marie (1955, cited in Wilson, 1975) developed the technique of surgically implanting disulfram tablets under the skin of the abdomen, so that its effects would continue for a much longer time, though in milder form, than the effects of orally ingested disulfram. Wilson, Davidson, and White (1976) compared the effects of implanted disulfram with placebo (sham operations) and found that while sham-operated subjects continued to drink after their first postoperative encounter with alcohol, 80% of the disulfram-implant patients remained abstinent following their experiences of a mild but prolonged and unpleasant disulfram-ethanol reaction. A subsequent placebo-controlled trial of implanted disulfram with a two-year follow-up (Wilson, Davidson, Blachard, & White, 1978) showed that disulfram produced significantly larger periods of abstinence than placebo.

A theoretically oriented study by Lamon, Wilson, and Leaf (1977) compared the effectiveness of nausea (produced by head movement in a moving visual field) with the effect of electric shock in the classical conditioning of aversion to drinking nonalcoholic beverages with distinctive flavors. As predicted, nausea proved significantly more effective than electric shock as an unconditioned stimulus.

The reader should not take the above emphasis on animal taste-aversion learning as an experimental model for the treatment of alcoholism to imply that other approaches are not being studied. On the contrary, research is being actively carried out regarding a number of other approaches involving both aversive and nonaversive procedures. For example, Lovibond and Caddy (1970), combining biofeedback training concerning blood-alcohol level and contingent electric shock for drinking alcohol when intoxicated, have presented evidence that they could train alcoholics to become moderate, controlled drinkers. Subjects receiving this type of training were significantly more moderate in their subsequent drinking than control subjects given noncontingent shocks during "conditioning" sessions. Other research has emphasized the use of cognitive self-control techniques, either alone or combined with electric-shock aversive conditioning (Caddy & Lovibond, 1976; Miller, 1978). In summary, treatments of alcoholism based on the use of aversive stimulation seem to be significantly more effective than placebo, though they are not the only effective treatments.

Deviant Sexual Behavior

There was once considerably more scientific and professional consensus than there is at present about what sexual behaviors should be regarded as deviant and thus in need of treatment. However, the ethical issues involved in changing adults' sexual orientation and preferences are usually dealt with in practice simply by working with clients who voluntarily present themselves for treatment and who give informed consent for the procedures employed.

The behavioral treatment of deviant sexual behavior has usually followed the experimental model of avoidance learning (Solomon *et al.*, 1953) rather than the Pavlovian model so influential in the treatment of alcoholics. The early studies were almost all uncontrolled case reports of the treatment of transvestites (e.g., Blakemore, Thorpe, Barker, Conway, & Lavin, 1963) or male homosexuals (e.g., Feldman & MacCulloch, 1964). Feldman (1966), in a review of this earlier literature, concluded that there was certainly not an "overwhelming case for the efficacy of any single aversion therapy technique in the treatment of any single sexual deviation" (p. 78).

Barlow, Leitenberg, and Agras (1969) described a controlled study of the use of "covert sensitization" in the treatment of pedophiliac behavior in one subject and homosexual behavior in another. First, a hierarchy of sexually arousing imagined scenes was first constructed for each subject. The highest six items in the hierarchy were chosen for "sensitization," by associating them with feelings of nausea and vomiting, also induced in imagination via instruction from the therapist. The ABAB design for each subject considered of baseline, acquisition, extinction, and reacquisition. The predicted systematic changes were demonstrated on the dependent measures, which included (a) daily records of incidents of sexual arousal of a deviant nature; (b) scores on the rated sexual-arousal value of particular scenes in the hierarchy; and (c) galvanic-skin-response scores when scenes in the hierarchy were imagined. Unfortunately, it was not possible to gather data of a more objective nature on the subjects' nonlaboratory sexual behavior. A later study by Callahan and Leitenberg (1973), also with a within-subjects design, found that covert sensitization was a more effective treatment for deviant sexual behavior than was electric shock presented contingent on the imagined scenes. The dependent measure sensitive to these treatment effects was daily records of incidents of sexual arousal of a deviant nature. Such records present the obvious possibility of biased reporting by subjects.

In a review of covert sensitization as a clinical procedure, Little and Curran (1978) concluded that there was promising evidence of its effectiveness as a treatment for sexual deviance, but not as a way of dealing with alcoholism, smoking, or obesity. Perhaps the reason is that imagery has a greater role in the development and maintenance of human sexual behavior, deviant or otherwise.

Obesity

At this point, the evidence is quite mixed as to whether treatments based on aversive stimulation are of any benefit in weight loss programs beyond the effects of nonspecific or placebo factors. On one hand, Janda and Rimm (1972) found that a covert sensitization treatment produced significantly more weight loss in overweight subjects than in subjects assigned to attention-control and untreated-control conditions. There was a correlation of .53 between the treatment's effectiveness and the discomfort produced by the imagined aversive scenes of nausea and vomiting when approaching a particular type of food to be eliminated from the diet. In contrast, Foreyt and Hagen (1973) found no differential weight loss between subjects in covert sensitization and placebo control conditions. Similarly, Elliott and Denney (1975) found that the subjects in all of their groups, placebo as well as covert sensitization, lost an equal amount of weight.

Smoking

It is also uncertain at present whether procedures based on aversive stimulation can help people stop smoking. Berecz (1972) had one set of subjects imagine smoking and then administer painful electric shock to themselves (i.e., the smoking was imagined, but the shocks were real). Another group actually smoked and gave themselves shock contingent on smoking, and a third group received a "placebo" manipulation with imagined shock as well as imagined smoking. For males who smoked heavily, at least, the imagined-smoking treatment was significantly more effective than the actual-smoking or placebo treatments. On the other hand, Carlin and Armstrong (1968) found that all their groups reduced their smoking significantly from baseline: conditioning (shock contingent on smoking) was no better than pseudoconditioning (shock received in an irrelevant situation) or control. And Conway (1977) found that none of the various treatment combinations used, whether involving avoidance conditioning or not, was more effective than control conditions in reducing smoking.

Stuttering

One of the most influential theories concerning how stuttering develops continues to be the one advanced by Johnson (1944) that stuttering originates from its own diagnosis, that is, from the child's self-conscious reaction to parental labeling and criticism of the child's normal nonfluencies. In the mature individual, stuttering is viewed as a self-maintaining process, the behaviors called stuttering consisting essentially of the struggling attempts in which the person engages in order *not* to stutter. Wischner (1952a,b) reformulated this view in learning theory terms, treating stuttering as an instrumental avoidance reaction motivated by anxiety and reinforced by anxiety reduction. (A review of some more contemporary views of the nature of stuttering is found in the chapter by Garber and Siegel in the present volume.)

Therapeutic approaches based on the views of Johnson and like-minded theorists focused on the need to reduce the individual's anxiety about stuttering. The individual might even be advised, "Go ahead and stutter. But learn to do so without fear and embarrassment" (Bloodstein, 1975, p. 308). According to this therapeutic philosophy, the paradox was that to the extent that the stutterer could accept his or her own disfluencies without anxiety, they would probably disappear. At least on the surface, these views would seem to suggest that aversive stimulation, by producing fear, would only make stuttering worse. A number of early studies were in line with this expectation. Porter (1939) found that stuttering rates increased with audience size, presumably because of the more numerous critical reactions the stutterer anticipated from the larger audience. Van Riper (1937) found that stuttering increased when stutterers were told that at the end of the session, they would receive as many electric shocks as the number of times they blocked in their speech.

However, Flanagan, Goldiamond, and Azrin (1958) demonstrated, using an ABA reversal design (no-punishment, punishment, no-punishment), that rates of stuttering were *decreased* by punishment (i.e., a 1-sec blast of a 6000-Hz tone at 105 dB presented whenever a subject stuttered). Note that in this study, the aversive stimulus was presented immediately after each disfluency rather than at the end of the session. Shames and Sherrick (1963) wrote a paper reconceptualizing stuttering and normal disfluency within an operant conditioning framework, giving an impetus to considerable further research on the effects of punishment on stuttering.

In a study of normal speakers, Siegel and Martin (1965) presented the tape-recorded word *wrong* to some subjects contingent on each disfluency and to others at random time. The contingent presentation of *wrong* sharply and significantly decreased disfluencies, while the random presentation had no discernible effect. The effect of contingent *wrong* was a temporary and reversible one. Using a multiple baseline design with three adult stutterers, Martin and Siegel (1966a), demonstrated not only that contingent electric shock would reduce stuttering frequency essentially to zero, but also that specific stuttering behaviors could be independently manipulated and that stuttering frequency could be brought under the control of a discriminative stimulus such as a nylon strap attached to the subject's wrist. Using a reversal design, Martin and Siegel (1966b) showed that the contingent presentation of the words *not good* (as contrasted to *good*) decreased the stuttering frequency of two adult stutterers. Siegel and Martin (1966) showed a clear effect of presenting the word *wrong* in reducing the disfluencies of normal speakers, whereas presenting the world *right* or a buzzer after disfluencies had less effect.

The effects of time-out on stuttering were studied by Haroldson, Martin, and Starr (1968). Using a reversal design with four adult stutterers as subjects, they illuminated a red light for 10 sec after each instance of stuttering as a signal that speaking was forbidden during that interval. Each of the subjects showed a marked decrease in stuttering in response to this contingency. Siegel, Lenske, and Broen (1969) demonstrated the suppression of normal speech disfluencies through a response-cost procedure in which points worth a penny each were subtracted when the subjects made interjections such as *er* or *um* or repeated sounds, syllables, or words. Martin and Haroldson (1979) found that the percentage of stuttering was decreased in adult stutterers by any of several experimental treatments: contingent time-out, noise, delayed auditory feedback, and a metronome condition.

Siegel (1970) reviewed the literature on the effects of punishment on stuttering and disfluency and concluded that the former conception, that punishment aggravates disfluency, was incorrect. Siegel considered at some length, without resolving it, the apparent paradox between traditional views of stuttering and modern demonstrations that punishment (i.e. contingent aversive stimulation) tends to decrease disfluency. Perhaps if one takes a broad view, there need be no contradiction between the views that a certain behavior, such as stuttering, may be both elicited by aversive stimuli and suppressed by punishment. For example, Azrin (1970) demonstrated that shock-induced aggression (biting) in monkeys could be suppressed by further response-contingent shock. Follick and Knutson (1978), who replicated this result with rats, showed that the effect was not due to the mere frequency and duration of the additional shock involved.

At this point, the effects of punishment on stuttering and disfluency are still at the laboratory demonstration stage. Although some attempts have been made to apply to these principles in the clinical treatment of stuttering (e.g., Martin, Kuhl, & Haroldson, 1972), we still await studies that adequately demonstrate generalization across settings, as well as long-term effectiveness.

PUNISHMENT AND INFORMATION PROCESSING

In the research reviewed up to this point, punishment has been regarded merely as a means of suppressing unwanted behaviors. This final section of the chapter weighs the merits of aversive stimulation as a possible facilitator of learning and problem solving. This has come to be one of the best-known uses of punishment in the psychological laboratory with both animal and human subjects, but its clinical and educational uses remain largely unexplored.

Research with Animals

The use of punishment to facilitate discrimination learning in animals has a long history. Yerkes and Dodson (1908) subjected mice to electric shock of varied intensities for the incorrect response in a discrimination box. The mice were given problems ranging from easy to difficult in terms of the relative brightness of the correct and the incorrect choice alternatives. The results of this study were stated as a principle that has come to be known as the *Yerkes–Dodson Law:* that performance on easy problems is facilitated by intense stimulation, whereas performance on difficult problems is impaired by intense stimulation and facilitated by weak stimulation. A study by Hoge and Stocking (1912) compared the value of giving rats punishment (shock) for the incorrect response with that of giving a reward (food) for the correct response in a discrimination box. A third group of rats was given both reward and punishment. It was found that the combination of reward and punishment was more effective than either alone, and that punishment alone was more effective than reward alone as far as the rate of learning was concerned. These findings were later replicated by Warden and Aylesworth (1927), who noted that the use of punishment tended to slow animals down at the choice point in the apparatus.

Paradoxical as it may seem, punishment for the correct response can also speed up learning. (A more detailed review of the following studies may be found in Fowler's chapter in the present volume.) Muenzinger (1934) observed the learning of rats in a *T*-shaped visual-discrimination box under three experimental conditions: shock for the incorrect response (shock-wrong), shock for the correct response (shock-right), and no-shock. All animals also received food for the correct response, and a correction procedure was used (i.e., the animals were permitted, via a return alley, to get back to the stem and choose again, and if incorrect, again, etc.) Shock-right resulted in significantly better learning than no-shock and was only slightly inferior to the shock-wrong condition. Muenzinger and Wood (1935) soon followed up this study with another comparing shock-wrong, shock-right, and no-shock procedures with one in which the animal was shocked for either response (shock-both) or was shocked on every trial before the choice point. The results showed that shock-both facilitated learning about as much as shock-wrong or shock-right. The no-shock groups and the group shocked before the choice point both performed poorly. Muenzinger and Fletcher (1936) suggested that shock-right and shock-both facilitated learning a discrimination because they induced the animals to slow down and engage in "vicarious trial and error" behavior at the choice point, moving their heads back and forth as if engaging in a careful comparison of the alternatives. However, shock *before* the choice point made the animals hasten past it without vicarious trial and error and was thus ineffective.

Not all investigators were able to demonstrate shock-right facilitation. Using a noncorrection procedure in which the rats were removed from the discrimination box after an incorrect choice, Wischner (1947), got results quite different from Muenzinger's. Shock-wrong produced faster learning than shock-right, and the latter did not differ in its effects from a no-shock condition. Muenzinger and Powloski (1951) then compared correction and a procedure they considered the equivalent of a noncorrection one, finding the facilitative effect of shock-right to be more apparent with the correction procedure. In an investigation of the intensity of shock, Wischner, Fowler, and Kushnick (1963) again found that with a noncorrection procedure, shock-wrong was the most effective condition; indeed, shock-right was even inferior to a no-shock condition. The greater the shock intensity, the fewer the errors made by animals in the shock-wrong condition that were confronted with an easy black–white discrimination, but animals in the shock-right condition made *more* errors.

An extremely important variable in whether shock-right facilitates visual discrimination learning turns out to be the level of difficulty of the problem. Difficulty is operationalized both by delays of reward and by the relative brightness of the correct and incorrect alternatives. Fowler and Wischner (1965), still using the noncorrection procedure, next varied problem difficulty by manipulating the relative brightness of the alternatives. They found that especially on the more difficult problems, both shock-right and shock-wrong facilitated learning relative to the no-shock controls. Fowler, Spelt, and Wischner (1967) did a factorial study showing that the amount of shock-right facilitation obtained varied regularly with levels of task difficulty, whether the difficulty was operationalized by the type of training procedure (i.e. correction vs. noncorrection) or by the relative brightness of cues. Spelt and Fowler (1969) showed that the important difference between the correction and the noncorrection procedures was whether delay of reward was imposed. (Intrinsically, correction provides a delayed reward for *incorrect* responses and thus promotes a more difficult problem.) Imposing an enforced and hence extended delay of reward following each error made the correction procedure more like the noncorrection one and reduced the magnitude of the shock-right facilitation obtained. Conversely, removal of the inherent delay (i.e., no reinforcement following an error) in the noncorrection procedure made it more like correction and increased the amount of shock-right facilitation obtained. Fowler, Fago, and Wischner (1971) showed that delay of reward was itself important in determining problem difficulty. In a noncorrection problem, longer delay of reward for the *correct* response made the discrimination more difficult and enhanced the effect of shock-right facilitation. Thus, the long-standing conflict between Muenzinger's and Wischner's results appears to have been resolved completely. The key point is that mild or even moderate punishment for correct responding is more likely to be helpful when the problem is more difficult. As Fowler's chapter in the present volume suggests, the Yerkes–Dodson Law needs to be replaced by a broader discriminability principle. One part of this principle states that aversive stimulation, like neutral or positively valenced stimulation, can facilitate discrimination learning when the alternatives are similar, by providing an additional distinctive cue to one of the stimulus compounds.

Research with Humans

Does punishment have effects on human learning and problem solving parallel to those seen in the animal learning literature just reviewed? The answer seems to be at least a qualified yes. In one of the earliest studies of this type, Bunch (1928) found that subjects learning a stylus maze learned it in fewer trials when they were shocked for incorrect responses than when no shock was administered. In a study of human maze learning, Feldman (1961) found that shock-right was the superior condition when shock intensity was low, while shock-wrong was superior when shock intensity was high. Freeburne and Schneider (1955) found that for human subjects learning a temporal maze, shock-right, shock-wrong, and shock-both produced significantly better performance than no-shock, paralleling the Muenzinger and Fletcher (1936) study with rats.

Most studies in the human literature on punishment have, however, used milder forms of aversive stimulation, most commonly the words *wrong* for incorrect responses alone or in combination with *right* for correct responses. Buss, Weiner, and Buss (1954) had subjects learn that each of a group of 2-inch-high blocks were to be labeled *Vec*. They were told at first: "You don't know what a *Vec* is now, but it will become clear to you as we go. To begin with you may have to guess" (p. 433). To some subjects the experimenter said *right* after a Vec response and *wrong* after a not-Vec response (right-wrong). Other subjects heard *wrong* after a not-Vec response (wrong-nothing), and others heard *right* after a Vec response only (right-nothing). The right-wrong and wrong-nothing conditions produced performance that was significantly superior to the right-nothing condition in terms of the steepness of stimulus generalization obtained on a second series of blocks of different heights. Buss, Braden, Orgel, and Buss (1956) found that right-wrong and wrong-nothing also produced significantly faster learning than right-nothing and interpreted this finding to mean that "*Wrong* is a stronger negative reinforcer than *Right* is a positive reinforcer" (p. 295). A similar superiority of right-wrong and wrong-nothing to right-nothing was found with the Wisconsin Card Sorting Test (Buss & Buss, 1956). In a discrimination learning study with children, Brackbill and O'Hara (1958) found that a reward and punishment condition (giving a candy for a correct response and taking back a candy for an incorrect one) was superior to reward only.

Reading through study after study in which punishment is more effective than reward, and reward has little or no effect on behavior, almost makes one have doubts that reward is important at all. Perhaps the most impressive findings of this type were those of Levine, Leitenberg, and Richter (1964), to which they gave the title, "The Blank Trials Law: The Equivalence of Positive Reinforcement and Nonreinforcement." They studied a two-trials-per-problem learning set, modified double alternation, contingent discrimination, and a guessing problem. In each of these problems, a series of blank trials (nothing said) would be inserted following a long sequence of right-wrong trials. It was found that such a blank trial had the same minimal effect as an equivalent trial on which the experimenter said *right*. However, even a single *wrong* by the experimenter in the series of blank or right trials markedly affected the subject's subsequent pattern of responses. In discussing their findings, Levine *et al.* stated that considering the critical role played by "positive reinforcement" in most contemporary theories of learning, it was strange to find that reinforcement and the absence of reinforcement had the same (minimal) effect on changes in response probabilities.

However, this superiority of punishment to reward does not hold up under other experimental conditions. For example, all of the above studies demonstrating the superiority of punishment to reward in human learning used two-alternative tasks, in which, for example, wrong-nothing would logically carry no more information than right-nothing. Buchwald (1962) showed that in a task with *four* alternatives, the results were quite different. In the four-choice task, when the experimenter said *right* on a given trial, the subject was likely to increase repetition of that response on the next trial, whereas saying *wrong* had little effect on the amount of response repetition. In a two-alternative version of the task, however, saying *wrong* led to a decrease in the amount of response repetition, while saying *right* had little effect. As already noted in discussing Thorndike's original work in this area, in a multiple-choice task, punishment for one of the incorrect choices does not convey as much information as reward for the correct choice.

Another important factor concerns whether subjects are fully informed about the meaning of *blank*. Spence, Lair, and Goodstein (1963) showed that in a simple two-choice verbal discrimination task, when the subjects were informed about what *blank* meant, the differences between wrong-blank, right-blank, and a full information condition vanished. In other words, in the original Buss *et al.* (1954) study and others reviewed, wrong-nothing may have been better than right-nothing simply because the subjects interpreted *nothing* to mean that they were correct and responded accordingly, whereas in right-nothing they did *not* interpret *nothing* to mean that they were wrong.

If having correct information about the meaning of *blank* were the whole story, the research just reviewed might be seen as having ended in a cul de sac.

This is not the case. On problems of greater difficulty, wrong-blank or other forms of punishment seem to facilitate performance even if the subject is fully informed about what *blank* means. A key experiment is that of Spence (1966), using a Taffel-type task where the subjects had to construct sentences using either first-person or third-person personal pronouns. The reinforcement combinations used were right-blank, wrong-blank, and right-wrong. These were combined factorially with instructions of three levels of informativeness: no instructions about the reinforcers (as in "verbal conditioning" research), minimal instructions of the type used by Buss and most other researchers already discussed ("it will become clear to you as we go along when you have made up the right kind of sentence"); and full instructions (e.g., that in the right-blank condition, when the experimenter said nothing, it meant the sentence was incorrect). Although increasingly explicit instructions facilitated performance, wrong-blank was consistently superior to right-blank in its effects under all three instructional conditions in the relatively difficult task Perhaps Tolman, Hall, and Bretnall (1932) were right all along when they spoke of a law of emphasis in explaining the effects of punishment. Perhaps the discriminability principle elaborated by Fowler in his chapter in this volume can be extended to apply to human as well as animal subjects. Considerable further research is necessary if we are to find out.

Research with Punishment and Information Processing in Clinical Populations

It is the thesis of this chapter that though punishment has a potential for misuse, it may also be a valuable technique for the clinician. At this time, unfortunately, only a few isolated studies may be cited exemplifying the role of punishment as a facilitator of information processing in clinical populations. The studies there are do nevertheless support the view that this is a promising area of investigation in the future, particularly with children.

Paris and Cairns (1972) gave a two-choice discrimination task to educable mentally retarded children and found that, as one might expect from the research already reviewed, saying *wrong* after incorrect responses had little effect. Study of the way such children's teachers used evaluative comments in the classroom suggested that they made positive remarks frequently and indiscriminately, and that their few negative remarks were highly informative in that almost every one was contingent on some particular response of an individual child.

Hemry (1973) identified first-grade children as either reflective or impulsive in terms of their scores on Kagan's Matching Familiar Figures Test (MFFT). On a discrimination learning task, Hemry found that all children performed most poorly under reward conditions and better under punishment and punishment-plus-reward conditions. Nelson, Finch, and Hooke (1975) compared the effects of token reinforcement and response cost on children's performance on the MFFT. Interestingly, impulsives made fewer errors under the response-cost procedure, whereas reflectives made fewer errors in the reinforcement condition. Firestone and Douglas (1975) compared the effects of reward ("That's good"), punishment ("That's not good"), and reward plus punishment on hyperactive and normal children's performance on a delayed-reaction-time task. Reward, but not punishment, led to a significant increase in hyperactive children's "impulsive" responses, such as intertrial responses and false starts. The study by Brent and Routh (1978) showing response cost to be more effective than reward with reading disabled children has already been described.

CONCLUSION

The traditional attitudes of psychologists against punishment as a child-rearing technique may be justified, at least in terms of our present level of knowledge. However, we need to know much more than we now do about the effects and the side effects of various forms of punishment and other forms of aversive stimulation. In the meantime, clinical use of at least the milder forms of punishment seems to be either quite worthwhile or at least worthy of further study in suppressing such unwanted behavior as self-injurious responses, ruminative vomiting, severe aggressive behaviors among the institutionalized retarded, bed-wetting, alcoholism, and deviant sexual behavior. Punishment effects on stuttering have been clearly demonstrated but have so far not been shown to have utility for treatment purposes. Thanks to the work of psychologists such as Professor Wischner and his colleagues, some of the uses of aversive stimulation in facilitating information, especially on difficult tasks, are well established in the animal behavior laboratory. Similarly, the facilitative effects of punishment are well-known phenomena in human experimental psychology. The clinical uses of aversive stimulation as an aid to information processing are thus an inviting area for future research.

ACKNOWLEDGMENTS

The authors wish to thank Sharon Garber, John F. Knutson, Gerald Siegel, and especially Harry Fowler for their helpful comments on an earlier version of this chapter.

REFERENCES

Akerley, M. S. Reactions to "Employing electric shock with autistic children." *Journal of Autism and Childhood Schizophrenia*, 1976, *6*, 289.
Altman, K., Haavik, S., & Cook, J. W. Punishment of self-injurious behavior in natural settings using contingent aromatic ammonia. *Behaviour Research and Therapy*, 1978, *16*, 85–96.

Anderson, L., Dancis, J., & Alpert, M. Behavioral contingencies and self-mutilation in Lesch-Nyhan disease. *Journal of Consulting and Clinical Psychology*, 1978, *46*, 529–536.

Azrin, H. N. Punishment of elicited aggression. *Journal of the Experimental Analysis of Behavior*, 1970, *14*, 7–10.

Azrin, N. H., & Foxx, R. M. A rapid method of toilet training the institutionalized retarded. *Journal of Applied Behavior Analysis*, 1971, *4*, 89–99.

Azrin, N. H., & Thienes, P. M. Rapid elimination of enuresis by intensive learning without a conditioning apparatus. *Behavior Therapy*. 1978, *9*, 342–354.

Azrin, N. H., Kaplan, S. J., & Foxx, R. M. Autism reversal: Eliminating stereotyped self-stimulation of retarded individuals. *American Journal of Mental Deficiency*, 1973, *78*, 241–248.

Azrin, N. H., Sneed, T. J., & Foxx, R. M. Dry-bed training: Rapid elimination of childhood enuresis. *Behaviour Research and Therapy*, 1974, *12*, 147–156.

Baer, D. M. Laboratory control of thumbsucking with withdrawal and representation of reinforcement. *Journal of the Experimental Analysis of Behavior*, 1962, *5*, 525–528.

Barlow, D. H., Leitenberg, H., & Agras, W. S. Experimental control of sexual deviation through manipulation of the noxious scene in covert sensitization. *Journal of Abnormal Psychology*, 1969, *74*, 596–601.

Barton, E. S., Guess, D., Garcia E., & Baer, D. M. Improvement in retardates' meal time behaviors using multiple baseline techniques. *Journal of Applied Behavior Analaysis*, 1970, *3*, 77–84.

Berecz, J. Modification of smoking behavior through self-administered punishment of imagined behavior: A new approach to aversion therapy. *Journal of Consulting and Clinical Psychology*, 1972, *38*, 244–250.

Blakemore, C. B., Thorpe, J. G., Barker, J. C., Conway, C. G., & Lavin, N. I. The application of faradic aversion conditioning in a case of transvestism. *Behaviour Research and Therapy*, 1963, *1*, 29–34.

Bloodstein, O. *A handbook on stuttering* (rev. ed.). Chicago: National Easter Seal Society, 1975

Brackbill, Y., & O'Hara, J. The relative effectiveness of reward and punishment for discrimination learning in children. *Journal of Comparative and Physiological Psychology*, 1958, *51*, 747–751.

Breger, L. Comments on "Building social behavior in autistic children by use of electric shock." *Journal of Experimental Research in Personality*, 1965, *1*, 110–113.

Brent, D. E., & Routh, D. K. Response cost and impulsive word recognition errors in reading-disabled children. *Journal of Abnormal Child Psychology*, 1978, *6*, 211–219.

Buchwald, A. M. Variations in the apparent effects of "Right" and "Wrong" on subsequent behavior. *Journal of Verbal Learning and Verbal Behavior*, 1962, *1*, 71–78.

Bunch, M. E. The effect of electric shock as punishment for errors in human maze-learning. *Journal of Comparative Psychology*, 1928, *8*, 343–359.

Buss, A. H., & Buss, E. H. The effect of verbal reinforcement combinations on conceptual learning. *Journal of Experimental Psychology*, 1956, *52*, 283–287.

Buss, A. H., Weiner, M., & Buss, E. Stimulus generalization as a function of verbal reinforcement combinations. *Journal of Experimental Psychology*, 1954, *48*, 433–436.

Buss, A. H., Braden, W., Orgel, A., & Buss, E. H. Acquisition and extinction with different verbal reinforcement combinations. *Journal of Experimental Psychology*, 1956, *52*, 288–295.

Caddy, G. R., & Lovibond, S. H. Self regulation and discriminated aversive conditioning in the modification of alcoholics' drinking behavior. *Behavior Therapy*, 1976, *7*, 223–230.

Callahan, E. J., & Leitenberg, H. Aversion therapy for sexual deviation: Contingent shock and covert sensitization. *Journal of Abnormal Psychology*, 1973, *81*, 60–73.

Carlin, A. S., & Armstrong, H. E. Aversive conditioning: Learning or dissonance reduction? *Journal of Consulting and Clinical Psychology*, 1968, *32*, 674–678.

Church, R. M. The varied effects of punishment on behavior. *Psychological Review*, 1963, *70*, 369–402.

Collins, R. W. Importance of the bladder-cue buzzer contingency in the conditioning treatment for enuresis. *Journal of Abnormal Psychology*, 1973, *82*, 299–308.

Conway, J. B. Behavioral self-control of smoking through aversive conditioning and self-management. *Journal of Consulting and Clinical Psychology*, 1977, *45*, 348–357.

Cook, J. W., Altman, K., Shaw, J., & Blaylock, M. Use of contingent lemon juice to eliminate public masturbation by a severely retarded boy. *Behaviour Research and Therapy*, 1978, *16*, 131–134.

Cunningham, C. E., & Linscheid, T. R. Elimination of chronic infant ruminating by electric shock. *Behavior Therapy*, 1976, *7*, 231–234.

De Palma, D. J. Effects of social class, moral orientation, and severity of punishment on boys' moral responses to transgression and generosity. *Developmental Psychology*, 1974, *10*, 890–900.

Doleys, D. M. Behavioral treatments for nocturnal enuresis in children: A review of the recent literature. *Psychological Bulletin*, 1977, *84*, 30–54.

Elliott, C. H., & Denney, D. R. Weight control through covert sensitization and false feedback. *Journal of Consulting and Clinical Psychology*, 1975, *43*, 842–850.

Epstein, L. H., Doke, L. A., Sajwaj, T. E., Sorrell, S., & Rimmer, B. Generality and side effects of overcorrection. *Journal of Applied Behavior Analysis*, 1974, *7*, 385–390.

Errickson, E. A., Wyne, M. D., & Routh, D. K. A response-cost procedure for reduction of impulsive behavior of academically handicapped children. *Journal of Abnormal Child Psychology*, 1973, *1*, 350–357.

Feldman, M. P. Aversion therapy for sexual deviations: A critical review. *Psychological Bulletin*, 1966, *65*, 65–79.

Feldman, M. P., & MacCulloch, M. J. A systematic approach to the treatment of homosexuality by conditioned aversion: Preliminary report. *American Journal of Psychiatry*, 1964, *121*, 167–172.

Feldman, S. M. Differential effects of shock in human maze learning. *Journal of Experimental Psychology*, 1961, *62*, 171–178.

Firestone, P., & Douglas, V. The effects of reward and punishment on reaction times and automatic activity in hyperactive and normal children. *Journal of Abnormal Child Psychology*, 1973, *3*, 201–216.

Flanagan, B., Goldiamond, I., & Azrin, N. H. Operant stuttering: The control of stuttering behavior through response-contingent consequences. *Journal of the Experimental Analysis of Behavior*, 1958, *1*, 173–177.

Follick, M. J., & Knutson, J. F. Punishment of irritable aggression. *Aggressive Behavior*, 1978, *4*, 1–17.

Foreyt, J. P., & Hagen, R. L. Covert sensitization: Conditioning or suggestion. *Journal of Abnormal Psychology*, 1973, *82*, 17–23.

Fowler, H., & Wischner, G. J. Discrimination performance as affected by problem difficulty and shock for either the correct or incorrect response. *Journal of Experimental Psychology*, 1965, *69*, 413–418.

Fowler, H., Spelt, P. F., & Wischner, G. J. Discrimination performance as affected by training procedure, problem difficulty, and shock for the correct response. *Journal of Experimental Psychology*, 1967, *75*, 432–436.

Fowler, H., Fago, G. C., & Wischner, G. J. Shock-right facilitation in an easy, noncorrection problem as effected by delay of reward. *Learning and Motivation*, 1971, *2*, 235–245.

Foxx, R. M., & Azrin, N. H. Restitution: A method of eliminating aggressive-destructive behavior or retarded and brain-damaged patients. *Behaviour Research and Therapy*, 1972, *10*, 15–27.

Foxx, R. M., & Azrin, N. H. The elimination of autistic self-stimulatory behavior by overcorrection. *Journal of Applied Behavior Analysis*, 1973, *6*, 1–4.

Foxx, R. M., & Shapiro, S. T. The timeout ribbon: A nonexlusionary timeout procedure. *Journal of Applied Behavior Analysis*, 1978, *11*, 125–136.

Freeburne, C. M., & Schneider, M. Shock for right and wrong responses during learning and extinction in human subjects. *Journal of Experimental Psychology*, 1955, *49*, 181–186.

Freud, S. The cases of "Little Hans" and the "Rat Man." In *Standard edition of the complete psychological works of Sigmund Freud*, Vol. 10. London: Hogarth Press, 1953–1974. (Originally published, 1909.)

Galbraith, D., Byrick, R., & Rutledge, J. T. An aversive conditioning approach to the inhibition of chronic vomiting. *Canadian Psychiatric Association Journal*, 1970, *15*, 311–313.

Garb, J. L., & Stunkard, A. J. Taste aversions in man. *American Journal of Psychiatry*, 1974, *131*, 1204–1207.

Garcia, J., MacGowan, B. K., Ervin, F. R., & Koelling, R. A. Cues: Their relative effectiveness as a function of the reinforcer. *Science*, 1968, *160*, 794–795.

Garmezy, N. Stimulus differentiation by schizophrenic and normal subjects under conditions of reward and punishment. *Journal of Personality*, 1952, *20*, 253–276.

Garmezy, N. The prediction of performance in schizophrenia. In P. H. Hoch & J. Zubin (Eds.), *Psychopathology of schizophrenia*. New York: Grune & Stratton, 1966.

Hald, J., & Jacobsen, E. A drug sensitizing the organism to ethyl alcohol. *Lancet*, 1948, *255*, 1001–1004.

Haroldson, S. K., Martin, R. R., & Starr, C. D. Time-out as a punishment for stuttering. *Journal of Speech and Hearing Research*, 1968, *11*, 560–566.

Harris, S. L., & Ersner-Hershfield, R. Behavioral suppression of seriously disruptive behavior in psychotic and retarded patients: A review of punishment and its alternatives. *Psychological Bulletin*, 1978, *85*, 1352–1375.

Harris, S. L., & Romanczyk, R. C. Treating self-injurious behavior of a retarded child by overcorrection. *Behavior Therapy*, 1976, *7*, 235–239.

Hart, R. J. Crime and punishment in the army. *Journal of Personality and Social Psychology*, 1978, *36*, 1456–1471.

Helfer, R. E., & Kempe, C. H. (Eds.). *The battered child* (2nd ed.). Chicago: University of Chicago Press, 1974.

Hemry, F. P. Effect of reinforcement conditions on a discrimination learning task for impulsive versus reflective children. *Child Development*, 1973, *44*, 657–660.

Hoffman, M. Conscience, personality, and socialization. *Human Development*, 1970, *13*, 90–126.

Hoffman, M. L. Moral internalization, parental power, and the nature of parent-child interaction. *Developmental Psychology*, 1975, *11*, 228–239.

Hoge, M. A., & Stocking, R. J. A note on the relative value of reward and punishment as motives. *Journal of Animal Behavior*, 1912, *2*, 43–50.

Janda, L. H., & Rimm, D. C. Covert sensitization in the treatment of obesity. *Journal of Abnormal Psychology*, 1972, *80*, 37–42.

Johnson, W. The Indians have no word for it: I. Stuttering in children. *Quarterly Journal of Speech*, 1944, *30*, 330–337.

Kagan, J. Reflection-impulsivity and reading ability in primary grade children. *Child Development*, 1965, *36*, 609–628.

Kagan, J. Reflection-impulsivity: The generality and dynamics of conceptual tempo. *Journal of Abnormal Psychology*, 1966, *71*, 17–24.

Kagan, J., Rosman, B. L., Day, D., Albert, J., & Phillips, W. Information processing in the child: Significance of analytic and reflective attitudes. *Psychological Monographs*, 1964, *78* (Whole No. 578).

Koegel, R. L., Firestone, P. B., Kramme, K. W., & Dunlap, G. Increasing spontaneous play by suppressing self-stimulation in autistic children. *Journal of Applied Behavior Analysis*, 1974, *7*, 521–528.

Kohlenberg, R. J. The punishment of persistent vomiting: A case study. *Journal of Applied Behavior Analysis*, 1970, *3*, 241–245.

Lamon, S., Wilson, G. T., & Leaf, R. C. Human classical aversion conditioning: Nausea versus electric shock in the reduction of target beverage consumption. *Behavior Research and Therapy*, 1977, *15*, 313–320.

Lang, P. J., & Melamed, B. G. Case Report: Avoidance conditioning therapy of an infant with chronic ruminative vomiting. *Journal of Abnormal Psychology*, 1969, *74*, 139–142.

Lefkowitz, M. M., Huesmann, L. R., & Eron, L. D. Parental punishment: A longitudinal analysis of effects. *Archives of General Psychiatry*, 1978, *35*, 186–191.

Leitenberg, H. Is time-out from positive reinforcement an aversive event? *Psychological Bulletin*, 1965, *64*, 428–441.

Levine, M., Leitenberg, H., & Richter, M. The blank trials law: The equivalence of positive reinforcement and nonreinforcement. *Psychological Review*, 1964, *71*, 94–103.

Linscheid, T. R., & Cunningham, C. E. A controlled demonstration of the effectiveness of electric shock in the elimination of chronic rumination. *Journal of Applied Behavior Analysis*, 1977, *10*, 500.

Little, L. M., & Curran, J. P. Covert sensitization: A clinical procedure in need of some explanations. *Psychological Bulletin*, 1978, *85*, 513–531.

Lovaas, O. I., Schaeffer, B., & Simmons, J. Q. Building social behavior in autistic children by use of electric shock. *Journal of Experimental Research in Personality*, 1965, *1*, 99–109.

Lovibond, S. H., & Caddy, G. Discriminated aversive control in the moderation of alcoholics' drinking behavior. *Behavior Therapy*, 1970, *1*, 437–444.

Luckey, R. E., Watson, C. M., & Musick, J. K. Aversive conditioning as a means of inhibiting vomiting and rumination. *American Journal of Mental Deficiency*, 1968, *73*, 139–142.

Lutzker, J. R. Reducing self-injurious behavior by facial screening. *American Journal of Mental Deficiency*. 1978, *82*, 510–513.

Martin, R., & Haroldson, S. K. Effects of five experimental treatments on stuttering. *Journal of Speech and Hearing Research*, 1979, *22*, 132–146.

Martin, R., & Siegel, G. M. The effects of response contingent shock on stuttering. *Journal of Speech and Hearing Research*, 1966, *9*, 340–352. (a)

Martin, R., & Siegel, G. M. The effects of simultaneously punishing stuttering and rewarding fluency. *Journal of Speech and Hearing Research*, 1966, *9*, 466–475. (b)

Martin, R. R., Kuhl, P., & Haroldson, S. An experimental treatment with two preschool stuttering children. *Journal of Speech and Hearing Research*, 1972, *15*, 743–752.

Matson, J. L., Ollendick, T. H., & Martin, J. E. Overcorrection revisited: A long-term follow-up. *Journal of Behavior Therapy and Experimental Psychiatry*, 1979, *10*, 11–13.

Measel, C. J., & Alfieri, P. A. Treatment of self-injurious behavior by a combination of reinforcement for incompatible behavior and overcorrection. *American Journal of Mental Deficiency*, 1976, *81*, 147–153.

Miller, W. R. Behavioral treatment of problem drinkers: A comparative outcome study of three controlled drinking therapies. *Journal of Consulting and Clinical Psychology*, 1978, *46*, 74–86.

Minton, C., Kagan, J., & Levine, J. A. Maternal control and obedience in the two-year-old. *Child Development*, 1971, *42*, 1873–1894.

Morris, E. K., & Redd, W. H. Children's performance and social preference for positive, negative, and mixed adult-child interactions. *Child Development*, 1975, *46*, 525–531.

Mowrer, O. H., & Mowrer, W. M. Enuresis: A method for its study and treatment. *American Journal of Orthopsychiatry*, 1938, *8*, 436–459.

Muenzinger, K. F. Motivation in learning: I. Electric shock for correct resonse in the visual discrimination habit. *Journal of Comparative and Physiological Psychology*, 1934, *17*, 267–277.

Muenzinger, K. F., & Fletcher, F. M. Motivation in learning: VI. Escape from electric shock compared with hunger-food tension in the visual discrimination habit. *Journal of Comparative and Physiological Psychology*, 1936, *22*, 79–91.

Muenzinger, K. F., & Powloski, R. F. Motivation in learning: X. Comparison of electric shock for correct turns in a corrective and non-corrective situation. *Journal of Experimental Psychology*, 1951, *42*, 118–124.

Muenzinger, K. F., & Wood, A. Motivation in learning: IV. The function of punishment as determined by its temporal relation to the act of choice in the visual discrimination habit. *Journal of Comparative and Physiological Psychology*, 1935, *20*, 95–106.

Nelson, W. M., III, Finch, A. J., & Hooke, J. F. Effects of reinforcement and response-cost on cognitive style in emotionally disturbed boys. *Journal of Abnormal Psychology*, 1975, *84*, 426–428.

Paris, S. G., & Cairns, R. B. An experimental and ethological analysis of social reinforcement with retarded children. *Child Development*, 1972, *43*, 717–729.

Parke, R. D., & Collmer, C. W. Child abuse: An interdisciplinary analysis. In E. M. Hetherington (Ed.), *Review of child development research;* Vol. 5. Chicago: University of Chicago Press, 1975.

Peterson, R. A., Wright, R. L. D., & Hanlon, C. C. The effects of extending the CS–US interval on the effectiveness of the conditioning treatment for nocturnal enuresis. *Behaviour Research and Therapy*, 1969, *7*, 351–357.

Porter, H. Studies in the psychology of stuttering: XIV. Stuttering phenomena in relation to size and personnel of audience. *Journal of Speech Disorders*, 1939, *4*, 323–333.

Roberts, P., Iwata, B. A., McSween, T. E., & Desmond, E. F., Jr. An analysis of overcorrection movements. *American Journal of Mental Deficiency*, 1979, *83*, 588–594.

Sajwaj, T., Libet, J., & Agras, S. Lemon-juice therapy: The control of life-threatening rumination in a six-month old infant. *Journal of Applied Behavior Analysis*, 1974, *7*, 557–563.

Shames, G. H., & Sherrick, C. E., Jr. A discussion of nonfluency and stuttering as operant behavior. *Journal of Speech and Hearing Disorders*, 1963, *28*, 2–18.

Siegel, G. M. Punishment, stuttering, and disfluency. *Journal of Speech and Hearing Research*, 1970, *13*, 677–714.

Siegel, G. M., & Martin, R. R. Verbal punishment of disfluencies in normal speakers. *Journal of Speech and Hearing Research*, 1965, *8*, 245–251.

Siegel, G. M., & Martin, R. R. Punishment of disfluencies in normal speakers. *Journal of Speech and Hearing Research*, 1966, *9*, 208–218.

Siegel, G. M., Lenske, J., & Broen, P. Suppression of normal speech disfluencies through response cost. *Journal of Applied Behavior Analysis*, 1969, *2*, 256–276.

Skinner, B. F. *The behavior of organims.* New York: Appleton, 1938.

Skinner, B. F. *Science and human behavior.* New York: Macmillan, 1953.

Solomon, R. L. Punishment. *American Psychologist*, 1964, *19*, 239–253.

Solomon, R. L., Kamin, L. J., & Wynne, L. C. Traumatic avoidance learning: The outcomes of several extinction procedures with dogs. *Journal of Abnormal and Social Psychology*, 1953, *48*, 291–320.

Spelt, P. F., & Fowler, H. Shock-right discrimination training: Effect of correction training with an enforced delay following an incorrect choice. *Journal of Experimental Psychology*, 1969, *79*, 504–508.

Spence, J. T. Effects of verbal reinforcement combination and instructional condition on the performance of a problem-solving task. *Journal of Personality and Social Psychology*, 1966, *3*, 163–170.

Spence, J. T., Lair, C. V., & Goodstein, L. D. Effects of different feedback conditions on verbal discrimination learning in schizophrenic and non-psychiatric subjects. *Journal of Verbal Learning and Verbal Behavior*, 1963, *2*, 339–345.

Spinetta, J. J., & Rigler, D. The child-abusing parent: A psychological review. *Psychological Bulletin*, 1972, 77, 296–304.

Tanner, B. A., & Zeiler, M. Punishment of self-injurious behavior using aromatic ammonia as the aversive stimulus. *Journal of Applied Behavior Analysis*, 1975, 8, 53–57.

Tate, B. G., & Baroff, G. A. Aversive control of self-injurious behavior in a psychotic boy. *Behaviour Research and Therapy*, 1966, 4, 281–287.

Thimann, J. Conditioned reflex as treatment for abnormal drinking: Principle, technic and success. *New England Journal of Medicine*, 1943, 228, 333–335.

Thorndike, E. L. *Animal intelligence*. New York: Macmillan, 1911.

Thorndike, E. L. *The fundamentals of learning*. New York: Teachers College, Columbia University, 1932.

Thorndike, E. L. *Selected writings from a connectionist's psychology*. New York: Appleton-Century-Crofts, 1949.

Toister, R. P., Condron, C. J., Worley, L., & Arthur, D. Faradic therapy of chronic vomiting in infancy: A case study. *Journal of Behavior Therapy and Experimental Psychiatry*, 1975, 6, 55–59.

Tolman, E. C., Hall, C. S., & Bretnall, E. P. A disproof of the law of effect and a substitution of the laws of emphasis, motivation, and disruption. *Journal of Experimental Psychology*, 1932, 15, 601–614.

Van Dyke, W. K., & Routh, D. K. Effects of censure on schizophrenic reaction time: Critique and reformulation of the Garmezy censure-deficit model. *Journal of Abnormal Psychology*, 1973, 82, 200–206.

Van Riper, C. The effect of personality upon frequency of stuttering spasms. *Journal of Genetic Psychology*, 1937, 50, 193–195.

Voegtlin, W. L., & Broz, W. R. The conditioned reflex treatment of chronic alcoholism: X. Analysis of 3125 admissions. *Annals of Internal Medicine*, 1949, 30, 580–597.

Warden, C. J., & Aylesworth, M. The relative value of reward and punishment in the formation of a visual discrimination habit in the white rat. *Journal of Comparative Psychology*, 1927, 7, 117–127.

Webster, D. R., & Azrin, N. H. Required relaxation: A method of inhibiting agitative disruptive behavior of retardates. *Behaviour Research and Therapy*, 1973, 11, 67–78.

White, G. D., Nielsen, G., & Johnson, S. M. Timeout duration and the suppression of deviant behavior in children. *Journal of Applied Behavior Analysis*, 1972, 5, 111–120.

Wilson, A. Disulfram implantation in alcoholism treatment: A review. *Journal of Studies on Alcohol*, 1975, 36, 555–565.

Wilson, A., Davidson, W. J., & White, J. Disulfram implantation: Placebo, psychological deterrent, and pharmacological deterrent effects. *British Journal of Psychiatry*, 1976, 129, 277–280.

Wilson, A., Davidson, W. J., Blanchard, R., & White, J. Disulfram implantation: A placebo-controlled trial with two-year follow-up. *Journal of Studies on Alcohol*, 1978, 39, 809–819.

Wischner, G. J. The effect of punishment on discrimination learning in a non-correction situation. *Journal of Experimental Psychology*, 1947, 37, 271–284.

Wischner, G. J. Anxiety-reduction as reinforcement in maladaptive behavior: Evidence in stutterers' representations of the moment of difficulty. *Journal of Abnormal and Social Psychology*, 1952, 47, 566–571. (a)

Wischner, G. J. An experimental approach to expectancy and anxiety in stuttering behavior. *Journal of Speech and Hearing Disorders*, 1952, 17, 139–152. (b)

Wischner, G. J., Fowler, H., & Kushnick, S. A. Effect of strength of punishment for "correct" or "incorrect" responses on visual discrimination performance. *Journal of Experimental Psychology*, 1963, 65, 131–138.

Wright, L. Aversive conditioning of self induced seizures. *Behavior Therapy*, 1973, 4, 712–713.

Yerkes, R. M., & Dodson, J. D. The relation of strength of stimulus to rapidity of habit formation. *Journal of Comparative Neurology and Psychology*, 1908, *18*, 459–482.

8 Intellectual Progeny of Seashore and Spence

Iowa Psychologists

DONALD K. ROUTH

INTRODUCTION

This chapter is a brief account of some individuals who were part of a stream of nearly 800 Ph.D. graduates of the Department of Psychology and the Institute of Child Behavior and Development (the former Child Welfare Research Station) of the University of Iowa, from 1897 to the present. Such an account is appropriate for a *Festschrift* volume such as the present one in that all of the contributors to the book have direct or indirect Iowa connections. As already noted, George Wischner, whose approaching retirement was the occasion for planning this book, was an Iowa Ph.D. under Wendell Johnson and Kenneth W. Spence. Wischner is also an academic descendent of Carl E. Seashore via Johnson and Lee Edward Travis.

The University of Iowa campus is located in Iowa City, in the east-central part of the state. It is just south of Interstate Highway 80, the road that connects New York, Chicago, and San Francisco. Iowa Avenue, the broadest street in town, was originally to have connected Old Capitol (the former state capitol building, which sits on a bluff overlooking the Iowa River) to a governor's mansion (which was never built). Here, on this street, at the eastern end of the university campus, stands a large five-story building named Spence Laboratories of Psychology. Connected to Spence Laboratories is an enormous, partly late nineteenth-century brick structure named Seashore Hall. Across the Iowa River

DONALD K. ROUTH ● Department of Psychology, University of Iowa, Iowa City, Iowa 52242.

on the west (medical) campus are the Wendell Johnson Speech and Hearing Center and, in a new wing of the present University Hospital, the Arthur L. Benton Laboratory of Neuropsychology.

THE GUTTMAN SCALE OF EMINENCE

The 770 Iowa psychology Ph.D.'s who obtained their degrees from 1903 through 1978 formed the basis of a quantitative study of "Correlates and Non-Correlates of Eminence in Psychology" (Routh, 1980). In this study, it was possible to define a Guttman Scale of Eminence in Psychology consisting of the following four items (in order of decreasing frequency of attainment): the presidency of the American Psychological Association, membership in the National Academy of Sciences, receipt of an honorary doctoral degree, and receipt of an honor from some scientific or professional organization. For example, in terms of this empirically derived scale, the most eminent Iowa graduate in psychology was found to be Walter R. Miles, a 1913 Ph.D. under Carl Seashore. Miles was president of the APA in 1932, was elected to membership in the National Academy of Sciences in 1933, and received an honorary Sc.D. degree from Earlham College in 1952, and among his honors were the Warren Medal of the Society of Experimental Psychologists in 1949 and the gold medal of the American Psychological Foundation in 1962. Miles was particularly interested in sensory and perceptual functioning: his Ph.D. topic was "Accuracy of the Voice in Simple Pitch Singing" and his best-known research formed the basis for the development of the red dark-adaptation goggles used by World War II pilots who had to be ready for night flying at a moment's notice. Among Miles's academic positions were professorships at Stanford and Yale. He was also at one time president of the Psychological Corporation.

Multiple-regression analysis identified the following nine variables as the most important correlates of eminence as measured by the Guttman scale: the presidency of some scientific or professional organization (other than the APA), the number of citations in the current *Social Science Citation Index*, a tenured faculty position in a major university, having published a book, having held a postdoctoral fellowship, membership in a government review group, the number of years since the Ph.D. was obtained, being a Fellow of the APA, and being the president of a company. Interestingly, among the variables that were *not* found to be correlates of eminence in this sample were the sex of the individual and the area of psychology in which the Ph.D. was received (general, experimental, clinical, or child). In other words, although women and men, and clinical and experimental psychologists, for example, differed significantly on many short-term criteria, such as publications and type of position taken, they did not differ on the long-term criteria, such as eminence or citations of their research.

The data, both for the above study and for much of the present chapter, were obtained from APA *Yearbooks* and *Directories*, from *American Men and Women of Science*, and from the directories of other scientific and professional organizations, such as the American Speech and Hearing Association (quite a number of Iowa psychology Ph.D.'s, especially from the 1920s and 1930s went on to become associated with that field). Cumulated *Psychological Index* and *Psychological Abstracts* volumes were examined, as well as selected articles and books written by the graduates. Information on the offices held in and the honors received from the APA and its divisions or regional or state affiliated organizations was obtained from APA *Yearbooks* and from issues of the *American Psychologist*. Citation counts were obtained from the 1978 editions of the *Social Science Citation Index* (SSCI), the *Science Citation Index* (SCI), and the *Arts and Humanities Citation Index* (AHCI).

OVERALL DESCRIPTIVE INFORMATION

Some of the descriptive data on the sample of 770 Iowa Ph.D.'s in psychology are presented here to provide an overview of the entire historical period under discussion. Then, the graduates reaching some level of eminence are described in sequence after the name of the faculty member who directed the Ph.D. The number of Ph.D.'s per year from the department of psychology and the institute averaged about 10, with a peak of 30 in 1951. The sample consisted of 594 men and 176 women (a 77:23 ratio), with a higher proportion of women among the graduates of the Institute for Child Behavior and Development. The mentors who supervised the most dissertations were Kenneth W. Spence, 75; Carl E. Seashore, 52; Arthur L. Benton, 46; Lee Edward Travis, 35; Don Lewis, 31; and I. E. Farber, 30. The mentor with the highest success rate in terms of eminence among Ph.D.'s supervised was Kurt Lewin, with 33%. In terms of the areas in which the Ph.D. was obtained, 239 were in clinical psychology, 174 general or unspecified, 150 in child or developmental, and 119 experimental psychology. There were 88 graduates in other areas, including social psychology, physiological psychology, counseling, the psychology of music, and the psychology of speech. Of the graduates, 73% published their dissertations, and 66% had publications beyond the dissertation. The mean number of citations in the SSCI was 8.16, the mean number in the SCI was 4.62, and the mean number in the AHCI .50. The individual with the largest number of citations in the SSCI was Albert Bandura (a 1952 Ph.D. under Benton); the one with the largest number of SCI citations was Herbert H. Jasper (a 1931 Ph.D. under Travis).

Twenty-two of the graduates (2.9%) had gone on to become editors of scholarly journals. Twenty-seven (3.5%) had been members of government review groups. For those who went into academic positions, the modal rank attained was full professor. Seventy-one of the graduates (9.2%) had held tenured positions in a university among the top 10 in the country as rated by the American Council on Education in 1957, 1964, or 1969. Seventy-two of the graduates (9.4%) had chaired academic departments. Twenty-seven (3.5%) had held positions as dean, vice-president, or president of a university. The university presidents among the graduates included George D. Stoddard (a 1925 Ph.D. under Giles Ruch), later Chancellor of the State University of New York, then President of the University of Illinois, and then Chancellor of New York University; and Glenn Terrell (a 1952 Ph.D. under Boyd R. McCandless and Charles Spiker), now President of Washington State University.

Of the graduates, 80% were APA members, and 27% were Fellows of the APA. Four were elected to membership in the National Academy of Sciences. Besides Walter Miles, there were Donald B. Lindsley (a 1932 Ph.D. under Lee Edward Travis), Leon Festinger (a 1942 Ph.D. under Kurt Lewin), and Benton J. Underwood (a 1942 Ph.D. under John A. McGeoch and Kenneth W. Spence).

Seventy-two of the graduates (9.4%) had been president of some scientific or professional organization. Thirty-five graduates (4.5%) had received an honor from a professional or scientific organization. Eleven (1.4%) had received honorary degrees.

Of the graduates, 32% had been licensed or certified as psychologists, and 14% were diplomates of the American Board of Professional Psychology, most commonly in clinical or industrial psychology. Also, 14% had been in private practice; 6.5% had been members of consulting firms; and 23 graduates (3%) had been president or had chaired the board of directors of a company.

Early History of the Iowa Psychology Department

Until 1927, when a separate department of psychology was established, instruction in psychology at the University of Iowa took place under the aegis of the department of philosophy. The first scientific instruction in psychology at the university was established in about 1888 by Professor G. T. W. Patrick, who at that time purchased some instruments from Germany. In 1895, J. Allen Gilbert came from Yale to Iowa as an assistant professor in order to teach the first formal laboratory course in psychology, in a building at 14 North Clinton Street. In 1897, Carl E. Seashore came from Yale to the University of Iowa as an assistant professor of psychology, replacing Gilbert. In 1901, a new psychological laboratory was completed and occupied in the Hall of Liberal Arts (the present Schaeffer Hall). In 1902, Seashore became a full professor of philosophy and psychology. It was in 1903 that Mabel Clare Williams (later Kemmerer) obtained the first Iowa Ph.D. in psychology, under Seashore's direction. This degree was also the second Ph.D. granted by the university. Dr. Williams continued to be associated with the psychology department as a faculty member, ultimately reaching the rank of associate professor at Iowa before moving to Mississippi. She was an active researcher and later published a popular book, *Some Psychology*, which went into a second edition. Like other members of her generation, she defined psychology as "the scientific study of mental life."

In 1905, Carl Seashore was made the head of the department and in 1908 began his many years of service as dean of the graduate college. Interestingly, he did not relinquish his position as department head when he became dean, and he continued to be actively involved in research and in research supervision in addition to his administrative duties. Seashore retired from the university in 1936, at age 70, but was then called back to serve as acting dean of the graduate college again during the wartime years 1942–1946. When the college of medicine and its hospital moved across the Iowa River to the west side of the campus, Seashore was responsible for securing the use of the building he named East Hall (now Seashore Hall) for the use of the psychology department, and this new psychological laboratory was dedicated in 1930. Seashore achieved the highest score on the eminence scale devised by Routh (1980), since he was elected president of the APA in 1911; was elected to membership in the National Academy of Sciences in 1922 (the first person in any discipline at the University of Iowa to be so honored); received a number of honorary doctorates, including one from Yale; and was the recipient of numerous awards.

INFORMATION ON INDIVIDUAL EMINENT GRADUATES

Seashore's Students

Nine of Seashore's Ph.D. students achieved some level of eminence as defined by the Guttman scale. The first of these was Daniel Starch, a 1906 Ph.D. whose dissertation concerned "Perimetry of the Localization of Sound." Starch taught at the University of Wisconsin and then at Harvard Business School but left academic life to found his own firm, Daniel Starch and Staff. He developed and applied methods of evaluating the impact of magazine advertising on readers, was an early president of the American Marketing Association, and won its Paul Converse Award in 1951. He received an honorary Sc.D. from Morningside College in 1949. After his death in 1979, it was learned that he had left money in his will to establish an endowed professorship at the University of Iowa.

Walter Miles has already been discussed.

Cordia C. Bunch was a 1920 Ph.D. under Seashore. His dissertation topic was "Measurement of Acuity of Hearing throughout the Tonal Range." He became the first psychologist in the otology department of the University of Iowa; was later professor of applied physics of otology at Washington University, St.

Louis; and was finally appointed research professor in the education of the deaf at Northwestern University. He did much to develop the audiometer for use in evaluating hearing loss and was honored by a special resolution of the American Speech and Hearing Association in 1942. His book, *Clinical Audiometry,* was published posthumously in 1943.

Donald A. Laird was a 1923 Ph.D. under Seashore. His dissertation consisted of "Studies Relating to the Problem of Binocular Summation." He taught at the University of Iowa, the University of Wyoming, and Colgate University, where he was head of the psychology department for 15 years. An American Board of Professional Psychology (ABPP) diplomate in industrial psychology, he was director of the Ayer Foundation for Consumer Analysis from 1938 to 1940. After 1940 he moved back to Dubuque, Iowa, and was self-employed writing psychology books, of which he wrote quite a large number. He received an honorary D.Sc. from the University of Dubuque.

Lee Edward Travis received his Ph.D. in 1924 under Seashore, in clinical psychology; his was the second Ph.D. so identified in the department (the first one having been granted in 1923). His dissertation was entitled "Test for Distinguishing between Schizophrenoses and Psychoneuroses." Actually, an abortive attempt had been made before this time to establish a program in clinical psychology in the department. A graduate student named Reuel H. Sylvester had received his M.A. in psychology from Iowa and was encouraged by Dean Seashore to go to the University of Pennsylvania to obtain his Ph.D. there under Lightner Witmer, the founder of the field of clinical psychology. By 1912, Sylvester had done so and came back to the University of Iowa to man the psychology clinic established in the department at that time. But Dr. Sylvester was not sufficiently involved in research to suit Dean Seashore and later left to become a faculty member at Drake University. To return to the main subject of this paragraph, Lee Travis was later singled out by Dean Seashore for a very special training program in which numerous departmental boundaries were breached (psychology, speech, physics, psychiatry, neurology, and otolaryngology), and a three-year postdoctoral fellowship from the National Research Council was made available to him. Travis was hired as an associate professor on the Iowa faculty in 1927 and was made a full professor the next year. In other words, Dean Seashore could not find the kind of clinical psychologist he wanted, so he trained his own and then hired him; but Seashore's idea of a clinical psychologist was more like what today would be called a speech pathologist. For example, Travis's research interest was in the neurophysiological aspects of stuttering, and that was the dominant theme in the clinical psychology program at Iowa during that era. In 1938, Travis left to become professor at the University of Southern California. Best known in the field of speech pathology, Travis was president of the American Speech and Hearing Association in 1935–1936 and received the Honors of the association in 1947. He also received an honorary D.S. degree in 1975 from Fuller Theological Seminary in California.

Clarence T. Simon received his Ph.D. in psychology in 1925 under Seashore, for a dissertation entitled "The Variability of Consecutive Wave Lengths in Vocal and Instrumental Sounds." He ultimately became professor of speech at Northwestern University. An ABPP diplomate in clinical psychology, he was also for many years director of the speech clinic at Northwestern. He was elected president of the American Speech and Hearing Association in 1946 and was awarded the Honors of the association in 1950.

Joseph H. Tiffin received his Ph.D. in psychology in 1930 under Seashore. The title of his dissertation was "Some Aspects of the Psycho-Physics of the Vibrato." Tiffin stayed on as a faculty member at Iowa for a time but ultimately went on to become professor of psychology at Purdue University. An ABPP diplomate in industrial psychology, Tiffin was elected president of the APA Division of Industrial and Organizational Psychology in 1958–1959. He received an honorary doctoral degree from the Northern Illinois College of Optometry in 1954. Tiffin published a text on *Industrial Psychology* that went into six editions.

Scott N. Reger received his Ph.D. in psychology in 1933 under Seashore, for a dissertation on "The Threshold of Feeling in the Ear in Relation to Artificial Hearing Aids." He stayed on at the University of Iowa in the department of otology (later otolaryngology) until his retirement as professor in 1969. He created the first workable model of the Bekesy audiometer available in this country. He was awarded the Honors of the American Speech and Hearing Association in 1969 for this and other accomplishments.

Claude E. Buxton received his Ph.D. in psychology in 1937 under Carl E. Seashore and C. H. McCloy. His dissertation topic was "The Application of Multiple Factorial Methods to the Study of Motor Abilities." He also stayed on at Iowa for a time but went on to become professor and chairman of the department of psychology at Yale. He was president of the Midwestern Psychological Association in 1950, president of the APA Division on the Teaching of Psychology in 1951–1952, and author of a book *College Teaching*, published in 1956. He received an honorary D.Sc. from Nebraska Wesleyan University in 1973.

Ruckmick's Students

Professor Christian A. Ruckmick had come to the Iowa faculty after receiving his Ph.D. from Cornell University in 1913. Two of his Iowa students met the criteria of eminence as defined by the Guttman scale.

Nancy Bayley received her Ph.D. in 1926 under Ruckmick's direction. Her dissertation was entitled "A Qualitative and Quantitative Study of Fear through Psychogalvanic Technique." For part of her career, Bayley was a research psychologist with the Institute of Human Development at the University of California, Berkeley; later she served as the Chief, Section of Child Development, Laboratory of Psychology, National Institute of Mental Health, Bethesda, Maryland. Known especially for her longitudinal studies of mental development and her origination of the Bayley Scales of Infant Development, she was elected president of two different APA divisions and of the Society for Research in Child Development. She was the recipient of the APA Distinguished Scientific Contributions Award in 1966 and of the G. Stanley Hall Award of the APA Division of Developmental Psychology in 1971. Bayley is also an ABPP diplomate in clinical psychology.

Ruckmick's other eminent student, Charles Van Riper, is discussed below under the heading of Lee Edward Travis, who was also a co-supervisor of his dissertation.

Knight's Best-Known Student

Professor Frederic B. Knight, who had obtained his Ph.D. at Harvard University in 1915, was on the Iowa faculty in both psychology and education. His best-known student was George H. Gallup, later of Gallup Poll fame, who received his Ph.D. in applied psychology in 1928. Gallup's dissertation title was "An Objective Method for Determining Reader Interest in the Content of a Newspaper." This was a survey of the readership of the *Des Moines Register* and the first such study ever made. Among other positions, Gallup was director of research for the Young and Rubicam Advertising Agency, professor in the Pulitzer School of Journalism at Columbia University, and founder and president of the American Institute of Public Opinion in Princeton, New Jersey. Among other awards, Gallup won the Christopher Columbus International Prize for achievement in communications in 1968. Among his many honorary doctoral degrees is an LL.D. from the University of Iowa in 1967.

Travis's Students

Lee Edward Travis supervised eight Ph.D.'s in psychology at Iowa who eventually achieved the criteria of eminence as defined by the Guttman scale.

The first was Bryng Bryngelson, a 1931 Ph.D. in clinical psychology. His dissertation title was "A Phono-Photographic Analysis of the Vocal Disturbances in Stuttering." Bryngelson went on to become a professor of speech at the University of Minnesota. He was elected president of the American Speech and Hearing Association in 1943–1944 and received the Honors of the association in 1963.

Herbert H. Jasper received his Ph.D. in 1931 under Travis. His dissertation title was "Chronaxie Studies of Stutterers and Psychiatric Cases." He went on to earn a Dr. es Sc. in physiology at the University of Paris. An authority on the reticular activating system in the brain, Jasper later became professor at the Montreal Neurological Institute and at the University of Montreal. In 1947–1949, he was the first president of the International Federation of Societies for Electroencephalography and Clinical Neurophysiology. He was founding editor-in-chief of the *International Journal of Electroencephalography and Clinical Neurophysiology*. He received honorary doctoral degrees from McGill University and from the universities of Marseilles and Bordeaux in France.

Wendell A. L. Johnson received his Ph.D. in clinical psychology under Travis in 1931. His dissertation topic was "The Influence of Stuttering on the Personality." Johnson spent the rest of his career at Iowa, at one time having joint appointments in the psychology department, the Child Welfare Research Station, and the department of speech. He was later named Louis W. Hill Research Professor in the department of speech pathology at Iowa, and, as already noted, after his death had that department's new building named after him. Although he was an ABPP diplomate in clinical psychology, Johnson was best known as an expert in speech pathology; his theory that stuttering often has its origins in the critical reaction of parents to their youngsters' normal disfluencies of speech was widely influential. Johnson was editor of the *Journal of Speech and Hearing Disorders* from 1943 to 1947, was voted the Honors of the American Speech and Hearing Association in 1947, and was elected president of that association in 1950. He was an author of a widely cited book on *Diagnostic Methods in Speech Pathology*.

Donald B. Lindsley received his Ph.D. under Travis in 1932, for a dissertation concerned with "Some Neuro-Physiological Sources of Action Current Frequencies." Later a professor of psychology at UCLA, Lindsley was elected a member of the National Academy of Sciences in 1952 and won the APA Award for Distinguished Scientific Contributions in 1959. Among other honorary degrees, he received an Sc.D. from Brown University in 1958. Lindsley, like Herbert Jasper, is regarded as an authority on the reticular activating system of the brain.

Charles Van Riper received his Ph.D. in psychology in 1934 under Travis and Ruckmick, his dissertation topic being "The Experimental Investigation of Laterality in Stutterers and Normal Speakers." Van Riper went on to become a professor of speech pathology and director of the speech clinic at Western Michigan University. He was voted the Honors of the American Speech and Hearing Association in 1956.

Herbert Koepp-Baker received his Ph.D. in clinical psychology under Travis in 1937, with a dissertation on "An Electrical Phonokinesigraph and Its Applications in the Study of Speech." He went on to become Distinguished Professor of Speech Pathology and Director of the Cooperative Cleft Palate Center at Southern Illinois University. He was elected president of the American Speech and Hearing Association in 1947 and voted the Honors of the association in 1965.

Margaret E. Hall (later Margaret Hall Powers) received her Ph.D. in 1938 in clinical psychology under Travis, her dissertation topic being "An Analysis of the

Role of Auditory Processes in Functional Disorders of Articulation." She became well known for her role in the organization and development of an outstanding program of speech correction in the Chicago school system, and for her advocacy of public-school speech correction as a part of graduate training in speech pathology. She was elected president of the American Speech and Hearing Association in 1954 and voted the Honors of the association in 1956. An ABPP diplomate in clinical psychology, she was active in getting psychology as well as speech correction into the schools, and in recognition of her efforts she was elected president of the APA Division on School Psychology in 1948.

Mack D. Steer received his Ph.D. in clinical psychology in 1934 under Travis. His dissertation topic was "Studies in the Psychology of Speech." An ABPP diplomate in clinical psychology, Steer went on to become director of the speech clinic at Purdue University and Distinguished Professor of Speech there. He was elected president of the American Speech and Hearing Association in 1951 and was voted the Honors of the association in 1958.

The Child Welfare Research Station and Wellman's Students

The Child Welfare Research Station was established by an act of the General Assembly of the State of Iowa in 1917 as an integral part of the university. Its mission was the conduct and dissemination of research on the normal child and the training of students (including those at the Ph.D. level) for these activities. The name of this unit was later changed to the Institute of Child Behavior and Development, and eventually, in 1973, it was disbanded, and its faculty were distributed to other departments including Psychology.

One of the faculty members in the Child Welfare Research Station (and its Director from 1949 to 1951) was Professor Beth L. Wellman. Herself an Iowa Ph.D. (in 1925, under Bird T. Baldwin, the first director of the Child Welfare Research Station), Wellman directed the work of two students who later met the criteria of eminence as defined by the Guttman scale.

The first of these students was Harold M. Skeels, who received his Ph.D. in 1932 for a dissertation entitled "A Study of Some Factors in Form Board Accomplishments of Preschool Children" Skeels stayed on at Iowa as a research associate and then as a faculty member and, together with George Stoddard, Beth Wellman, and Marie Skodak, carried out the "Iowa Studies" of the adverse impact of institutional care on the mental development of children. His most cited publication was a *Monograph of the Society for Research in Child Development* in 1966, a long-term follow-up study of some of these children. In 1968, Skeels received the G. Stanley Hall Award of the APA Division on Developmental Psychology for this research. Skeels finished out his career working for the National Institute of Mental Health in Bethesda, Maryland.

George G. Thompson received his Ph.D. in 1941 from the Iowa Child Welfare Research Station under Beth Wellman. His dissertation topic was "The

Social and Emotional Development of Preschool Children under Two Types of Educational Programs." Thompson went on to become professor of psychology at Syracuse University. His book on *Child Psychology* went into a second edition in 1962. He received commendation from the American Psychological Association for contributions to psychology.

Tiffin's Students

It was previously mentioned that Professor Joseph Tiffin stayed on as a faculty member of the psychology department at Iowa for some time before moving to Purdue. Two of the Iowa Ph.D. students he supervised met the Guttman scale criteria for eminence.

The first of these was Don Lewis, who received his Ph.D. in 1933 for a dissertation entitled "Studies in Timbre." Lewis worked as assistant director of the Operations Research Staff for the War Department during 1942–1945 and received a War Department Commendation for meritorious civilian service. Before and after the war, he remained on the Iowa psychology faculty until his retirement in 1968. In 1960, he published a book on *Quantitative Methods in Psychology.*

Grant Fairbanks received his Ph.D. in psychology in 1936 under Tiffin's supervision, his dissertation title being "The Relationship between Eye-Movements and Voice in Oral Reading of Good and Poor Silent Readers." He went on to become a professor at the University of Illinois. Although he was an ABPP diplomate in clinical psychology, he was best known for his work in the field of speech and hearing, for example, his research on the effects of delayed auditory feedback on speech. The *Voice and Articulation Drillbook,* which Fairbanks first published in 1937, was widely used in the field. He was editor of the *Journal of Speech and Hearing Disorders* from 1949 to 1954 and was voted the Honors of the American Speech and Hearing Association in 1955.

Reger's Best-Known Student

As noted above, Professor Scott N. Reger stayed on the Iowa faculty, in the department of otolaryngology, throughout his career after receiving his Ph.D. He supervised several doctoral students in psychology, among whom was Noble H. Kelley, a 1936 Ph.D. whose dissertation topic was "A Comparative Study of the Response of Normal and Pathological Ears to Speech Sounds." Later a research professor at Southern Illinois University, Kelley was for over 20 years secretary-treasurer, executive officer, and trustee of the American Board of Professional Psychology (then known as the American Board of Examiners in Professional Psychology). He was president of the APA Division of Consulting Psychology in 1966–1967. Kelley, known affectionately to many as "Mr. ABPP," was given the APA Award for Distinguished Professional Contributions in 1974.

A Student of Williams

For a number of years, Professor Harold M. Williams, a 1928 Ph.D. in psychology, stayed on as a faculty member of the Child Welfare Research Station. One of his students, Melvin S. Hattwick, meets the Guttman scale criteria for eminence. Hattwick received his Ph.D. in 1934, and his dissertation topic was "A Genetic Study of Differential Pitch Sensitivity." After working many years in the commercial advertising world, for such firms as Batten, Barton, Durstine, and Osborn, he became professor of marketing at Colorado State University. One of his books (published in 1960) was entitled *The New Psychology of Selling*. In 1969, he received the G. D. Crain Award for Contributions to Advertising Education.

A Student of Irwin

Another member of the faculty of the Child Welfare Research Station was Professor Orvis C. Irwin, who received his own Ph.D. at Ohio State University in 1929 before coming to Iowa. The student of his who met the Guttman scale criteria for eminence was Marion A. Wenger. Wenger's 1935 Ph.D. dissertation bore the title "An Investigation of Conditioned Responses in Human Infants." After working for several years in psychophysiology at the Fels Research Institute, Wenger moved to UCLA, where he eventually became professor and chairman. In 1964, he was elected president of the Society for Psychophysiological Research, and in 1970, he received an award from the Society for his research contributions. Currently, the most cited item among his publications is his 1972 *Handbook of Psychophysiology*.

Lewin's Students

During the 1930s, Professor Kurt Lewin was no doubt the best known of the faculty members at the Iowa Child Welfare Research Station. His record of producing outstanding doctoral students certainly preceded his move to Iowa. For example, among his Ph.D. students at the University of Berlin was Bluma Zeigarnik (for whom the Zeigarnik effect is named). And at Iowa, Lewin had postdoctoral fellows working with him who later became well known, such as Roger Barker. It is thus no surprise that 4 of his 12 Ph.D. students at Iowa attained the criteria of eminence used here.

Daniel L. Adler received his Ph.D. in 1939 under Lewin at the child Welfare Research Station, with a dissertation on "Types of Similarity and the Substitute Value of Activities at Different Age Levels." Adler's most recent academic post was that of professor at San Francisco State University. He was a winner of the Biven Foundation Award.

C. Edward Meyers received his Ph.D. in 1941 under Lewin at the Child Welfare Research Station. His dissertation topic was "Child Behavior under Conflicting Authority and Different Types of Commands." An ABPP diplomate in school psychology as well as a developmental psychologist, Meyers has been most active in research with the mentally retarded. In 1972, he was named editor of the *Monographs of the American Association on Mental Deficiency*. In 1977, he received the Education Award from the American Association on Mental Deficiency.

Undoubtedly, Lewin's best known Iowa Ph.D. was Leon Festinger, who received his degree in 1942 from the Child Welfare Research Station. His dissertation topic, "An Experimental Test of a Theory of Decision," bears an obvious relationship to his subsequent influential work on the phenomenon of cognitive dissonance. Festinger is Staudinger Professor of Social Psychology at the New School for Social Research. He received the APA Distinguished Scientific Contribution Award in 1959, was elected president of the APA Division of Personality and Social Psychology in 1962–1963, and was elected to membership in the National Academy of Sciences in 1972. There seems to be a greater breadth of citation of his work than of that of any other Iowa Ph.D. in that his 1978 citations include not only 376 in the *Social Science Citation Index* and 69 in the *Science Citation Index,* but also 24 in the *Arts and Humanities Citation Index*.

Beatrice A. Wright received her Ph.D. in 1942 under Lewin's supervision at the Child Welfare Research Station. Her dissertation topic was "Fairness and Generosity: An Experiment in the Development of Ideology." Currently a professor of psychology at the University of Kansas, she is probably best known for her 1960 book, *Physical Disability: A Psychological Approach*. She won a research award from the American Personnel and Guidance Association in 1959, and the Book Award of the Child Study Association of America in 1960, and she was elected president of the APA Division on Rehabilitation Psychology in 1962–1963.

Spence and His Students

The arrival of Kenneth W. Spence at the University of Iowa from Yale in 1938 coincided rather closely with the end of one era and the beginning of another very much identified with his name. As already noted, Dean Seashore had retired in 1936. After an interim period, John A. McGeoch was brought in as head of the psychology department, but then McGeoch died in 1942, and Spence took over the department, serving as its head until he left for the University of Texas in 1964. One notable difference between Seashore and Spence was in their attitudes toward animal research. Seashore never developed animal laboratories in the department of psychology, feeling that these were more appropriately located in departments in the biological sciences. Spence, of course, felt quite otherwise and immediately encouraged his students and colleagues to do animal experiments. Professor Spence directed or codirected 75 Iowa Ph.D.'s. Many of these graduates are, of course, still engaged in making their scientific contribtuions and are only now beginning to reach the age at which some of the honors labeled here as evidence of eminence begin to be bestowed. The discussion here is limited to the four who have already risen above threshold, so to speak.

Sidney W. Bijou received his Ph.D. in 1941 under Spence for a dissertation involving "A Study of 'Experimental Neurosis' in the Rat by the Conditioned Response Technique." Bijou retired as Professor at the University of Illinois and has taken a postretirement academic position in Arizona. Although he is an ABPP diplomate in clinical psychology, Bijou regards his main area of research as developmental psychology. He was founding editor of the *Journal of Experimental Child Psychology* and has made many contributions to the field of behavior modification, with handicapped as well as normal children. He was elected president of the APA Division on Developmental Psychology in 1965–1966 and won the division's G. Stanley Hall Award in 1980.

Benton J. Underwood received his Ph.D. in 1942 under John A. McGeoch and Kenneth W. Spence. His dissertation was concerned with "The Effect of Successive Interpolations on Retroactive and Proactive Inhibition." Professor Underwood has been on the faculty of Northwestern University since 1946 and is well known as a prolific experimentalist. Currently, the most frequently called item in his bibliography is his 1960 book (with Rudolph W. Schulz), *Meaningfulness and Verbal Learning*. He received the Warren Medal of the Society of Experimental Psychologists in 1964, and the APA Distinguished Scientific Contributions Award in 1973, and he was elected to membership in the National Academy of Sciences in 1970.

Margaret Kuenne (later Margaret K. Harlow) received her Ph.D. in 1944. Her degree was from the Child Welfare Research Station, but the dissertation was supervised by Kenneth W. Spence. This was a classic piece of research, and the published version is still the most cited item in her bibliography: "Experimental Investigation of Transposition of Response in Young Children." The G. Stanley Hall Award she received from the APA Division on Developmental Psychology in 1972 recognized not only work published under her own name but also the appreciable contributions she had made to the research program of Harry Harlow concerned with the affectional systems of nonhuman primates.

Abram Amsel received his Ph.D. under Spence in 1948. His dissertation topic was "Experimental Studies of Drive Combustion and the Role of Irrelevant Drive Stimuli in Animal Learning." He is now professor of psychology at the University of Texas. The item of his that is most frequently cited is his 1958 *Psychological Bulletin* article on "The Role of Frustrative Nonreward in Noncontinuous Reward Situations." He served as editor of the journal *Animal Learning and Behavior* from 1972 to 1976, and in 1980 he won the Warren Medal of the Society of Experimental Psychologists.

A Student of Meier

Professor Norman C. Meier was himself an Iowa Ph.D. (under Seashore, in 1926) who stayed on as a faculty member throughout his career; his particular specialty was the psychology of art. One of his students, Earl F. English, met the criteria of eminence used here. English had worked as a reporter and as a high-school journalism instructor before coming to graduate school, and his 1944 dissertation topic was "A Study of the Readability of Four Newspaper Headline Types." He went on to become professor and dean of the University of Missouri School of Journalism, one of the oldest and most highly respected journalism programs in the country. He was the author of a book, *Introduction to Journalism Research,* was the holder of numerous offices, and was the winner of a large number of awards in the field of journalism.

A Student of Farber

Professor I. E. Farber was himself an Iowa Ph.D. (1946, under Spence) who stayed on as a faculty member for many years, moving to the University of Illinois at Chicago Circle just after Spence left Iowa for Texas. One of Farber's students who has attained the criteria of eminence as used here is Norman Garmezy, whose 1950 Ph.D. was in clinical psychology. Garmezy's dissertation topic was "Stimulus Differentiation by Schizophrenic and Normal Subjects under Conditions of Reward and Punishment." He is now professor of psychology at the University of Minnesota, was elected president of the APA Division of Clinical Psychology in 1978, and received the Stanley Dean Award in 1967. The item in Garmezy's bibliography (1974) that is currently most frequently cited is his 1974 review of the research literature on children at risk for schizophrenia in adulthood.

A Student of Benton

Professor Arthur L. Benton originally came to the University of Iowa in 1948 to head the program in clinical psychology and later accepted a joint appointment in the department of neurology. One of Benton's students who attained the criteria of eminence used here is Albert Bandura, whose 1952 doctoral dissertation was "A Study of Some of the Psychological Processes Associated with the Rorschach White Space Response." Bandura is currently professor of psychology at Stanford University. He was elected president of the APA in 1974 and received the APA Award for Distinguished Scientific Contributions in 1980. In 1979, he received an honorary D.Sc. degree from the University of British Columbia. He has the largest number of current citations in the *Social Science Citation Index* of any Iowa Ph.D., the most frequently cited item being his 1969 book on *Principles of Behavior Modification*. His best-known research concerns modeling and imitation.

A Student of McCandless and Spiker

Professor Boyd R. McCandless was an Iowa Ph.D. (1941, under Ojemann in the Child Welfare Research Station) who later returned to direct the Institute of Child Behavior and Development from 1951 to 1960. Professor Charles C. Spiker was an Iowa Ph.D. (1951, under Orvis C. Irwin in the Institute of Child Behavior and Development) who stayed on and was the director of the institute from 1960 to 1971. A joint student of McCandless and Spiker who has attained the criteria of eminence used here is Glenn Terrell, whose 1952 doctoral dissertation was "An Investigation of Conditions Affecting Transposition Behavior of Preschool Children." Terrell is currently president of Washington State University in Pullman, Washington, and became commissioner of the Western Interstate Commission on Higher Education in 1968. He received an honorary LL.D. degree from Davidson College in 1969.

A Student of Bechtoldt

Professor Harold P. Bechtoldt came to the University of Iowa in 1948. His Ph.D. was from the University of Chicago. An Iowa Ph.D. student of his who has attained the criteria of eminence used here is Paul A. Games, whose 1957 doctoral dissertation was "A Factorial Analysis of Verbal Learning Tasks." Games is currently a professor at Pennsylvania State University. Like his mentor, Professor Games is well known as a statistician and methodologist. He won the Johnson Award of the American Educational Research Association in 1973.

DISCUSSION

The great influence of "professional age" (time since the Ph.D.) on the present criteria of eminence is very likely responsible for the fact that only 4 of the 39 individuals whose careers are described above obtained their degrees after 1949, and none since 1957. There are also a number of individuals whose untimely deaths probably prevented their ultimate receipt of honors that otherwise would have been bestowed on them. Among the Iowa Ph.D.'s who showed great promise but did not live long enough to attain recognition, the author would list the following: Robert H. Seashore (Ph.D. 1925, under the supervision of his father, Carl E. Seashore) at the time of his death in 1951 was professor and chairman of the department of psychology at Northwestern University and had been president of the APA Division of General Psychology and of the Midwestern Psychological Association. Beth L. Wellman (Ph.D. 1925, under Bird T. Baldwin of the Child Welfare Research Station), at the time of her death in 1952, had served as professor and director of the Iowa Child Welfare Research Station and had played a prominent role in the "Iowa Studies" on the effects of institutionalization on children. George A. Kelly (Ph.D. 1931, under Seashore and Travis), at the time of his death in 1967, was a professor at Brandeis University and had served as president of the APA divisions of both clinical and consulting psychology. Kelly's classic 1955 book on *The Psychology of Personal Constructs* inspired a great deal of research by others and continues to be heavily cited. Harold G. Seashore (Ph.D. 1933, also under the supervision of his father, Carl E. Seashore), at the time of his death in 1965, was vice-president of the Psychological Corporation and had served as president of the APA Division of Counseling Psychology. And Boyd R. McCandless (Ph.D. 1941, under Ojemann of the Child Welfare Research Station), at the time of his death in 1975, was a professor at Emory University. He had served as the founding editor of the journal *Developmental Psychology*. The APA Division of Development Psychology has named its annual Boyd R. McCandless Young Scientist Award after him. It seems a greater honor to have such an award named after oneself than merely to receive the award.

Finally, this chapter would not be complete without recognition of the fact that many activities of psychologists, though highly valued and indispensable to the field, are not as highly visible as those that lead to rapid eminence. Among these are excellent undergraduate teaching, departmental administration, peer review activities, direct service delivery, and research supervision. The present chapter has provided considerable recognition of the research supervision activities of the Iowa Ph.D.'s who stayed on as faculty at Iowa but has necessarily neglected the same kinds of contribution on the part of Iowa Ph.D.'s who went elsewhere.

Professor George J. Wischner, who spent much of his teaching life as a faculty member at the University of Pittsburgh, was one such excellent research supervisor. It was from him that the author learned the craft of scientific research in psychology and, also by his example, that of supervising the research of students. For this, I cannot thank him enough, but I hope that putting together this *Festschrift* volume conveys some of my personal appreciation.

ACKNOWLEDGMENTS

The author wishes to thank Dewey Stuit for his comments on a preliminary draft of this chapter.

REFERENCES

Garmezy, N. Children at risk: The search for the antecedents of schizophrenia. Part 1, Conceptual models and research methods. *Schizophrenia Bulletin*, 1974, *8*, 14–90.

Routh, D. K. *Correlates and non-correlates of eminence among psychologists*. Unpublished manuscript, University of Iowa, 1980.

☐ Index